BATH SPA UNIVERSITY
LIBRARY

the Teaching for Social Justice Series

William Ayers
Series Editor

Therese Quinn
Associate Series Editor

Editorial Board: Hal Adams, Barbara Bowman, Lisa Delpit, Michelle Fine,
Maxine Greene, Caroline Heller, Annette Henry, Asa Hilliard, Rashid Khalidi,
Gloria Ladson-Billings, Charles Payne, Mark Perry, Luis Rodriguez,
Jonathan Silin, William Watkins

A School of Our Own:
Parents, Power, and Community at the East Harlem Block Schools
TOM RODERICK

The White Architects of Black Education:
Ideology and Power in America, 1865–1954
WILLIAM WATKINS

The Public Assault on America's Children:
Poverty, Violence, and Juvenile Injustice
VALERIE POLAKOW, Editor

Construction Sites:
Excavating Race, Class, and Gender Among Urban Youths
LOIS WEIS and MICHELLE FINE, Editors

Walking the Color Line:
The Art and Practice of Anti-Racist Teaching
MARK PERRY

A Simple Justice:
The Challenge of Small Schools
WILLIAM AYERS, MICHAEL KLONSKY, and GABRIELLE H. LYON, Editors

Holler If You Hear Me:
The Education of a Teacher and His Students
GREGORY MICHIE

D1344222

B.S.U.C. - LIBRARY

00218645

UNIVERSITY

A School of Our Own

PARENTS, POWER, AND COMMUNITY
at the
EAST HARLEM BLOCK SCHOOLS

TOM RODERICK

Foreword by William C. Ayres

Teachers College
Columbia University
New York and London

BATH SPA UNIVERSITY
COLLEGE
NEWTON PARK LIBRARY

Class No.

379.973 ROD

DISCARD

Dawson

Some of the writing in the early chapters was previously published in
Celebrating Diverse Voices: Progressive Education and Equity (Frank Pignatelli
and Susanna W. Pflaum, Editors). Copyright © 1993 by Corwin Press, Inc.
Reprinted with permission from the Publisher.

The poem *Dreamers* is reprinted by permission of the author. Copyright ©
1977 by Douglas Worth.

Copyright © 2001 by Teachers College, Columbia University

All rights reserved. No part of this publication may be reproduced or
transmitted in any form or by any means, electronic or mechanical,
including photocopy, or any information storage and retrieval system,
without permission from the publisher.

Library of Congress Cataloging-in-Publication Data

Roderick, Tom.
    A school of our own ; parents, power, and community at the East
Harlem Block Schools / Tom Roderick ; foreword by William C. Ayres.
        p. cm. — (The teaching for social justice series)
    Includes bibliographical references and index.
    ISBN 0-8077-4156-6 (pbk.) — ISBN 0-8077-4157-4 (cloth)
    1. East Harlem Block Schools (Organization)   2. Community and
school—New York (State)—New York.   I. Title.   II. Series
    LC221.3.N38 R63 2001
    371.19'09747'1—dc21   2001037753

ISBN 0-8077-4156-6 (paper)
ISBN 0-8077-4157-4 (cloth)

Printed on acid-free paper
Manufactured in the United States of America

08   07   06   05   04   03   02   01   8   7   6   5   4   3   2   1

To Hayes Jacobs,
with warmth and gratitude

Dreamers

who ached beyond
mere drudgery of subsistence
urging the possible
a little further
than at first it had wanted to go

Douglas Worth, 1977

Contents

Foreword

Because we are living in a time of unapologetic selfishness and mean-spirited individualism, a time of greed triumphant, of unchecked militarism and the glorification of technological weaponry, of rapid retreat from a traditional faith in education as a means to a better life in favor of a no-holds-barred discipline-and-punish approach to policy and practice, of slippery subterfuges and novel justifications for the enduring evil of racism, of politics reduced to a soap opera or a mocking and diversionary infomercial—because we are living in such a time, Tom Roderick's story of the East Harlem Block Schools rings with urgency and energy on every page.

A School of Our Own recalls the birth and development of parent-run neighborhood schools beginning in 1965. Part policy, part curriculum, touching on teaching but also on organizing, it is at once a story of struggle and hope, conflict, pain, loss, and desire. Tom Roderick takes us there—into that moment, into that place—and provides a vivid, nuanced account, allowing us to draw our own lessons and conclusions from the complex dilemmas and choices faced by people who challenged the world as they found it, and created something new with their own hearts and heads and hands.

There is a certain brilliance on display when educators and organizers come together in pursuit of social justice. After all, teaching at its best and community work at its best share important common edges. Both enterprises believe that every human being possesses deep capacities to learn, to make decisions, to participate fully. The message of both is, you can change your life, and you can change the world. Enter a classroom, knock on any door, and the assumption of the teacher or the organizer is that before them stand three-dimensional creatures, centers of meaning-making energy fully capable of thought, dreams, and action. Teachers and organizers at their best assume that the people with the problems are also the people with the solutions.

Teaching and organizing encourage people to ask critical questions of society, perhaps most centrally, to struggle with the dynamic question, Who am I in the world? What will I become? And each seeks to expand the choices and the chances available as people move toward deeper and wider ways of knowing, of seeking.

Any system of injustice, of course, relentlessly seeks justification; every sustained wrong masks its meaning. In America popular beliefs about the poor float along on an ocean of ignorance, a near-total disconnection from first-hand experience. Tom Roderick takes us into the shops, street corners, and kitchens of East Harlem—vital places filled with human possibility, trembling and real. He lifts the veil and shows us smart, caring people in the active pursuit of a better life for their children. The dream of social justice will simply not be killed.

William Ayers

Acknowledgments

Many people have contributed generously of their time and wisdom to make this a better book.

The late Hayes Jacobs, director of writing programs at the New School for Social Research, believed in the book from the beginning and helped me shape it.

Peter Friedman, Jo Garfield, Sally Huxley, Dick Karlin, Candy Schulman, and other members of Hayes's Advanced Seminar at the New School during 1977–82 were my first audience. Having no tolerance for jargon, they insisted that I write in plain English and bring out the inherent drama and humanity of the story by working the interview material into vivid scenes.

My parents, George and Frances Roderick, and Block Schools' staff member and supporter Peggy Crawford provided financial support for the project in its early stages.

The following people granted me interviews, sharing the stories and observations on which the book is based: Margaret Adams, Florence Ali, Connie Arevalo, Donna Benton, Brooke Bushong, Happy Byers, Margaret Capaz, Rhonda Carloss Smith, Peggy Crawford, Vivienne Dyce, Robert Egan, John Eyrrick, Robert Gangi, Lois Goldfrank, Carmen Gonzalez, Alice Graves, Marjorie Grosett, Joe and Rosie Gueits, Elinor Guggenheimer, Debbie Henry, Micaela Hickey, Adelaide Jacquet, Shirley Johnson, Susan Kosoff, Trude Lash, Georgia McMurray, Jim Meier, Dianne Morales, Millie Lopez, Judi Macaulay, Sonia Medina, Liz Muhlfeld, Antonia Perez, Dorothy Pitman Hughes, Lydia Rios, Anna Rivera, Blanche Saia, Peter Sauer, Barbara Slemmer, Dorothy Stoneman, Rosie Tirado, Ethel Velez, Peggy Walton, Carmen and Tony Ward, Gardenia White, Lelia Wigaysire-Rickin, and Rosalind Wiener.

The following people read portions of the manuscript in its early stages and gave me their reactions and ideas: Patricia Allen, John Bell, Susan Berresford, Richard Boone, Dorothy Bloomfield, Ann Cook, John D'Emilio, Tom Draeger, Jane Lee Eddy, Barbara Finberg, Lyn Fine, Norm Fruchter, Ellen Galinsky, Colin Greer, Mark Kesselman, Madeline Lee, Herb Mack, Anitra and Carter Mehl, David Nasaw, John Niemeyer, Maxine Phillips, Margaret O'Brien Steinfels, and Doug and Karen Worth.

During the past four years, as I brought the project to completion, these people read the manuscript, gave me their suggestions, and cheered me on: Bill Ayers, John Bell, Larry Garvin, Laura McClure, Dianne Morales, Maxine Phillips, Theresa Quinn, Anna Rivera, Alan Shapiro, Dorothy Stoneman, and Carmen and Tony Ward.

Through our weekly co-counseling sessions, Mike Bucci, my dear friend and counselor, has given me crucial emotional support through all of the ups and downs of the past ten years. Without him, it's likely that the uncompleted book would still be gathering dust in storage.

Photographer Eric Maristany captured many wonderful images of the Block Schools on film. Most of the photographs in the book are his.

Elizabeth Groden did a excellent job of transcribing a number of the interviews I conducted in the past few years.

On a number of occasions, Molina Porter at Child Care Inc. made arrangements for me to examine archival material in the organization's files.

The main branch of the New York City Public Library was an invaluable resource, especially its microfilms of newspaper articles about the antipoverty program and the campaign for community-controlled day care.

The carrels at the Bank Street Library have been a perfect place for concentrating on the writing during the past two years.

My colleagues on the core staff of Educators for Social Responsibility Metropolitan Area—Barbara Barnes, Iara Benton-Molina, Lillian Castro, Leslie Dennis, Larry Garvin, Laura McClure, Nino Nannarone, Marisol Ramos, and Heather Smith—helped keep the organization running full-speed while I devoted a portion of my time and attention to finishing the book.

My wife, Maxine Phillips, my children, Emma Rose and Anne Marie, and my sister, Anne Roderick, have shown extraordinary patience with me for the many weekend and vacation hours I have devoted to the book.

Susan Liddicoat, my editor at Teachers College Press, appreciated the power of my story while guiding me gently to align it more closely with the interests of a contemporary audience. In this way she helped me write just the book I wanted to write.

My greatest debt, of course, is to the children, parents, and staff of the East Harlem Block Schools, whose decency, courage, persistence, and humor continue to inspire me. May this book be worthy of them.

Introduction

In the summer of 1966, Anna Rivera was running a candy store on a tenement block in East Harlem and living with her husband, her two young children, and her nephew in a tiny apartment separated from the store by a curtain. Running the store suited her better than the factory work she'd done after dropping out of high school. But the strain of keeping it going and caring for her family was dangerously aggravating her diabetes and high blood pressure—and she felt trapped. "I was a very quiet, withdrawn, alone kind of person," she recalls. "I didn't have any close friends. I was really heavy, and felt very ashamed of myself. I thought I had nothing to offer."

Then one day while shopping, Anna saw a sign advertising the Block Nurseries. She had no idea that by enrolling her son, she was beginning a new life. Drawn in by the warmth of the teachers and other parents, she began spending time at the school and participating in school activities. During the next 10 years, as parent coordinator and then assistant teacher, she earned a reputation as a wise and trusted counselor. After receiving her B.A. degree in 1978, she served for three years as director of the schools' college program, and then became head teacher of the three-year-olds at one of the Block Nurseries, a post she held until her retirement in 1998.

Through the Block Schools, Anna found schools for her children, teachers who listened to parents, and work she enjoyed. She also found community. "Looking back," she says, "I can see that I needed a body of people real bad. Before I got involved, it was just my kids, my husband, and me. That was my whole life. My parents were in Puerto Rico. I had no family here except my own. So I attached myself to the schools."

The support Anna Rivera got from that "body of people" was the key to her dramatic personal growth. "My husband used to discourage me in everything," she explains. "He wanted to keep me the way I was when I first came to the schools, so that he could control me. He was to be the main one. I was to be a mother, wife, and housekeeper—that was all."

"At the schools, it was different. When I'd say, 'I can't go on,' people would say, 'Oh yes you can. You can do it, Anna. Where do you need help?' And I'd say, 'I don't really need help—I just need you to tell me that I can do it.' And they did. Constantly. That's why I'm still here."

Throughout 1999, *The New York Times* ran a series of articles entitled "Life After Welfare." The series aimed to assess the impact of the major "welfare reform" law, which Congress passed and President Clinton signed in 1996, by seeing how it was playing out in Wisconsin, a state that the *Times* claimed had come as close as any to "ending welfare." In the final story, "Bold Effort Leaves Much Unchanged for the Poor" (December 30, 1999), reporter Jason DeParle wrote: "After dozens of visits and hundreds of interviews inside a welfare revolution—at public-aid offices early in the morning and in slum-district homes late at night—the real surprise is how rarely a life seems truly transformed."

Why was the reporter surprised? Apparently, he accepted the argument, advanced by proponents of "welfare reform," that welfare had become a major cause of poverty (by encouraging dependency) and that when the meager payments it provided were taken away and poor people were forced to take jobs, their lives would change dramatically for the better. Jason Turner, the administrator Mayor Rudolph Giuliani imported from Wisconsin to end welfare in New York City, is a true believer in this strategy. During a televised discussion of the city's welfare-to-work program, he gushed about the virtues of work. "Work makes you free!" he exclaimed. Viewers pointed out that a German version of the same phrase—"Arbeit macht frei"—was printed on the gates of concentration camps like Auschwitz.

I don't mean to disparage work. I love the work I do, and wish that all people could have jobs they enjoy. But as the concentration camps remind us, not all work is freeing. Not all work leads to growth and learning. Some work is tedious, mind-numbing, demeaning, exhausting, and alienating. Most of the jobs available to poor people in our economy are of this kind; and, on top of that, they often don't pay a living wage.

People seriously interested in creating the conditions for poor people to change their lives will have to look beyond "welfare reform." One place to look is the East Harlem Block Schools. At the Block Schools, low-income parents found satisfying employment as assistant teachers and teachers; they became engaged in the affairs of their neighborhood and city; and they built an organization that has served their community for more than 35 years—all while taking part in a common effort to improve the education of their own and their neighbors' children.

The most effective strategies for eliminating poverty are comprehensive approaches that strengthen families, build neighborhood institutions, provide living-wage jobs, and engage people in public life. *A School of Our Own* is an action-portrait of a neighborhood effort that did just that. It's the story of a remarkable community organization started by a group of Puerto Rican women in 1965 with federal antipoverty funds. The book takes readers into the world of these mothers and housewives, and shows how they created schools for their children, built a community that enabled them and many others to change their lives, battled "the system" to protect the integrity of their schools, and became key players in a grassroots campaign for day care reform.

"He's allowed me to go to the mountain," Martin Luther King, Jr., proclaimed in the speech he gave on the evening before his assassination. "And I've looked over, and I've seen the promised land." Millions of people during the 1960s shared in the exhilaration and sense of possibility King expressed. The East Harlem Block Schools were a product of that "mountaintop time"—a period when grassroots organizing was challenging racial injustice all over the country and the federal government was responding with such measures as the Voting Rights Act and the War on Poverty.

The 1960s were a long time ago—in more ways than one. Stunning changes have occurred in the decades since then, including the collapse of the Soviet Union and the end of the Cold War; the AIDS epidemic; the end of apartheid in South Africa; the personal computer and the Internet; and the rapid globalization of the economy. The civil rights movement gave way to a succession of other grassroots movements, each with substantial impact, including the movement to end the war in Vietnam, feminism, gay liberation, environmentalism, the anti-nuclear power movement, and the nuclear freeze movement. In what they hope will coalesce eventually into a new movement for economic justice, activists in 2001 are challenging sweatshops, rising income inequality, and symbols of globalization like the World Trade Organization. Meanwhile, the United States has become more multiracial and multicultural than ever before, as millions of immigrants have arrived from Central and South America, Asia, and Eastern Europe.

The federal government's attitudes and policies about poverty have shifted substantially as well. Far from Martin Luther King's mountain, we're slogging along in a valley—and a dark one at that. A low point came in 1996 with passage of the punitive, mean-spirited "reform" of welfare. The law ended welfare as we knew it (to no one's regret) but failed to replace it with the resources low-income families need to raise themselves out of poverty, including living-wage jobs, training, health insurance, and child care.

What can a story from the "mountaintop time" of the 1960s offer in a "valley time" more than 30 years later? A great deal, I believe. I was there.

I arrived in New York City in the summer of 1965 in the midst of John Lindsay's successful first mayoral campaign. White and middle class, the son of a prominent lawyer in Akron, Ohio, I had gone off to Yale in 1960, and had become involved in the civil rights movement. Working with the Northern Student Movement, an organization founded by a Yale dropout and initially based on campus, I had organized volunteer tutoring programs for African-American children, first in New Haven, and then in Akron and Philadelphia. Those experiences led me to choose education as a career, and I came to the city at the age of 22 to enroll in the master's degree program at Bank Street College.

After my year at Bank Street, I taught third graders for two years at Public School 92 in Central Harlem. But when I took a job with the East Harlem Block Schools in 1968, I found my true New York City home. P.S. 92 had been a decent school. The adults were generally committed to their work and friendly enough. But in class all day with my 34 children, I'd found it hard to connect with the other teachers. Isolation was not an issue at the Block Schools. My first year there I taught second grade with a warm and devoted parent assistant teacher, Millie Lopez; my friend Dorothy Stoneman taught first grade with her wonderful parent assistant, Carmen Clemente. We were all together with our first and second graders in one big room in a former store space on Madison Avenue near 113th Street. Our surroundings were shabby, our salaries low. But the classes were small; the children had plenty of warm, smart, caring adults to help them; and parents and teachers worked closely together, striving to create a school that would be different—and better. Here was a place where a teacher could *really* make a difference! My WASP reserve melted. I experienced a thrilling sense of camaraderie with the talented, diverse group of people who were sharing the adventure with me. And I discovered energies in myself I didn't know I had. During the next seven years, I threw myself into the effort to build the Day School into a full eight-grade elementary school.

As the years went by, my love for the people grew. I knew at the time that this was special: We were *living* the "beloved community" we'd heard Martin Luther King talk about. I was also aware that it hadn't come about by accident. The founding parents and their first executive director, Tony Ward, had done something right in setting up their parent-controlled schools. *A School of Our Own* is my attempt to put my finger on what that was. In telling the Block Schools' story, the book aims to capture what happened there, to explain why these schools had such a powerful impact on people's lives, and to distill the lessons for today's educators, organizers, advocates, and policy-makers.

The Block Schools continue to this day, but the book focuses on the period from 1965 to about 1980. During that time, the Block Schools created and ran two nursery schools, an elementary school, and a college program, and launched the Youth Action Program (which would become the model for the national YouthBuild Movement). Funding came from an array of governmental and private sources. The guiding principle was that the people being served by the organization would govern it; and so the schools were parent-controlled. But wanting the best for their children, the parents hired and worked closely with professional educators committed to sharing their knowledge and skills. With people of diverse backgrounds working together toward a common goal, the schools provided an ideal setting for learning. When erratic federal policy and a rigid, paternalistic city bureaucracy threatened to undermine the qualities that made the schools effective, the Block Schools fought back and advocated effectively for substantial changes in day care policy.

A notable current example of the Block Schools' approach to education and organizing is YouthBuild USA, which in 145 sites around the country is engaging young adults in rebuilding housing for low-income and homeless people, improving their academic skills, and taking leadership to improve their lives and their communities. YouthBuild grew directly out of the Block Schools, and represents a conscious effort to adapt the Block Schools' model of neighborhood organizing to work with young people. My hope is that *A School of Our Own* will speak to people working in a variety of other settings as well—from battered women's shelters and AIDS clinics to schools and after-school programs—who will benefit from seeing how the Block Schools combined high-quality service with empowering education and advocacy.

In researching the Block Schools' story, I have relied primarily on interviews, documents from the Block Schools' files, and newspaper accounts.

As I did the interviews (mostly between 1978 and 1981), I was struck by the fullness of people's remembrances, often rich in detail and full of dramatic dialogue. Where possible, I have attempted to verify these stories by getting corroboration or corrections from other people present and by checking them against minutes of meetings, letters, newspaper articles, and other documents. Where there are divergent points of view on an event or issue, I have tried to present the various perspectives fairly. Although I interviewed a number of people outside of the Block Schools who provided their perspectives—sometimes laudatory, sometimes critical—*A School of Our Own* is primarily from the Block Schools' point of view. It represents the collective memory of key players in the Block Schools' community, the story of their triumphs and struggles as they saw it—in short, a "people's history." For most people referred to in this book I use real names, but I have changed names in some cases.

In 1975 I left the Block Schools for a year of teaching and traveling in England. When I returned, I found the organization struggling with the New York City "fiscal crisis." While the nurseries suffered substantial cuts, the situation turned out to be most devastating for the elementary school. After years of supporting the school by raising private funds, we had successfully negotiated for the Day School to become an alternative public school. Unfortunately, its first year as a public school (1975–76) coincided with the layoffs of 10,000 New York City teachers. Since the Day School's teachers lacked Board of Education tenure, they were among the first to go. As a result, we lost virtually the entire professional teaching staff we had built over the years.

These discouraging events highlighted the contradiction between the liberating community of the Block Schools and the perverse governmental policies that seemed intent on undermining and destroying it. Why should we have this contradiction, I asked myself, in a country where government was supposed to be "of the people, by the people, and for the people"? Wrestling with that question, I resolved to write this book. I wanted to understand the meaning of the Block Schools' experience and share its wisdom with other educators and activists. Above all, I wanted to give the Block Schools' people their due—to ensure that their voices would be heard and their story told.

As my work on the project unfolded, I decided that a focus on the nurseries was the best vehicle for telling what needed to be told about the Block Schools. Since my work was with the elementary school, *A School of Our Own* is not directly about my experiences. It's about the people who created the nurseries, struggled for their survival, and fought the good fight for better day care for all the city's children. It's their story, and for the most part they tell it in their own words.

1

Beginnings

The East Harlem Block Schools began in 1965, the happy result of two marriages and much luck. One marriage had joined Tony Ward, a White community organizer, and Carmen Maristany, a Puerto Rican woman with four children. The other brought together two worlds: the radical social vision inspired by the civil rights movement and the traditional culture of 111th Street between Park and Madison Avenues, an "urban village" in the heart of New York City's Spanish Harlem.

Today a six-story tenement and an abandoned brownstone are the only residential buildings still standing on the block. But at the time of the 1960 census, it was home to 3,000 people. According to one long-time resident: "The block was people—people in the street, people on the sidewalks, people all over the stoops, people leaning out the windows, people on the fire escapes, just people everywhere."

When I first saw the block in the summer of 1968, what impressed me most was the sheer energy of the place . . .

A low-flying jet roars overhead on its descent into LaGuardia Airport. As the plane disappears in the distance behind the 20-story orange boxes of the James Weldon Johnson Housing Project, a commuter train bound for Grand Central Station clacks along the elevated tracks above Park Avenue. Before the train's rumble dies away, a painful squeaking of brakes announces the arrival of an enormous tractor trailer rig with a delivery for Marichal-Agosto, one of the two tropical fruit companies on the block. With shouts and gestures, several men start helping the driver back the rig up to the loading dock.

A young woman, shopping cart in hand, walks by with two small children on her way to the famous Park Avenue Market (*La Marqueta*), then the largest enclosed market in the city, extending from 111th to 116th Streets under the railroad tracks. There she will shop amid dozens of wooden stalls for meat, canned goods, fruits, and vegetables at low prices.

Across the street near *La Marqueta*'s 111th Street entrance, a dark-green garbage truck is crushing and grinding empty crates and rotting vegetables in its huge maw. Stretching past the garbage truck, a line of cars grows steadily—their path blocked by the rig. Suddenly the drivers lose their patience and an angry chorus of blasting horns fills the air. Shouting and dodging amid all these cars, trucks, and people, children play chasing games.

Toward evening, the mood changes. People stream onto the sidewalks, the stoops, and the street. The open fire hydrant is an endless source of fun, as boisterous children drench themselves in its powerful spray or turn it mischievously at cars and passersby. Using tables and chairs fashioned from milk crates, men sit out on the sidewalks playing dominoes, drinking beer, and listening to baseball on the radio. Stickball games fill the street. Firecrackers blast the night air—for weeks before the Fourth of July, and weeks after. The pungent smell of food frying in oil and heavily seasoned with garlic and oregano wafts from open windows and mingles with the sounds of Latin music blaring from a social club. Playing and arguing, laughing and crying, dancing and fighting—it is all going on, not within apartment walls but on the street for everyone to see . . .

If the residents gave 111th Street its color and energy, the block owed its characteristic rhythm to the work that went on there daily—the grunting, laughing, cursing work of maneuvering the huge trucks and handling the heavy crates.

Illegal work played its part as well. There was a brisk business in parts from stolen cars. Several times a week, the morning light would reveal yet another carcass of a late-model car, brought to the block and stripped the night before. The block was also a major crossroads in the East Harlem drug traffic. Pushers and addicts, seldom residents of the block themselves, came to buy, to sell, to wait, to shoot themselves high.

The drug dealing gave the block a "Wild West" aspect, and made it a place of sudden death. In the course of a year, two or three people would be shot and killed in disputes over money or territory related to drugs.

But if 111th Street had its share of evil, it was never burdened with hypocrisy. Life hung out raw, like the slabs of meat that stocky men in bloody white aprons pushed on wooden dollies from the meat wholesaler, Alberto y Rafael, at 111th and Madison, to *La Marqueta*. Living at the edge of poverty, the people did not need philosophers to remind them that life is too short and too dear to waste in covering things up.

And most people living on the block over the years had nothing to do with crime or drug addiction. They did their best, in harsh conditions, to live their lives, do their work, and raise their children. One of them was the founder of the Block Schools.

Carmen Maristany was born in 1938 in New York City, one of eight children in a family where only Spanish was spoken. When she was 12 years old, her father died, leaving her mother to raise the family on a meager seaman's pension.

The going was rough for the Maristanys as well as for most other families on East 111th Street. But during the 1950s, there was a real spirit of camaraderie on the block. "I didn't have any money, because my mother didn't have money," Carmen recalls, "but that wasn't so important. The block was good and alive and people cared. The kids used to keep pigeons and fly kites from the roofs. The people all knew each other and knew each other's kids. If an adult would say something to the kids, they would all listen and respect that person. During those years, we didn't even lock our doors."

The block's residents—many of whom had come from the vicinity of Mayaguez, on the western coast of Puerto Rico, during the 1930s and 1940s—tended to confine their lives to the block and the close community it offered. "I had never taken a subway ride until I started high school," Carmen admits. "My first train trip at age 14—and I was petrified! I never read the papers. What did all that have to do with me? I didn't know that there was a whole other world."

After graduating from Julia Richman High School, Carmen got married. For the next few years, she had her hands full caring for her four young children and enduring her marriage, which became increasingly intolerable because of her husband's penchant for drugs and other women. It got so bad that Carmen finally moved back in with her mother, adding her own children to her seven brothers and sisters already living in the tiny apartment.

By 1960, Carmen was more than ready for a change, and she decided to look for work—a step that was possible because her mother was willing to help care for the children. With only a high school diploma, she talked her way into a job as a counselor in a children's shelter at 104th Street and Fifth Avenue.

The job was a turning point. It gave her financial independence, got her out of the house, and enabled her to use her talents to do work she enjoyed. For the first time since her marriage, she began to feel that she had "a life."

At the same time, changes had come to the block. "When I was growing up," Carmen observes, "the people involved with drugs were the old-timers—like the seamen. They were all very discreet, and the whole subject of drugs was hush-hush. You never, never saw anybody shooting up. Every once in a while you'd hear about a killing or something, but you never *saw* anything. After my generation, though, it began to hit the kids. I saw it happen right before my eyes. Young kids started getting hooked—children of people I knew—I was afraid for my own kids too."

By the early 1960s, nodding junkies had become a familiar sight on the corners and in the hallways. People bought expensive metal grates and police locks, and bolted their windows and doors. In that atmosphere, the camaraderie so cherished by the block's residents began to evaporate into suspicion and fear.

Although nothing could compensate the people of 111th Street for these tragic changes, the mood was not entirely bleak. For the late 1950s and early 1960s brought not only drugs to 111th Street, but awareness of a national upheaval. "John F. Kennedy and Martin Luther King were the symbols," Carmen explains. "Lots was happening, and we felt alive. I can't really say it was hope, but we started thinking it was possible that something might happen, that things in our neighborhood might begin to change for the better. It was like we felt we finally had somebody in our corner."

Community organizations, large and small, were springing up all over East Harlem. The American Friends Service Committee (AFSC) provided the most important link between the changing national climate and Carmen's world. The AFSC sponsored projects in a number of cities on the East Coast. In 1958, they opened their "East Harlem Project" at 94 East 111th Street near Park Avenue (later the location of the Block Schools' central office).

The East Harlem Project drew in a number of young middle-class social activists, who supported themselves with outside jobs while living and working in the neighborhood. Although Carmen did not participate directly in the activities of the East Harlem Project, she got to know the people who worked there. One of them was Tony Ward.

Tony was born in 1940 in New York City, became a Quaker during high school, and attended the University of Rochester, where he was active in a disarmament organization and was a charter member of the campus NAACP. After graduation, he spent a year in South America, teaching and acquiring fluency in Spanish. In 1962, he came to East Harlem, full of the idealism that characterized the times. When he first moved onto the block, he refused, as a matter of principle, to put locks on his doors. Only when he had been completely relieved of his possessions over a period of several months did he reluctantly secure his apartment.

To support himself, Tony had intended to teach in the public school system, but his refusal to sign the loyalty oath then required of all teachers meant that he had to look elsewhere for work. He was hired by the AFSC to develop its tiny informal tutoring program on 111th Street. By 1964, he had 120 volunteer tutors coming each week to work with children in their homes.

Carmen and Tony were married in August 1964. Over the next year, Tony continued to run the tutoring program, and Carmen, who had left her job at the children's shelter, found a new channel for her energies as board member and volunteer with the Block Development Project (BDP), a community organization engaged in block organizing.

Through the BDP, Tony and Carmen became good friends with BDP's director, Dave Borden, and his wife, Vivianna, who happened to be the daughter of Luis Muñoz-Marin, a former governor of Puerto Rico.

Vivianna had the idea of starting a babysitting co-op on 105th Street between Second and Third Avenues, where she lived. From her block she brought together about eight parents—primarily middle-class people—to explore the idea further. During the winter of 1964–65, the group held a number of meetings in which Carmen took part. Gradually, the idea evolved from a babysitting co-op to a storefront nursery run by parents. No single person could claim credit for the idea. It was rather a natural meeting of the minds at a time when slogans like "parent control" and "grassroots democracy" were in the air.

Outlining the idea in a rough proposal, Vivianna went to Aspira, a social and cultural agency. As the most influential Puerto Rican organization in the city at that time, Aspira was being asked by federal officials to recommend Puerto Rican programs for funding as part of President Lyndon Johnson's War on Poverty. Aspira's response to Vivianna's proposal was positive.

While the 105th Street group continued to refine the idea, Vivianna set to work revising the proposal. Tony helped with the writing, although he made it clear that his work with the tutoring program would prevent him from getting further involved.

The proposal, submitted to the Office of Economic Opportunity (OEO) early in April, requested funds "to establish and maintain two nurseries," whose purpose would be to overcome the "environmentally induced handicaps" of children in East Harlem. Aimed primarily at Puerto Rican children, the schools would "wisely utilize both languages" (Spanish and English) to help the child develop as an effective "bilingual person." A major priority would be "to bring parents into the educational process." To this end, assistant teachers would be from the neighborhood and the parents would act as a board of directors. Every effort would be made "to assure that real decision-making power and control over the school [were] lodged with the parents and no one else."

Even as the idea evolved and funding was virtually assured, Vivianna's group on 105th Street was dwindling. Its middle-class members, who had no long-term commitment to stay in the community, were simply not willing to invest the time and energy necessary to start a school. Then Vivianna herself decided to withdraw for personal reasons. The venture was on the verge of collapse when Vivianna asked Carmen if she would take over.

Carmen was both excited and hesitant. She had never done anything like this before. Her own children were now too old to participate in a nursery program. On the other hand, East Harlem desperately needed nursery schools. And Carmen was intrigued by the concept of parent control. "I used to go to the public school, and ask the teachers to do more for my kids," she explains. "They were polite, but I got no results. Then I married Tony, and the whole thing changed. I became one of their peers, because they were talking to Tony, who was one of their peers. They became very concerned, and started to expect more of the kids. They'd call home. They'd tell us about this special program and that special program. I always felt frustrated if my mother had to go to school for my kids because she just didn't get the respect. I wanted to see a school where none of that nonsense would happen, a place where the teachers would be people *we* had invited."

Finally, Carmen decided to go ahead. Eager to involve her friends and neighbors from 111th Street, she began knocking on doors. "We have the chance to start a bilingual nursery school, where *our* language and culture will be respected," Carmen would say. "It will help get the children ready for first grade. Parents are going to be able to make all the decisions about their children's education. I'm wondering if you're interested and what you'd like to see in something like this."

By June, Carmen had found six to eight people who were enthusiastic. Although Tony was busy organizing the summer tutoring program, he had decided to help, and perhaps even to apply to be director. Funding seemed assured as long as a definite group with adequate community representation was there to receive it.

On a Saturday early in June, Carmen called on the people who had been most responsive, invited them to a meeting, and gave each a copy of the proposal. Sonia Medina was one of the people Carmen visited that day. "When Carmen knocked on my window—she always knocked on my window, not on my door—she tingled with excitement," Sonia recalls. "The only thing that got me excited about that proposal was her happiness and exuberance about it."

The meeting took place that evening in Carmen's mother's apartment. Attending were Sonia; Connie Arevalo, Carmen's closest childhood "buddy" and godmother of her children; Rosie Gueits, an acquaintance of Connie's; Florence Ali, Carmen's sister; Marguerita Maristany, Carmen's mother; Ramona Harvey, Lucy Vasquez, and Frances Crespo, neighbors; Carmen Bess, the only person left from Vivianna's group; and Tony and Carmen Ward.

Sipping rich Spanish coffee served by Carmen's mother, the women listened while Tony gave a brief summary of the proposal. Carmen looked around nervously at people's faces for reactions. Maybe the women would think she was just trying to set something up for her husband. Maybe they would simply be reluctant to get involved.

After answering a few questions, Tony left, and Carmen asked people to say what they were thinking. Any fears she had about their interest evaporated instantly. Far from agonizing over whether to make a commitment, they plunged right into discussing what the school would be like, and what to do first. "There was so much to be learned," recalls Sonia, "so much that was new, so many new directions. All of a sudden we were going to start something new, and we didn't know how. I had to remind people that we didn't have space, we didn't have money, we didn't have staff, and we didn't have the children. Only enthusiasm kept people in the program. We weren't asked to sign any papers. None of us knew that we would one day be able to work for the program. No one had any idea for themselves. It was pure, it was honest, and it was for somebody else."

There was one rather sharp exchange, which Sonia triggered by making what she thought was an innocent suggestion. "Do you want the children to have uniforms? You know, like a little dress a child may wear and they're all alike so you don't know who's the child that's got money, and who's the chi—"

"*Ay Dios Mio!*" Connie burst in. "You must be crazy! I went to Catholic School for eight years with uniforms—that same blouse and jumper for eight years! There's no way I'm gonna have my two sons dressed alike, and no way I'm gonna wash the same pants and shirts for eight more years!"

As soon as Connie stopped, everyone started talking at once, and Carmen had to calm the hubbub. "Let's give Sonia a chance to finish," she said.

"I have a son in public school," Sonia continued. "The kids who go with broken shoes or the button that's missing—I see how those kids get labeled, even on their report cards. A uniform is something that a child can wear and the parents don't have to pay much money."

When Sonia was done, the others had their chance. Speaking in English (while Rosie translated for Lucy), they shared their views. Most did not like the idea of uniforms. "We want our school to be different," Connie argued. "We want to treat our kids on an individual basis. How can we do that if they all look the same?"

When the controversy about uniforms had run its course, the women went on to such matters as where to begin looking for space, how to recruit children, and how to let people in the neighborhood know. Rosie admits that they went into a number of other topics as well, which had nothing to do with starting a school.

Finally, around 11:00, the meeting ended. Carmen wasn't sure if she had somehow managed to assemble a group of unusually daring and energetic people, or if they just didn't know what they were getting themselves into. But one thing was clear: Their enthusiasm went beyond her wildest expectations. That evening, the East Harlem Block Schools were born.

On June 18, word arrived from the New York Council Against Poverty that the grant had been approved. "Can this be for real?" the parents wondered. They had no office, no credentials, and no experience running early childhood programs. Yet the federal government was about to give them $65,411 to establish and run two nursery schools.

During July, the group met a couple of times, and people kept in touch. Although they felt like "just a group of neighbors," they began to call themselves a board of directors in their communications with OEO officials, who preferred to deal with some kind of formal entity.

One important task was to maintain good communication with Aspira, whose initial recommendation had been crucial in winning approval for the proposal. The person who agreed to serve as liaison with Aspira was Sonia Medina. A woman of unusual dignity, whose strength is leavened by a warm smile and a great capacity for enthusiasm, Sonia was born in Puerto Rico and spent the first 18 years of her life there. Her father, an architect and an exile from fascist Spain, died when she was six, but not before he had helped his daughter develop a strong sense of pride and a lively curiosity. "My father always gave me an explanation for everything," Sonia recalls.

In 1965, at 32, Sonia had lived on 111th Street for seven years, but still thought of Puerto Rico as her true home. "As a child," she says, "I was raised to have tremendous respect for every living thing. I spent many days at the beach. When you spend many days by the ocean, you never forget it, you never give it up." Those memories helped feed her excitement about the Block Nurseries. She saw that the schools were an opportunity for her to bring some of the warmth and beauty she knew from her childhood in Puerto Rico to the streets and tenements of Spanish Harlem. They were a chance to create "a piece of 'the island' in *El Barrio*."

Sonia was the perfect person to deal with Aspira. For one thing, she seldom finds herself at a loss for words. And she doesn't let herself be pushed around.

Almost immediately a conflict arose over who should be the executive director of the Block Nurseries. The parents wanted Tony. Officials at Aspira insisted that they had better candidates.

Although the parents met and talked with these people, they didn't like them. Aspira's favorite, a Puerto Rican psychologist, provoked an especially strong reaction from Rosie Gueits. "I found him snotty and arrogant," she recalls. "He had an aura about him that said, 'I'm better than you—like, *my* shit don't stink.'"

The issue came to a head early in August. At a meeting in her office, Aspira's director told Sonia that the parents would be making a big mistake if they hired Tony, because he was too young, lacked the necessary training and experience, and was not Puerto Rican.

When Sonia explained why the parents liked Tony, the woman said firmly that she could accept only a Puerto Rican with an advanced degree and experience in early childhood education. She suggested that if Mr. Ward cared so much, he might take a position as assistant to the director.

Sonia had the last word. "We appreciate the help you gave us in getting the proposal approved," she said in Spanish. "But that proposal says very clearly that our school is parent-controlled. You can't dictate to us. *Our* decisions and *our* procedures will make the difference."

As she returned to East Harlem on the Lexington Avenue subway, Sonia felt disgusted. She was convinced that Aspira was trying to manipulate the situation so that they could keep the program as "their baby." She was also angry with their insistence on "total professionalism."

As a result of her firsthand experience with East Harlem schools and hospitals, Sonia did not share Aspira's regard for professionals. Once her son Richie came home from school, saying that his teacher had hit him. Entering his classroom the next day, Sonia told the teacher of Richie's complaint. "These children!" the woman exclaimed, wringing her hands. "When I get mad, I lose my temper, and I just can't control myself."

"Well, I would like to make a suggestion, if you don't mind," Sonia told her politely. "Please try a littler harder to control yourself, because if you lose control of yourself again with my child, I might lose control of myself too—and break your neck!"

Sonia did not encounter teachers like that every day, but the incident had removed any illusion that there was magic in a degree or a professional certificate.

As soon as she arrived home from the meeting at Aspira, Sonia called the parents to her apartment for an emergency meeting. (Carmen declined to attend, since Tony would be a major item on the agenda.) After indignantly explaining what had happened, Sonia paused, and then went on solemnly: "This evening, we have a very important decision to make—a decision that will influence the whole future of our school. The decision is, do we want Tony for director?

"Let me explain to you why *I* like Tony. Number one, he lives around our block, and he knows the problems that we all face. Number two, he cares. Number three, Tony helped write the proposal, and he's done work already without pay. Number four, the top salary in our program is $7,000 and the people Aspira wants are asking for $12,000 or more."

After a short discussion, Sonia passed out ballots. "You don't have to agree with me," she continued. "If you don't want Tony as director, all you have to do on your ballot is write 'No.' If you want Tony, all you have to do is write 'Yes.'"

Every ballot came back with a "yes" on it. "Tony was who we wanted," explains Connie Arevalo. "There were no two ways about it. If Tony couldn't be director, then we didn't want to go through with it." The parents did not see Tony as an outsider. He spoke fluent Spanish. For three years he had been living in the neighborhood. Through his work with the tutoring program, he had become a familiar figure on the block. And he was Carmen's husband. He had, in short, become part of the community. In choosing him, the parents felt they were choosing one of their own.

But if the decision was not difficult, it did mark an important step in the development of the Block Nurseries. In going through the decision-making process, the "group of neighbors" coalesced into a board of directors. No longer dependent on Carmen's organizing efforts, the parents under Sonia's leadership had made a major decision. With one stroke, this new board established its independence from its "parent" agency and its role within the Block Nurseries as the ultimate source of authority. As Sonia put it, "After we hired Tony, that's when we began to get serious."

On August 15, two days after his summer tutoring program came to an end, Tony began work as executive director of the Block Nurseries. The contract with OEO (finally signed on August 23) lasted only through the end of January. Tony feared that the agency might withdraw its support if the program was not in operation by then. That meant he and the parents had only five months to create a school—from scratch.

Fortunately, they now had a base of operations. Having phased out the East Harlem Project, the AFSC agreed to let Tony and the parents use the brownstone at 94 E. 111th Street. But classrooms were another matter. Most of the buildings in the neighborhood were decrepit tenements built at the turn of the twentieth century. It would be difficult to find space that could be made adequate for children at a reasonable cost. As a first step, the parents fanned out over East Harlem to see what was available.

At the same time, Tony began to put together a staff. His guiding assumption was that the parents initially could not create entirely by themselves the kind of school they wanted. They would need the help of professionals for at least several years, and they ought to have the best. The success of the school would depend on maintaining a delicate balance between the parents and these professional people.

The method for selecting teachers would be fundamental in defining the meaning of "parent control." But deciding on a hiring process didn't seem momentous to Tony at the time. He knew he could not make the final choice. But he did not want people teaching at the schools whom he strongly disliked. So he decided to do an initial screening. The candidates he thought he could work with would go to the board, which would make the final choice.

By the first week in September, candidates began to meet with the board. "We were scared as hell," recalls Rosie Gueits. "We felt, 'Damn, these are professional people, and we're just housewives.'"

The first time was especially awkward. "We met in Rosie Gueits's living room," Tony recalls. "At that time, Rosie had nine children, and her apartment was just four rooms. I had written out questions for the parents on yellow paper, with carbon copies. The first candidate came in and sat down. I said a few words of introduction, and then waited. There was complete silence. A couple of people cleared their throats. Finally, Sonia summoned the courage, and haltingly read off the first question, her eyes glued to the yellow sheet."

That interview was also memorable for the candidate. A small, soft-spoken White woman with 13 years of experience as a teacher of young children, Alice Graves had learned of the position through an ad in *The New York Times*. "I had never met a Puerto Rican before," she admits. "It was all so new to me. I had grown up on Staten Island, and before the interview I'd never been that far uptown. My family felt it was horrible for me to go up there, but I was desperate. I needed the money."

After the interview, Alice was even more convinced she wanted the job—and not just for the money. "I felt an immediate closeness with the people," she says. "They were genuine. I could see that they were really trying to put together a school based on caring about children."

The parents were acute in picking up even subtle expressions of class and racial prejudice, and the setting itself was part of the screening process. Says Tony: "Many of the interviews were in Sonia's apartment. The person being interviewed sat in her tiny little living room, packed in there with the whole committee. The people waiting were crammed into the kitchen, which was just three feet away from the living room. The radio was playing. The two dogs were barking. Babies were crying next door. It was a good way of weeding out teachers who didn't have the guts to take East Harlem."

By the third week of September, the board had hired four people (including Alice Graves) to fill the professional positions of director and three teachers for one nursery. Two were African-American; one was Filipino; and one was White. One was an advocate of the Montessori method. The others espoused some version of "progressive education" in the tradition of John Dewey. Two were experienced, and two were just starting out. Decision-making was by consensus. Observes Carmen: "They weren't sure what they wanted except to get people they liked."

Tony and the parents had every reason to feel good about the progress they were making, except for one thing. Serious snags had developed in the search for space. To get a permit to operate a nursery school, they would need facilities that met Department of Health standards. Tony and the parents had no problem with that. But how could they meet those standards while staying within their budget and their neighborhood?

Of the four spaces the parents had found so far, three were in old buildings, and the costs of renovating them would be prohibitive. That left only two adjoining storefronts in Franklin Plaza, a middle-income co-op, as a possible site for one of the centers. The location—on a commercial block amid high-rise apartment buildings—was not ideal, and renting and renovating them would be expensive. But Tony and the parents decided they had better put in an application to Franklin Plaza, while continuing their search for something more to their liking.

Pushing his worries about space to the back of his mind, Tony now turned his attention to another crucial matter: hiring the parent staff. This was a bit awkward, for the only parents involved so far were the board members. Because they had come in at the beginning, and had already done much work with no pay, they had earned first crack at the jobs. But what procedure could be devised to enable the board to hire itself? This was a dilemma that Tony found impossible to solve neatly. He ended up simply telling the board members at one of their meetings late in September that if they wanted jobs in the program, they could have them.

All of the people on that original board insist that their reaction to Tony's announcement was complete surprise. But most of them jumped at the chance. Rosie's reaction was typical. "From the beginning," she says, "I knew this was what I wanted to do. When I was younger, I had worked. Then when I got married, I stayed home all the time. It didn't bother me, being a housewife. I just felt maybe this would be a change of pace: Let me get out there and do something! The idea grabbed me immediately."

And so Sonia, Rosie, Romona, and Florence went on staff as assistant teachers. Connie Avevalo, now board chair, was hired as a clerk-typist. To get applicants for the two remaining assistant teacher positions, the parents put out word in the neighborhood.

Meanwhile, the lack of space was beginning to create a logjam. Tony delayed putting the newly hired teachers on the payroll as long as he could. Hoping that a breakthrough on space would come soon, he was concerned to save as much money as possible for future emergencies. But by mid-October Tony decided that he could put off his staff no longer without the risk of losing them. On October 19, the teachers and assistant teachers officially began work by taking part in a three-week training program.

For help with training, Tony turned to Bank Street College, a leader in child-centered education. Blanche Saia, a child psychologist from the College, coordinated a week of lectures and workshops on child development, room arrangement, equipment, art, and children's literature. The week gave the staff a good dose of Bank Street's philosophy, which appealed to Tony because of its attention to all aspects of a child's growth—emotional, social, physical, and intellectual.

During the next two weeks, the staff made visits to some of the best private schools in the city. The parents learned a lot just from making the arrangements. According to Rosie Gueits: "Tony would ask who would like to go to such and such a place. Then he'd say, 'Here's the number. You set up the appointment.' It was scary, making the phone calls and going downtown to talk to people. It was something I hadn't done before, and I wondered if I was speaking correctly, if I was saying things right."

Rosie describes the discussions that followed each day of visits: "When we'd come back, we'd give feedback about what happened, what we saw that we liked, what we didn't like, how people treated us and whatnot. We'd all bring that out, and then we'd say, 'Let's make sure *this* doesn't happen or *that* doesn't happen in *our* school.'

"We noticed that in a lot of those places, you didn't feel comfortable. You felt funny, you felt out of place. And another thing, it was cold at that time. Sonia used to say, 'There's no coffee in this place. People don't offer you a cup of coffee.'

"So we said, 'Okay, the first thing we're going to do when we open up our school is to make sure we have coffee. Even if we don't have the money for donuts, we're going to have coffee, and a place where people can sit down and stay for a while and talk.' We said we'd try to keep a smile on our face regardless of how we were feeling. If we're having a hard time, it doesn't mean we have to have a puss on our face. And we said, 'Our school will be different from those other schools. It will be a place where everybody—kids, parents, and even people who aren't parents in the school—can feel at *home*.'"

While school visits continued well into November, the parents also began recruiting children in earnest. It would have been possible to fill the schools several times over with no effort, just by opening them up to the middle-class residents of Franklin Plaza. But the parents wanted to reach the children who needed a nursery school most. And so, armed with masking tape and flyers, they went into the tenements, plastering up notices and knocking on doors.

Like the school visits, canvassing was something new for most of the parents, and it was scary. Before they went out, they did role-playing. To give each other additional support, they went in pairs. "We were shocked at some of the things we saw going on in the families," says Connie Arevalo. "Some of the people really opened up to us. They told us all kinds of personal things—about their health problems, about what they were going through with their husbands, and about how desperate they felt sometimes with their children. When they told about some of the things they'd gone through in their lives, I could hardly believe it. I'd seen it in movies, but I hadn't realized it happened in real life. And the saddest thing was that they thought they just had to sit and take it. They had no one to talk to, no place to go."

The experience of canvassing helped shape the schools. "We'd come back to the office after a day of canvassing," Connie remembers, "and we'd talk about what happened. Right away, we saw that we couldn't just have a nursery for children. We realized that we had to figure out a way to help the whole family. We weren't sure exactly *how* at first. But we knew we had to find a way."

November—and still no space. It was beginning to look as though the parents might get something even more innovative than they had bargained for, a sort of "school without walls"—or ceilings, or windows, or floors.

Then, on November 24, good news came from Franklin Plaza. The co-op's board had approved the Block Nurseries' application! One Block Nursery had a home at last.

Elated as he was, Tony also felt uneasy. The bareness of the two huge adjoining rooms reminded him of the gloomy fact that had been obscured by the desperate scramble to find some place—*any* place—to house the school: It would take thousands and thousands of dollars to make the former stores into decent places for children. Where would the money come from?

He had already raised the matter with the board. Like him, they could see no choice but to take the spaces, if the program was to open at all. According to Tony: "Their attitude was, 'If we have to do it, we have to do it. We'll worry later about the consequences. They'll have a harder time shutting us down if we are running and have children than if we have nothing and are asking.' And so it was 'Damn the torpedoes, and full steam ahead!'"

December was a whirlwind. Intense feelings of frustration and excitement, pent up by weeks of anxious waiting, burst forth and swept everyone along. Orchestrating the complex situation and helping to channel the energy was Tony, who was determined to get the school open by the end of the month.

The biggest challenge was preparing the space. Through his contacts at the AFSC, Tony had enlisted the services of architect Jack Hall, who agreed to provide his services *pro bono*. But architect's drawings were only the first step in a lengthy process. Both the Buildings and Health Departments had to approve the plans, which would then have to be let out to contractors for bids. Sometime before work got underway, Tony would have to clear up the little detail of where the money was going to come from to pay for it all.

There was no way all this could be accomplished in a month. Faced with this reality, Tony, the parents, and the teachers decided to concentrate on one of the two rooms, and do what they could to make it adequate—if only barely—for temporary use.

First came cleaning. The two vast rooms (each 25 feet wide by 100 feet deep) were filthy, having lain unused for a year and a half. Everyone pitched in to help. "We put a light bulb on an extension cord and hung it down from a big ladder," says Connie, "and then we all helped mop the bare concrete floor—with cold water, because we didn't have any hot water in the place."

The work was the kind to make people friends for life, if they made it through the first day. "We would work all morning, and by lunchtime we'd be starving," Rosie recalls. "We used to go out and buy food from the restaurant, or maybe if we didn't have any money, we'd cook at home and bring in the leftovers. We had no plates or anything, so we used to rip up paper bags. We'd sit there and eat with our hands and talk and laugh.

"Everybody used to look through the windows at us. They thought we were crazy. They used to stand and look at us like we were some kind of freaks or something. So we covered the whole front window—all the windows in the front—with newspapers. That was our shade."

Marisol Gutierrez, hired as an assistant teacher, had been on staff for a week. While people swept and scrubbed and mopped and polished, it fell to Marisol to clean a toilet. When she objected, she got a fast reaction from the other parents: "Who do you think *you* are—a princess or something? In this school we don't talk about 'it's not proper for an assistant teacher to do this' or 'a director shouldn't have to do that.' No way!" Marisol and the Block Nurseries parted company immediately—by mutual consent.

Walls and ceilings needed painting, and that brought in some of the fathers. Rosie's husband, Joe, describes a common routine: "I'd go out and buy two or three cases of beer. Someone else would bring paint, brushes, and so on. After a six pack, one wall was done. Next thing you'd know, it was 2:00 in the morning, and we'd be sitting around bullshitting. We got to be very close."

Every day saw some new development. Bright-yellow curtains replaced the newspapers on the large plate glass windows. A carpenter began constructing shelves for toys and cubbies for the children's belongings. Men from a small flooring company started to cover the bare concrete floor with tiles.

Meanwhile, the teachers, working in classroom teams of one professional with two parent assistants, began setting up their rooms. Members of each team also made visits to the homes of the children who would be in their class.

Christmas approached, and the curriculum became the major topic of discussion. Here the parents felt on shaky ground. But their fears were balanced by the fact that deep down they trusted their impulses and knew that they could draw on their experiences with their own children. Sonia describes her feelings: "I was a little uncomfortable because I didn't know how the children would react. But I felt they need respect, to be secure, to be loved and understood. Once you give them that, you've passed a little bit of the test. I knew there'd be no harm in letting a child sit on my lap and holding him, like a mother."

December 20: Workmen finished laying the tiles.

December 23: The carpenter put the final coat of paint on the cubbies.

December 27: The children's chairs arrived.

And on December 28, the school opened!

It opened not because it was ready to open, but because Tony and the parents just could not bear to put it off any longer. As Carmen said, "I kept expecting more things to happen so that the school would open, and then, all of a sudden, it just opened!"

Three classrooms and an office were jammed into the one large room, with cubbies and shelves as the only partitions. The lighting came from the front wondows and a naked light bulb hanging on an extension cord from a ladder. As a result of a delivery delay, the children's tables were plywood boards on milk crates. But a Block Nursery was happening at last.

"We all got there early," says Connie, remembering the first day. "Everything was spic and span. My desk was the divider between the office and the classrooms. I had to sit there—right next to the classrooms—and type and answer phones. We had given the parents times to bring their kids in, like every 15 minutes. I was so nervous that my hands were cold. I wanted everything to be just right. I couldn't believe it was finally the moment to greet new parents and children into our school.

"Everyone was fighting to get the first kid. The kids looked so cute and nice. As they came in, we'd say 'hello' and start to talk to them. Some would just walk right into the classroom. Others were shy. If they looked scared, we'd tell them they could wait with us. It was like a family. We left it all up to feelings. We greeted the parents too, and offered them coffee. We wanted them to stay, to make sure the kids got adjusted. I was proud that people were calling me 'Mrs. Arevalo,' even though as soon as they'd say it, I'd tell them, 'Call me Connie. We use first names here.'

"When I saw everything running so smoothly, when I saw that it was gonna work and our dream was coming true, tears started to come down. I remember Rosie coming and hugging me, and all of us hugging and kissing each other. We had a wonderful feeling of accomplishing something, of doing something beyond ourselves."

The sense of victory and the spirit of camaraderie that Connie experienced set the tone for the day. But not everyone shared completely in Connie's exuberance. "I remember being nervous, and it going well," Tony says. "But I hardly had time to appreciate the victory. Things were still such a mess, and I could see it going on and on. The books were screwed up, and I couldn't pay the bills. The place wasn't renovated yet, and we still had another school to get open, and nothing was settled. I was exhausted."

And Sonia, who had envisioned holding a child on her lap "like a mother," found that her first day in the classroom was not exactly what she had expected.

"His name was David," she recalls, "and he was four, going on fourteen. We were greeting the children as they came in, and I said to David, 'Hi, my name is Sonia. Welcome to your new classroom!'

"He said, 'So what? So what?' (He would repeat everything twice.)

"I went on: 'This is going to be my first—'

"'Big deal! Big deal!' he said.

"He turned, and looked at me from top to bottom. 'Want me to kiss you, and say everything's all right?' he asked.

"'No,' I answered, trying to be very casual, 'not yet—because we haven't developed that kind of uh . . . relationship, relationship.'

"'So what! So what!' he said.

"He sat there and looked around the class. After a little while, he said: 'The only thing goin' on here is a buncha little kids.' Then he started questioning everything, and making fun of it at the same time.

"When it was time to go, he looked up at me. 'This is it? This is it?' he asked."

What could Sonia say? Yes. This *was* it—for the first day. But many more days would follow, and in them would be some surprises—even for David.

2

Our Children Have Their Own School

Late in January, less than a month after opening day, the Block Nursery on 106th Street welcomed a delegation of officials from Washington. "At first, I was worried," Tony recalls, "but as I showed them around, I realized that they were not just liking the school—they were absolutely delighted with it."

The visit gave Tony some much-needed perspective. "For the first time," he says, "I had the chance to get my eyebrows above water, and look at the school through someone else's eyes. And I said to myself, 'We do look good! This *is* nice!' It was the whole atmosphere more than anything else—the sense of a well-ordered, well-run place with a good feeling among the community people."

The work of setting up the other nursery was moving ahead quickly: The board hired staff, Tony arranged for training, parent staff members canvassed for children, and everyone pitched in to clean and paint. In February 1966, the second Block Nursery opened in a storefront Sonia had found on Madison Avenue.

Just five months after receiving their first money, Tony and the parents had their entire program in operation. But in doing that, they had, according to Tony, "broken every rule in the book." They had ignored OEO regulations about nepotism and conflict of interest. With their storefront spaces that were not yet renovated, they did not qualify even for a temporary permit from the Department of Health, and therefore were operating illegally. Most risky, though, was the matter of the "revolving funds"—cash advances totaling $40,000 that OEO gave the Block Nurseries to meet ongoing expenses.

Tony assumed that without major renovations the schools eventually would be closed down. Jack Hall, the architect, estimated the cost at $30,000—far more than the amount provided in the budget. But Tony was having trouble getting approval for even slight modifications in the budget, and federal guidelines had strict limits on spending for renovations. The revolving funds gave the schools a way out of this Catch-22 situation—at least for the time being.

What Tony did, essentially, was to use the revolving funds to pay for renovations. The process began as early as December 1965, when the architect started drawing up the plans. Within the next few months, the drawings were completed, contractors hired, and materials ordered. With all the classes of the 106th Street nursery crowded into one room, work began on the other room. Cabinet work was done and lighting installed during weekends and school vacations. The major jobs, such as putting in the kitchen and building the interior walls, were scheduled for the summer, when the schools would be closed.

Tony did everything he could to cut costs. Robert Egan did the legal work for free. Jack Hall, the architect, worked *pro bono* as well. The New York Friends' Group helped Tony locate the best and cheapest contractors. And the parents did all the painting and cleaning.

But when Tony had to spend money, he did. Although some of those expenditures showed up in the reimbursement requests, others did not. Sure that they would be disallowed, he did not even request reimbursement for them. As a result, the revolving funds, instead of remaining at their level of $40,000, went down and down and down.

Of course, some day OEO would want its revolving funds back. But that was the future. The children were there now. "We decided to go ahead and do it," says Tony, "and deal with the problem when it came up, by which time we'd have some reputation and some political clout. That's how things worked out, though much, *much* more painfully than we had hoped."

In fact, Tony and the parents spent little time brooding over the decision. "Although I was expending large sums of money," Tony admits, "I probably didn't have more than an average of 10 minutes a week to consider how I was doing it." The question of how the bills got paid seemed trivial, compared with the challenge of creating excellent schools for the children.

In a park behind the 106th Street nursery, children's shouts and laughter fill the air. Three boys are swarming over a jungle gym, while a fourth hangs upside down by his knees, as still as an opossum. Some girls are jumping rope, while Florence Ali, a parent teacher, looks on. *"Dos y dos son cuatro/Cuatro y dos son seis/Seis y dos son ocho/Y ocho, dos y seis,"* they chant as they take their turns.

The other parent teacher, Toni Perez, is sitting on a park bench, helping a little boy with a jammed zipper. And Lois Goldfrank, the professional teacher, is playing "monster" with half a dozen boys and girls. The children taunt the "monster," and then run away screaming as Lois hunches her shoulders, growls, and stalks off after them.

"That's all for now," Lois says finally. A graduate of Bryn Mawr with a master's degree from Bank Street College, the slender, brown-haired young woman is in her second year of teaching. Panting, she sits down on the bench, and a stocky five-year-old boy runs up to her, his brown corduroy winter coat flapping open.

"Teacher, look what I found," he yells.

"Oh, Wayne, those are crabapples," she says, looking at the small green fruit in his hand.

"Are they alive?"

"No. Once they fall off the tree, they're dead."

"But if I put them on the tree again, they'll be alive, won't they?"

"Why don't we try it, and see what happens. Where's the tree?"

Wayne grabs his teacher's hand, and pulls her to the spot where he found the crabapples. A few minutes later, Lois, Wayne, and two survivors from the monster game go inside to get some scotch tape.

So begins a month-long exploration of living and dying in the five-year-olds' classroom . . .

It is rest time—the hour after lunch when the children nap on their cots. Today is Lois's turn to put them to sleep, and she is with them in the classroom. Florence and Toni are sitting on a couch in the parents' lounge, drinking coffee and talking with Millie Rabinow, a psychiatric social worker who recently has come on staff as a part-time mental health consultant. "How are things going so far?" Millie asks.

"It's scary for me," says Toni. "I feel like all eyes are on me." Having started working as an assistant teacher in September, she is only in her second month of teaching. Florence and Millie reassure her. The discussion ranges from Toni's fears to the curriculum to individual children.

Finally, after about 45 minutes, Millie asks, "Wasn't Lois supposed to join us?"

"Oh shit!" Toni exclaims. "We forgot all about her!"

At that moment, the door to the classroom opens, and out comes a flustered, red-faced Lois. "I can't do it! I just can't do it. I've tried being firm with them. I've tried rubbing their backs. Nothing works. I no sooner get one to sleep than another pops up."

"We forgot all about you," Florence says, grinning. "Why didn't you tell us sooner you were having a hard time?"

A dark-skinned woman, short and powerfully built, Florence walks over to the classroom, and stands in the doorway with her arms folded, looking into the darkened room. *"Baja la cabeza y trata de dormirte* [Put your head down and try to sleep]," she says in a calm, firm tone. The buzz of conversation stops immediately. Two boys hiding behind a bookcase go to their cots. Three minutes later, Florence joins Lois, Toni, and Millie for the rest of the meeting . . .

The morning work period is in full swing. Skyscrapers are rising in the block area where Lois is working with six children. A lavish, if imaginary, breakfast is being prepared in the dollhouse corner. The rabbit is earning his carrots, enduring his daily round of cuddles and strokes. Florence is with three children who are playing with water, using funnels, tubes, and containers of many shapes and sizes. And Toni is simply bewildered.

Having just set out juice and cookies for the snack that will follow the work period, the 30–year-old mother of three looks around the room. Water play, block building, painting, rabbits—it's all so different from what she did in school. The jobs she held after dropping out of high school—assembler in a toy factory, mail clerk—certainly didn't prepare her for this either. Besides, in her family, she was always "the stupid one, the ignorant one." What am I doing here anyway? she wonders.

"Toni, draw me a picture of a doll," whines Karen, a chubby light-skinned girl with big brown eyes and two pigtails of straight dark-brown hair.

Toni puts her own thoughts aside, and follows Karen to a table where several children are drawing. She makes an outline of a doll for Karen. "Now you color it in," she says smiling.

As Karen sets to work, Toni feels a light tapping on her shoulder. It is Florence. "Can I talk to you for a minute?"

"Sure," says Toni, standing up. "What did I do wrong now?" They walk a few steps away from the table, and Florence whispers, "Don't do their drawing for them. If you do, they'll try to copy your drawing. If it doesn't come out the same, they'll get frustrated, and say they can't draw. So let them try to do it themselves."

Toni is still thinking about what Florence said when Lois comes up to her. "Toni, would you watch the block area for a few minutes? I'll be right back."

I wonder what trouble I can get into here, Toni says to herself as she enters the block area. The children's work is impressive. Two elaborate buildings, over four feet high, are nearing completion. Then Toni notices Nuncio, a wiry little boy, working by himself. While she watches, he tries twice to start a building. Both times it comes tumbling down. When on the third try, a wall of the building collapses once again, Nuncio angrily pushes the whole building down and starts kicking the rubble.

Toni freezes. What to do? She knows why his building is falling, and she wants to help. But should she? Suddenly, she hears a quiet voice behind her. It is Alice Graves, the educational director of the 106th Street nursery. "Go ahead, Toni," Alice says. "Go over and give him a hand." Toni goes over and shows Nuncio how to place the blocks so that they won't fall . . .

During the two-year period from 1966 to 1968, the Block Nurseries, with adequate funding and relative freedom from bureaucratic interference, created an excellent educational program for young children. Each of the schools' six classrooms had unique characteristics, but common to all was a distinctive approach to early childhood education. That approach—child-centered, but incorporating the perspectives of parents from East Harlem as well as those of middle-class professionals—jelled within a year after the nurseries opened. Its features come through clearly in the recollections of Lois Goldfrank, Florence Ali, and Toni Perez, who worked together with the five-year-olds at the 106th Street nursery during the 1966–67 school year.

"The block area was the center of our curriculum," recalls Lois, who as the professional teacher had major responsibility for planning children's activities. "That was where we did most of our work in social studies." The block area took up a quarter of the classroom, and extended into the dollhouse corner to encourage girls as well as boys to get involved. In the beginning of the year, Lois would get down on the floor with the children and help them build. By talking with them about their buildings, appreciating their work, and providing accessories (like rubber people, dollhouse furniture, little scraps of carpet), she engaged their interest and showed them the possibilities. Says Lois: "It wasn't long before they were building really fantastic hotels and apartment buildings. Some of the constructions were six feet high."

As the year went on, the play became more and more sophisticated. Ideas often came from the children. They built runways, houses, and even cities for the rabbit. One boy decided to build an animal of blocks. Other youngsters picked up on the idea, and for a while the block area was a menagerie of imaginary animals.

The teachers also made suggestions and helped the children relate blocks to other things they were learning. Lois cut pictures of buildings from magazines and put them up in the block area. The class went on trips—to such places as La Guardia airport, the Fulton fish market, the Guggenheim Museum—and looked at various kinds of buildings. Upon returning to the classroom, the youngsters would discuss what they had seen. Usually, a group of six or eight would decide to represent the experience in the block area.

Although block building, social studies, and science were Lois's favorite activities, the curriculum she developed with Toni and Florence also included painting, clay, water play, and cooking. The teachers spent time with children individually, teaching them words and numbers. The children did lots of dramatic play, acting out stories the teachers read them. Recalls Lois: "I can still see Nuncio shouting, 'Caps for sale! Caps for sale!'"

Some parents took issue with Lois on the teaching of reading. "A lot of people wanted me to teach five-year-olds reading right away," she says. "They felt that poor children in particular needed to learn to read early— and the earlier, the better. Other parents disagreed. They had heard of the philosophy of letting kids get ready to read, of not pushing them into reading. We argued about it strongly in class meetings.

"I compromised on the issue. I explained how activities like blocks and trips help get kids ready for reading. I brought in articles about the dangers of pushing kids into reading too early. But at the same time I also did a lot of reading activities. Some of the parents wanted formal instruction with primers. I certainly didn't do that. But I did things like making alphabet lotto, which taught them the alphabet through a game. I did much more with reading than I would have if left on my own, but I found ways to meet the parents' requests without compromising my principles."

When Lois thinks back on the children, her clearest memories are of the most difficult ones. "Emilio was a real concern of mine," she says. "In the course of the year, I must have visited his home 10 times. He was a tall boy, good-looking but poorly coordinated, hyperactive, and immature.

"When a kid gets to be five years old, you start thinking about what is going to happen to him in first grade. It was clear that Emilio was going to have a lot of trouble. He didn't speak in complete sentences in English, and his Spanish wasn't that great either. He went around making strange noises and strange faces. He had a lot of trouble playing with other kids, and had terrible temper tantrums.

"I remember that early in the year, some kids got interested in playing cowboys. I supported that for a while, and got Emilio involved. But he became the sheriff and started arresting everybody by running around and knocking them down. That was the day he threw the most incredible temper tantrum of all, when I stopped him from making all those 'citizen arrests.'

"One embarrassing thing for me was that I found out on a home visit that his mother gave him a bottle three times a day. I thought that was really awful—I was sure that was why he was so infantile. But then Toni told me that it was not unusual for Puerto Rican parents to give their kids bottles at that age, that it was a cultural custom. So that couldn't be the reason he was so infantile.

"Later I found out that he had been in the hospital for eight months when he was small. When he came out, his parents had babied him. They did too much for him, and didn't have the same expectations for him that they had for their other children.

"So I worked with his parents, trying to get them to stop pampering him. In the classroom, I spent time alone with him, helping him master skills like cutting, hammering, and using crayons. I taught him words and number concepts, and encouraged him to express his fears and aggressive feelings through drawing, painting, and block building rather than by hurting other children.

"He improved in many ways. His English got better, and that helped his relationships with the other kids. He felt proud of the new skills he was learning. By the end of the year, he was drawing a lot and talking out his fantasies. He would draw pictures of monsters in the doorway that were going to get him. We wrote books together. That was a big improvement because in dictating the stories, he was really relating to me. In the beginning of the year, he hadn't related to anyone. He even got to the point where sometimes he could tell me what was upsetting him instead of throwing a tantrum."

But whether the children were difficult or not, Lois's main strategy for reaching them was the curriculum. "I didn't do a lot of psychologizing," she says. "I spent time helping kids deal with feelings, but my clear priority was to have lots going on. With a room full of exciting activities, I found that problems other teachers had just didn't come up."

Although Lois provided the leadership in developing the curriculum, she was only one-third of the classroom team. Unlike at many schools, where parent "aides" are relegated to housekeeping chores, the parent teachers at the Block Nurseries had major classroom responsibilities. That was true even for someone like Toni, who was just starting out.

Toni has good memories of her year with Lois and Florence, although as a first-year teacher she had a lot to learn. Most difficult was knowing when to intervene in children's activities and when not to. "Being a mother,

I had a tendency to do everything for them," she admits. "I had to learn to step aside, and to let them be creative."

It helped that she had good models. "I learned from seeing how Lois talked with kids and what she did with them," Toni recalls. "I was impressed by the way she'd sit on the floor with them. At first, I thought it was strange. But then I asked myself: 'Why do I always have to be above them? Why not come down to their level sometimes?' I loosened up and started to play with them more.

"I learned better ways of dealing with children. I was very rough with my own kids before I got involved with the Block Nurseries. After I started teaching, I began to understand children better. I learned that when you discipline a child, you have to say why. If you tell a child to sit down for 10 minutes, you've got to explain the reason. If you don't, he won't know any better the next time. It's the same thing when a kid gets mad at another kid and hits him. You stop the fight, but you let them talk it out.

"I learned my way of disciplining from Florence. I used to watch everything she'd do and then try out her techniques. They worked. When the kids were all in an uproar, she would talk to them in a firm, but loving way. They knew they couldn't pull no shit over her, because she wouldn't allow it. But they knew she cared for them too."

Toni doesn't remember any disagreements with Lois over curriculum. "At first I had my doubts about water play," she admits. "But then I saw how it was helping the kids learn measuring. I would always ask, 'Why are we doing this?' And Lois would always give me an explanation. She encouraged me too. She'd say, 'Toni, if you want to try something, tell Florence and me, and we'll help you.' That really got me to try my own things."

One of Toni's "own things" was cooking. "One day a group of about six kids and I walked over to *La Marqueta*," she recalls. "We went from stall to stall, looking at the different kinds of Spanish vegetables and saying their names. '*Es un aguacate!*' they shouted. '*Son pimientos!*' Then we bought plantains, avocados, peppers, onions, rice, and sausages.

"When we got back to the classroom, some of the kids cut up the avocados. Others cut up the onions and peppers—for the rice, to give it taste. And we made *arroz con salchichas, plantanos fritos, y aguacates.*"

Another high point for Toni was helping Lois and the children build a model of 106th Street from First Avenue to Central Park. "We took walks with the kids along 106th Street between the East River and Central Park," she explains. "When we came back to the classroom, we got them to talk about what they'd seen. Then they decided who would make what. They built the model on a big piece of cardboard on a table. The kids painted in the streets and playgrounds, built the elevated train tracks that cross 106th

Street at Park Avenue, and used small wooden blocks to make the build-ings. It took two or three weeks to make the whole thing."

Although all three teachers spoke Spanish, Toni had the best command of the language. Her bilingual work was probably her greatest contribu-tion that first year.

"Most of the kids in the class were Spanish-speaking," she says. "Their parents wanted them to learn English because they'd soon be going to first grade. So teaching the kids English was one of our main goals. But we didn't do it through a structured program. We talked with the kids in English most of the time. We used Spanish when a child didn't seem to understand. If I said, 'Go get me a book,' and the kid gave me a dumb look, I'd say, '*Vete buscarme un libro.*' Then I'd repeat the English again.

"When we noticed that some kids weren't following the stories Lois was reading, I started taking a group of kids to another part of the room and reading them stories in Spanish. Or if I didn't have a Spanish book, I'd use an English book and translate it into Spanish as I went along.

"We put up signs around the room in Spanish and English—blocks, *bloques*; sink, *lavador*; and so on—and we sang Spanish songs. We had a rhyme the kids used to love that went '*Pollito*, chicken, *gallina*, hen/*lapiz*, pencil, *pluma*, pen/*ventana*, window, *puerta*, door/*maestra*, teacher, *piso*, floor.' Those were the kinds of things we used to do. The kids picked up English very fast."

In contrast to Toni, who spent much of the year struggling with self-doubt and insecurity, Florence was perfectly clear about what should hap-pen in a classroom and did not hesitate to say so. "I battled with Lois Goldfrank," Florence says, "and we got very close.

"Lois had to realize that she couldn't teach the kids middle-class edu-cation. It didn't make any sense to stand up there and talk about daddy, when some of the children had never seen a daddy. I felt, 'No. We don't even discuss daddy. We discuss mom and where mom is coming from and how to stabilize mom.'

"I'd grown up in the neighborhood. I knew what the problems were, because I was one of the examples. I'd grown up without a father, and I didn't have a 'father image.' Lois couldn't tell me that I didn't live the way I did.

"She had her master's degree, and there I was, without a high school diploma, saying things like, 'Why do you let Wayne treat you that way?'

"'Well, he's a very angry boy, and he needs a place to let that anger out.'

"'Come on now, Lois. When you say things like that, you're coming from Boston. I was born and raised here, and I know it's not right for him to hit you and curse at you that way.'

"We just battled until she saw the need of what I was saying. One day she came to me and said, 'How do *you* think we should deal with Wayne?' We discussed it, and finally she agreed with me. 'I'll be real clear that he can let his anger out by screaming or hitting a pillow if he wants to,' she said, 'but I won't let him hit me.' I could see that she wasn't coming from Boston. So I said, 'Okay, that's cool. Let's try it.' And it worked."

Florence also had differences with Lois over how certain children should be expected to relate to the group activities. "Some kids were withdrawn," Florence explains, "and you tried all different ways to motivate them into the play areas, but it just didn't work. Lois and I argued about what to do. She felt we should just bring those children into the activities with the other children. She had set up the curriculum, and she felt all the kids should tackle block building, water play, painting, and so on. I said, 'No. We should motivate those children where they are. There are three people in the classroom. Why should I be in block building or some other activity when a child is sitting over there by himself? By not joining the group, that child is saying, 'Help me! Don't leave me alone!'

"Gradually, Lois came around to seeing what I was saying: that we had to do something special with those children. And I was able to do it. I was able to come to a child who wasn't fitting in and find a way to communicate. I read to them. If they wanted to talk, I listened. I became their shelter. Eventually, once they came to trust me, they opened up and started to get involved."

Nicky was such a child. He hadn't talked all through his previous year in the four-year-olds' classroom, and now he wasn't talking in the "fives," either. Although he sometimes took part in activities like painting and block building, he remained absolutely silent.

All three teachers agreed to give him special warmth and support, to stop other children from teasing him, and to encourage him to develop friendships. They made a point of including him, asking him questions, and making sure other children did not answer before he had a chance. But Florence was the teacher who got most involved.

One day, while she was with him at rest time, he finally spoke. "The lights were out, and all the other kids were asleep," she recalls. "Nicky just leaned over and whispered in my ear. I was so excited! Within a few minutes, the phones all over the school were ringing with the news that Nicky had talked.

"From that day on, we had long conversations every day at rest time. He never did talk to the other kids, but he would whisper to us. It turned out that he knew everything: the words to our songs, the names of the colors, the different kinds of trucks. He was aware of everything that was going on."

Florence also got involved with the children who had frequent outbursts of temper, broke the limits for classroom behavior, or acted out in destructive ways. "I had all the humdingers," she says. "I always had to deal with the kids who had the most problems. And I did. Once they understood there were certain things I just wouldn't allow, we got along fine. They saw I wasn't trying to be mean to them, but that I was just being fair—and firm."

Her work with Nydia is an example. "Nydia was a tough little street kid," Florence recalls. "I used to bring clothes for her from home. She was always testing the limits.

"One day, we took the kids out. As we were waiting to cross the street on our way back, she broke away and ran across by herself. A car was coming—thank God it didn't hit her!—and I was very upset. I walked into the school with Nydia in my arms. 'She's not coming back to school no more,' I said.

"'What happened?' Lois asked.

"'Don't ask me nothin'. I ain't even gonna discuss it. She's just not comin' to school.' I was still nervous and shaking.

"'So now you're going to direct the school?' Lois said. 'You're going to put people out?'

"'I don't care. She ain't comin' back.'

"I carried her home—she lived on the top floor—and I told her mother what she had done. 'She can't come back to school for a week,' I said. 'Until a week is up, I won't accept her in.'

"A week went by, and then another week, and she didn't show up. During the third week, I made a home visit to see how she was doing. She was glad to see me, and I knew she had missed school. 'You can come tomorrow,' I said.

"She came back, and I never had any more problems with her—not with crossing the street, not with anything. Lois saw this. Nydia wasn't my child—I couldn't put her on my lap and spank her. But she had to learn that there were certain things she just couldn't do."

This, then, was the Block Nurseries' approach to early childhood education. The educational philosophy was "the Bank Street model": child-centered, experience-based, informed by the latest research in child development. Equally important was parent control: institutional arrangements designed to ensure that the perspectives of the children's parents would shape classroom practice as well.

Each classroom had three teachers—a professional (from "Boston" or elsewhere) and two parents (from East Harlem). Each of the adults had unique strengths, and, despite differences in class, culture, and education, they strove to work together on the basis of equality and mutual respect.

Every day, after the children left at 3:00, the classroom team met to wrestle with issues of curriculum and individual children and to plan the next day's activities. In the process, the three teachers became close and learned from each other. The professional teacher was not the unquestioned authority. She was expected to provide leadership, but her influence depended on her powers of persuasion and the effectiveness of her work with the children, not on the prerogatives of her role. She did not jealously guard her expertise, but shared it with her co-teachers, as they shared theirs with her. The result was that the children got the full benefit of the talents, skills, and wisdom of all three people.

The founding principle of the Block Nurseries was that this kind of close collaboration between parents and professionals was absolutely necessary to provide the best possible education for the children. To make that idea a reality in classrooms was the main focus of the Block Nurseries during their first two years.

"He's not going to drive me insane!" Sonia had told herself after her encounter with David, the four-going-on-fourteen-year-old she had met on her first day of teaching. "Somehow I'm gonna think faster."

But David pushed her to the limit. "I felt like taking that kid and killing him," she recalls. "He used to look at me from top to bottom like he was undressing me, and make me feel so uncomfortable. With the other kids, he went through a whole routine of acting tough. He'd call them stupid. He'd talk to them, but when they'd talk to him, he'd say, 'That's it! That's it!'

"'David,' I said, 'it can't be like that—you doing all the talking and shutting everyone else up.' So I started talking to him.

"Now it happened that Jeffrey lived in the same building that David lived in. I could tell that David wanted to be friends with Jeffrey, but David was getting out of proportion being cute. Nobody wanted to be with David because he was using being cute as a negative gesture to put people off. So I said, 'David, since you want to be funny—but funny in a way that you are not going to have any friends—I'm going to help you. I want to be your friend, if you'll let me. And even if you don't let me, I'm still going to be your friend.'

"One day, the class was getting ready to go to Central Park. 'Are you ready to go to Central Park?' I asked David.

"'Central Park?'

"'Yes, Central Park.'

"'I've never been to Central Park,' he said. I was shocked. How could a family live so close to Central Park and never take their kid?

"Well, we went, and I made a big deal of it. He was so happy! My God! He ran; he touched; he asked questions; he was the picture of happiness. When we came back, I said, 'Want to tell me a story about the park?' And the story he told was about how big Central Park is, and about how he had seen bicycles and grass and trees and cars and squirrels and how he had loved the swings. He was so happy that he forgot to be cute when he talked to me.

"That trip to the park was the turning point. He got to be friends with Jeffrey, and he started changing. He opened up to me. He said his parents were very strict, and probably had never been to Central Park either. 'They aren't interested,' he said.

"In June 1966, my son Richie was graduating from junior high. His graduation was the same day as a party we were having for the kids in the school. I said, 'David, I won't be here early tomorrow morning because I have to go to my son's graduation.'

"'You have to?' he asked.

"'Yes,' I said.

"'Nobody's going to be here with me. My mother isn't coming to the party. No one in my family is coming.'

"'Don't worry,' I said. 'I'll be here.' What I did was to take Richie's picture ahead of time. The minute the graduation was finished, I took a taxi to the school. When I walked in, there was David, sitting alone in his white shirt and his tie, holding back the tears.

"'This is the time you come! This is the time you come!' he said. (He was repeating himself, just the way he had on the first day.)

"'I told you I'd be late,' I said, 'but I promised you I'd come—and here I am. Come and hold my hand.'

"Until the last child was gone, he held my hand close. He and Jeffrey were the only ones whose parents didn't come to the party. I could see they were upset that their parents didn't come. But I also could tell that they felt secure, knowing I was there."

Sonia and David were not the only ones who struggled during the Block Nurseries' opening months. Only one of the professionals originally hired by the parents survived past June 1966. But despite the turmoil and the turnover, the period saw two developments that would shape the future of the Block Nurseries: The parents made a clear decision about the kind of education they wanted for their children, and they found an educational director who knew how to make it happen in classrooms.

The original group of teachers did not represent a consistent philosophy of education. To decide on an approach, the parents would have to see what actually worked best in their schools. It was partly a process of elimination. The person hired as director of the 106th Street nursery struggled from the beginning. On Tony's recommendation, the board asked "the crying director" for her resignation, and she left in February 1966.

To fill the position, Tony recommended Alice Graves, teacher of the three-year-olds and the first person the parents had interviewed. According to Tony: "Alice expected a lot, but she was loving and soft-spoken. She balanced the line between firmness and very gentle support."

She also got along well with the parent teachers, who called her "Alice," not "Mrs. Graves," and liked the way she shared what she knew from her 13 years of experience as a teacher. "I'm embarrassed to say it, but back then I didn't even know how to make play dough," admits Rosie Gueits. "I learned that and lots of other things from Alice. No matter how simple a thing was, she never made you feel like a dummy that you didn't know it. She was compassionate and inspiring. She taught so you wanted to keep on learning. She was a worrier, but she encouraged people. 'Keep trying,' she'd say, 'and you'll do it.'"

In March the board hired Alice to be director of the 106th Street nursery. The shy, gentle demeanor of the new director was deceptive. "She was an easy person, but very firm," says Rosie Gueits. "She hardly ever raised her voice above a whisper. But when she needed to, she could put you in your place with just a few well-chosen words." Soon she would clash with a teacher whose ideas about early childhood education were very different from her own.

A charming young Filipino woman, Estelle Estrada was just completing a course of training in the Montessori method when she came for her original interview with the board in September 1965. Although Estelle spoke with great enthusiasm about the approach, the parents remained skeptical. "We liked Estelle," explains Connie. "She was nice, and open. But we hired her with reservations about the method. We felt it might be too strict for young children."

Estelle was competent, and her classroom ran smoothly. But Rosie Gueits, one of the parent teachers in the classroom along with Sonia, soon decided that the approach was not for her. "She got along better with Sonia," Rosie explains. "I found it too strict."

When Rosie complained that the children weren't developing their language because Estelle had them doing so much quiet work on their own, Estelle brushed off her concern, saying that it was the Montessori method.

Estelle's attitude also put people off. "She was very formal, very professional," Tony observes. "She insisted on being called 'Miss Estrada.'"

The board asked Alice for her views. "Montessori puts great emphasis on work," she replied. "The children have to sit down and work at specific tasks designed by adults. I don't think that's the best way for children to learn. I believe in the importance of *play*. And by 'play' I mean an activity that's really open-ended—one in which children can use their own ideas, feelings, and imaginations."

Estelle's days at the school were numbered. In April, after a run-in with Alice, she resigned, and the Block Nurseries' brief experiment with Montessori came to an end. Several things explain the parents' preference for Alice and what she called the "child development approach" over Montessori, a method originally designed specifically for working-class children. Tony favored Alice's approach, and he was influential, of course; but equally important was Alice's effectiveness in the classroom. As Tony put it, "I felt the classrooms should be a certain way. Alice showed they could be *good* that way. The parents had Estelle's moderately competent Montessori classroom to compare with Alice's superb progressive class-room." Alice's style and methods also supported the founding parents' basic impulses, as expressed by Connie in their initial meeting ("We want to treat our kids on an individual basis") or by Sonia who, as the first day of school approached, pictured herself "letting a child sit on my lap and holding him, like a mother." Finally, while Estelle acted as though her professional training made her superior to the parents, Alice related to people as a peer, relatively free of class bias.

But if choosing Alice represented progress, the parents still faced serious challenges in their effort to create good schools. Foremost among them were recruiting and holding professional teachers.

By the end of June 1966, when the centers closed for summer vacation, the Block Nurseries did not have a single professional teacher. Alice had left the classroom to become educational director of the 106th Street nursery; Estelle had resigned; another had quit; and two had been fired.

Both firings grew out of incidents in which teachers hit children. Lydia Rios, board member and parent teacher, describes what happened in the case of Arlene, a professional teacher at the Madison Avenue nursery.

"Arlene had a lot of trouble handling the kids. One day I saw her drag a little girl named Sarah across the room. Sarah was screaming, and Arlene was being very rough with her. When I saw it, I got sick. I couldn't believe that a teacher would do that to a child. I went to Tony and told him.

"'What do you think we should do?' he asked.

"'I think she should be fired immediately,' I said. 'Our kids shouldn't have to suffer. We started our own school so that this wouldn't happen. If we're going to allow it anyway, we might as well put our kids in public school.'

"But Tony felt it was important to follow procedures. 'Let's wait, and give her another chance,' he said. He talked with her and told her that if she did anything like that again, she was going to be out.

"Meanwhile, I couldn't work any more. I stayed home, because I couldn't work with a teacher who treated children like that. About two weeks later, it happened again. She got mad at Joey and slapped him. That's when we took steps and fired her."

Although no one doubted the need to fire Arlene, her difficulties (and those of the other teachers) did not stem only from incompetence. Noise, interruptions, and lack of privacy in the makeshift storefront classrooms were constant sources of frustration. And during those first months (January through June 1966), classroom work was hampered also by tension between parents and professionals. According to Joe Gueits: "In the early days, there was a definite separation of classes. After the kids went home, the staff would break up, and you'd see the parents on one side and the professionals on the other side. The friction came out of disagreements over the roles of professional teachers and assistant teachers. Some professionals felt the assistants were only there to wipe noses and clean. Some assistants felt they knew more because they had four or five kids and the professional was an unmarried woman just out of college."

Ironically, firing Arlene was a significant step toward resolving the situation, for one source of the tension was uncertainty about who was really in charge. Although the Block Nurseries were parent-controlled on paper, many parents harbored suspicions that "parent control" would prove to be an empty slogan.

Lydia's behavior illustrates the point. When Tony refused to fire the teacher immediately, she stayed home. Tony might be right that procedures had to be followed, but how could she be sure that he wasn't just siding with the professional against the parents? Time would tell. Meanwhile, Lydia was not about to make a fool of herself. In a sense, it was a test: "Will parents *really* be listened to?" If so, Arlene would have to go. If not, Lydia had better things to do with her time.

As it turned out, the firing of Arlene established two important principles. The first was that teachers who didn't live up to the Block Nurseries' standards would indeed be fired. The second was that although teachers could be fired, fairness required an orderly process.

Tensions and principles aside, the troubles of the professional teachers meant that in the early months major responsibility for keeping the classrooms running smoothly fell on the parent teachers. Fortunately, they were equal to the challenge.

Almost all of the parent teachers were Puerto Rican women in their twenties, mothers of young children. They had grown up in East Harlem, the children of immigrants from Puerto Rico. A few had high school diplomas, but the majority did not. Although they were housewives, most also had worked outside the home, as sales clerks or factory workers. Some had been welfare recipients. Among them were extraordinarily talented and energetic people who not only brought great gifts to the classroom, but also didn't give up easily.

Lois Goldfrank remembers Florence: "She and I were both 25 years old. But I had just gotten married and had no children. Florence was the mother of five girls, ages ten, nine, eight, seven, and six. She got up every morning, got those kids dressed, braided their hair, made their breakfasts, and got them off to school. Then she came to school and worked the same hours I did in the classroom. After school, she went home and did all the cooking and cleaning. As a board member she often came back to the school for meetings in the evening. For a time, she was going to school four days a week in the evening to get her high school equivalency. As if that were not enough, her marriage was breaking up, and she was going through a lot of stuff around that. She was simply a phenomenal person."

It was no accident that people like Florence found their way to the Block Nurseries. East Harlem was (and still is) full of women with strength and ability whose paths have been blocked by racism and sexism. Potential professionals or executives, artists or activists, they languish as factory workers or sales clerks. For women such as these, teaching at the Block Nurseries offered a special opportunity.

But although the parents managed to hold the schools together, the situation was far from ideal. If the schools were going to be outstanding, the board would have to find and hire some professional teachers who were imaginative, competent, and committed to working with parents. Fortunately, during the summer of 1966, they accomplished that. Their success in hiring professional teachers that summer was due to their greater clarity about what they were looking for. They also had better candidates to choose from. Word about the schools had fallen on the ears of young people who, touched by the civil rights movement, were looking for ways to join in the struggle for racial justice. In the summer of 1966, the Block Nurseries' board found itself choosing teachers from the cream of a generation.

The people they hired were middle-class women in their early twenties. One was Black; the rest were White. One was married; the others were single. Only one had grown up in New York City; the others had come from small towns and suburbs. All were graduates of elite colleges; all but one had done a year of postgraduate work at Bank Street College of Education. All had been involved in some kind of political activity in college (on peace or civil rights issues) and saw a parent-controlled school in East Harlem as a place where they could continue to act on their commitment to social justice. As Lois Goldfrank put it, "The Block Nurseries were a way for me to bring my work and my politics together."

fall of 1966, the elements of an outstanding program were be- to come together at the Block Nurseries, but there was still a long to go. The young teaching staff had to master a demanding approach to early childhood education. Equally important, they had to learn to work together, and that meant dealing well with class differences.

"I felt like another kid in there learning," says Lydia Rios, recalling her first year as a parent teacher in the Madison Avenue nursery. "Nobody knew I felt that way, but I did. Water play, blocks, clay—I would do exactly what the kids were doing. I found it fascinating. It was the first time I had had those experiences myself.

"It helped me with my kids at home. Before, I'd always said, 'You can't play with water—you might make a mess.' Now, I began to put out water for them. I'd get clay. We'd make play dough. What I learned at the school I'd bring home to do with my kids, and they enjoyed it."

From September 1966 to June 1968, the Block Nurseries enjoyed a set of conditions that made them ideal for adult learning. The staff were receptive, enthusiastic about the novelty of the schools and the new opportunities the situation offered them. Working conditions were favorable: Classrooms were newly renovated; funding for educational equipment and supplies was adequate; educational directors, unburdened by paperwork, could spend 80% of their time in classrooms; with the school day lasting only until 2:30, classroom teams could meet for an hour daily.

There was tight accountability. The staff was accountable to the parent board, and the classrooms were like fishbowls with Tony, the educational directors, and parents frequently dropping in and always nearby. "I was not only allowed to be the best kind of teacher I could be, I was supported in being it," observes Susan Kosoff, a professional teacher. "When I had taught in a public school on Cape Cod, the principal had never come to visit my class—not once, during the whole year. At the Block Nurseries, Tony came by; Eileen, who taught in the classroom next door, gave me lots of support; and the parents always challenged me, because I felt so accountable to them. Lots of jobs would have been more comfortable, but to grow, sometimes you have to inconvenience yourself."

In this climate of excitement, ideal working conditions, and accountability, Alice Graves and Margaret Adams (director of the Madison Avenue nursery) trained their staffs in the child development approach. Like Lydia, all the teachers learned just from being in the classrooms with each other and with the children. But Alice and Margaret exerted strong leadership. "The schools moved in the direction they did because we had meetings every single day to talk over what was happening," observes Alice. "If we had not met regularly, we never could have done it."

Alice's work with Sonia illustrates the process. "I suggested that the children in Sonia's class do some painting," Alice recalls. "Sonia asked, 'What should we have them paint?'

"'Little kids don't necessarily want to paint anything in particular,' I said. 'They just want to put paint on paper.'

"'I think they want an idea from us about what to do,' she replied. 'We should draw the outline of something for them to paint in.' I said I disagreed, Sonia launched into one of her long speeches, and we were off to the races. Around and around we went.

"Fortunately, Rosie Gueits was there, and she didn't argue with me. She argued with Sonia. Sonia was able to listen to Rosie, and the two of them agreed that we'd try to do it. I told them to watch very carefully, and listen to what the children were saying.

"When we met the next day, I asked, 'How do you think it went? Did the children seem to be having fun?'

"'Yes, they were excited,' Rosie and Sonia agreed.

"'Tell me exactly what you saw,' I said.

"'They were really putting the paint on very carefully,' Rosie began. They went on to describe how they'd seen the children experimenting with various colors and trying hard to control their brushes. On the basis of their own observations, Rosie and Sonia acknowledged that the activity was worthwhile."

While Alice helped children's strengths come out through exciting curricula, Millie Rabinow's tools were a thorough knowledge of child psychology and a finely tuned sensitivity to people. A social worker with clinical training, Millie served the Block Nurseries as a part-time mental health consultant from 1966 until her death from leukemia in 1968. A frail, gray-haired woman in her late fifties, Millie was soft-spoken, nonjudgmental, and always willing to go out of her way to help people. Loved and respected by everyone, she provided personal counseling, ran workshops on child-rearing and child development, trained and supervised the parent coordinators, and helped teachers find better ways of dealing with difficult children.

Adelaide Jacquet, an African-American woman who served as a professional teacher at the nurseries from 1966 to 1968, was one of many deeply influenced by Millie's work: "Millie helped me with lots of kids, but the one who stands out is Julio. Julio was hyperactive, loud, and sometimes uncontrollable. He would go around making strange sounds like 'rat-tat-tat' and 'pow!' If some blocks fell down, he might stand still, looking shocked, and then dive under a table. He was in a world of his own. His mother was a nervous older woman, anxious and overprotective."

"'Julio is a very strange little boy,' I told Millie in a meeting one day. 'But I guess if I had a mother like his, I'd be strange too.'

"'Let's not make any judgments until we know more about what's going on,' Millie said."

Millie guided the classroom team through a process of observation and discussion to determine what was causing Julio's strange behavior. The breakthrough came on a trip to nearby Ward's Island. Talking excitedly to Carlos, a Spanish-speaking parent teacher, Julio said that Ward's Island with its grass and trees reminded him of the Dominican Republic. It turned out that Julio and his mother had been traumatized by violence they had witnessed during the revolution there.

"Once we realized that," recalls Adelaide, "we could provide reassurance. We encouraged his mother to come around more, and she started feeling more comfortable. We also wondered why we hadn't figured it out sooner. It seemed so obvious. But that's not unusual. A kid does things that annoy you, and you immediately jump to conclusions. In thinking about children Millie took great time and care. Since we respected her so much, we started thinking about kids that way too. Mostly because of her, the schools became places where people thought about individual kids and how to relate the program to their needs."

While striving to create an effective child-centered curriculum and address the needs of individual children, staff members also were trying, quite consciously, to bring out the best in each other across barriers of race and class. That's what made the Block Schools' brand of progressive education distinctive.

The founders of the Block Nurseries believed that reversing the usual power relationships by investing decision-making authority in a parent board was a necessary condition for dealing well with class and racial differences. But they soon realized that this was not sufficient. They also needed strong leadership, willing to confront people when they acted out of old patterns and then to support them in trying new behavior.

Alice's work with Rosie Tirado, a new parent teacher, illustrates this. Alice noticed that Judy, the professional teacher, would come in on Monday with the week's plan, including specific tasks assigned to Rosie and Ellie (the other parent teacher). It wasn't that she never gave the parents anything important to do, but she was making all the decisions. "It's fine with me," Rosie told Alice. "I don't know how to plan anyway."

"Of course you don't—because you haven't been involved in it," said Alice. "In our society, middle-class people write the directions, and poor people are supposed to follow them. But we're changing that. Here we all share everything."

With Alice's support, Rosie began working in various areas of the classroom, not just the doll corner where she felt most comfortable. If she was assigned to an activity like cooking, then she, not Judy, decided what to cook, bought the food, and wrote up the recipe. The three teachers began to take turns doing the weekly plan. When it came time for her week, Rosie knew she could get help from Alice, Judy, and Ellie, but she also knew *she* was responsible for it.

Rosie came into conflict with Judy over cleaning. "After lunch, I'd go and clean up everybody's table," Rosie recalls. "Ellie would tease me: 'There goes Rosie with her sponge and Ajax.' Alice didn't like it. She felt I should be with the kids at that time. But I wasn't going to put the kids to sleep, leaving all that mess.

"One day Judy said, 'It's okay, Rosie. I already cleaned it.'

"'Judy, that's the thing. You never clean the table right. It's filthy, Judy.' Then when the kids get up, they have to play in that mess. And look at all the food under the table.'

"'Oh, okay, okay,' she said. Then she looked at me. 'You're mad at me, aren't you.'

"'No, Judy. It's just that first of all you shouldn't let the kids play with the food. And then when lunch is over, you shouldn't leave all that mess.'

"We got close, and she started helping more. She got so she'd take the broom away from me when I was sweeping the classroom. 'Let me do it, Rosie!'"

Every day, when the children were taking their afternoon nap, the teachers would meet to share what they'd done that morning and to think about the next day. To Alice, a "break" was a time to talk about children and learning.

Alice told the teachers to encourage the children to use the names of things when they asked for them. "But I don't know the names of all the things myself," Rosie protested.

"That's where the three of you need to work together," Alice insisted. "By next week, I want you to know everything in this classroom by name—all the kitchen things, the block shapes, the kinds of paper, and so on. If you don't know what something is called, ask Judy or Ellie. And let's put labels on things all over the room. Children don't come to nursery school just to play and take a nap."

Many of the parents had deeply engrained tendencies to put themselves down. To begin to share their talents in the classroom, they needed, above all, to feel respected and listened to. Toni Perez describes one of the turning points for her in that process. "We were having a staff meeting with Millie Rabinow," she recalls, "and along came the word 'masturbation.' I didn't know what the hell they were talking about. After it had gone on for about 15 minutes with me just listening, I gave Rosie Gueits a funny look.

"'What?' she asked.

"'What is masturbation?' I whispered.

"She just looked at me. 'Toni, you mean you don't know what masturbation is?'

"'No, I've never heard of the damn word,' I said. So she explained it, using words familiar to me.

"Millie noticed that we were whispering and asked what we were talking about. 'Don't say nothing!' I whispered to Rosie.

"But Millie just waited. Finally, Rosie said, 'Toni has something to say.'

"'Oh my God, Rosie!' I said. 'Why did you have to say that?'

"I was embarrassed as hell, but I explained that I hadn't understood what they meant by the word 'masturbation.' I knew what it was—I had my own word for it—but I didn't know the word they were using.

"Though I felt embarrassed, Millie didn't laugh at me. 'If you've got something to say,' she said, 'don't be afraid. Don't say it just to me or to one person; say it to everybody so that everybody can hear what you have to say.'

"When Millie said that, I felt more confidence. It made me feel that people would really listen to me without putting me down. I had never been one to talk in staff meetings. I never used to say a word. After that, I started talking. They couldn't shut me up."

It was myriad incidents like these with Rosie Tirado and Toni Perez that opened up new kinds of working relationships between parents and professionals at the Block Nurseries. As a result, a tremendous amount of learning took place, and strong bonds of friendship formed across class and racial lines.

Reality fell far short of the vision. Professional teachers were still paid considerably more than parent teachers and took more than an equal share of responsibility. Some professionals put lots of energy into training their assistants, but others did so only when pushed. Some parents eagerly sought new responsibilities, but others withdrew at the slightest excuse.

But the Block Schools' relative sophistication in dealing with race and class distinguished them from many other social change organizations of the time, which were weakened or destroyed by turmoil along these societal fault lines. And although serving as parent teachers was a significant form of parent participation, there were many more.

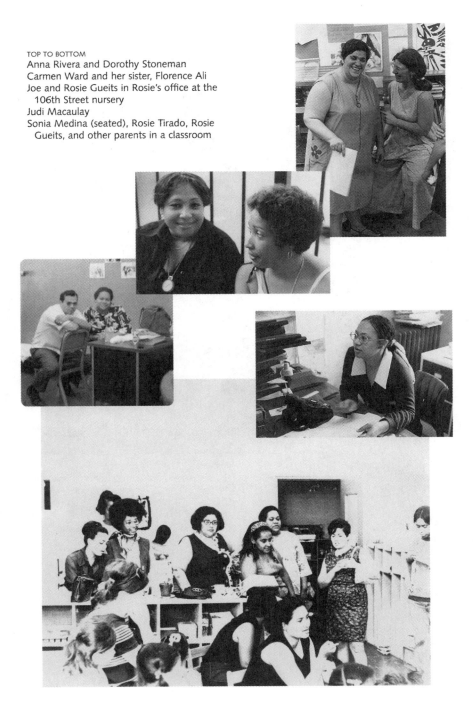

TOP TO BOTTOM
Anna Rivera and Dorothy Stoneman
Carmen Ward and her sister, Florence Ali
Joe and Rosie Gueits in Rosie's office at the
  106th Street nursery
Judi Macaulay
Sonia Medina (seated), Rosie Tirado, Rosie
  Gueits, and other parents in a classroom

TOP TO BOTTOM
Tony Ward
Rosie Tirado and the author
The author teaches a lesson to second
  graders while Lydia Rios looks on
Rosie Gueits on the day she received her
  bachelor's degree from Goddard College
Carmen Ward

3

Power to the Parents

It's rest time, and the three-year-olds are lying quietly on their cots. Barbara Slemmer, their teacher, is tiptoeing toward the classroom door when she hears a faint whimper. The young woman with long red hair pauses and listens. One of the children has started to cry. Making her way toward the sound in the semidarkness, she sees that it's Eduardo. Sitting down on the edge of his cot, she begins rubbing his back. "What's wrong?" she whispers.

"I want my Teddy bear," whines the boy.

"Maybe your mother will let you bring it tomorrow. I'll talk to her when she comes to pick you up today." She continues to rub his back gently. As he drifts off to sleep, she thinks about the shy, frightened little boy. He's hardly talked to anyone since starting school a week ago. Why hasn't he brought his Teddy bear? she wonders. On a home visit, she learned that Eduardo has a new baby sister. Knowing that the boy would be going through two major adjustments—to school and to the new baby—she suggested that he bring along a favorite toy for the first few days. But he has brought nothing.

"I think Eduardo misses his Teddy bear," Barbara tells his mother when she comes to pick him up that afternoon.

"Yes, I know," says Nilda Ramirez, a small woman with delicate features. "But my husband won't let him take it to school. He says it's too childish." After a brief conversation, Mrs. Ramirez agrees to talk to her husband. "I'll try," she says, "but I don't think he's going to change his mind."

When Eduardo comes in the next day without his Teddy bear, Barbara asks Lydia Rios, the parent coordinator, for help. "Oh yes. I've known Nilda and Sam for a long time," Lydia says. "They live on my block. I'll see what I can do."

Lydia phones Nilda, who admits that she hasn't discussed it yet with Sam. Lydia pushes her. Two hours later Nilda calls Lydia back. "We talked for a long time," she says. "He didn't change his mind, but he said he'd talk to you today when he picks up Eduardo."

At 3:00, Lydia, Barbara, and Sam sit down on tiny children's chairs in the classroom. In Spanish, with Lydia occasionally translating for Barbara, they discuss Eduardo's Teddy bear. "My son almost died at birth," says Sam, a husky man with short, curly black hair. "He was born fighting for his life, and if he's going to make it in this world, he's going to have to keep right on fighting. That's why I tell my wife she's got to stop babying him. I don't want him to go soft on me. He's not a baby anymore. It's time for him to grow up."

"Sam," Lydia says smiling, "with you for a father, he'll be a fighter all right! You don't have to worry about that!" Sam laughs. "We're not saying you should baby him. But don't forget he's only three. This is the first time he's been away from home. Lots of kids bring a favorite toy with them when they first start school."

By the end of the 45–minute meeting, Lydia has managed to persuade Sam to allow his son to take the Teddy bear to school and not to belittle him for "childish" behavior. As Barbara anticipated, the security provided by the Teddy bear helps the boy make a successful adjustment to school.

Connie Arevalo (whom we met in Chapter 1) was the Block Nurseries' first parent coordinator. An outgoing young Puerto Rican woman, Connie was one of Carmen Ward's original 111th Street group. As a mother of two small boys, she had taken immediately to Carmen's idea of starting nursery schools. "I wasn't working then," she explains, "and I got very excited about it. I started reading books about preschool, and going to meetings. Before long, I was hooked. I used to sleep the school, eat the school, and think the school—it took over my whole life."

Connie became chair of the board of directors, helped canvass for children, took part in the staff training sessions, and began to spread the word about the schools. She talked with dozens of people—friends, neighbors, families she met in her canvassing, and complete strangers who dropped in off the street. Barely able to contain her enthusiasm, she had no trouble drawing them in.

Although Connie was officially on payroll as a clerk-typist, everyone soon recognized her effectiveness with parents, not only in promoting the schools but in listening and lending support. By following her natural inclinations, she was creating a new job that was obviously needed. In January, not long after the opening of the 106th Street nursery, Connie left her position as clerk-typist to become "parent coordinator."

Nobody sat down and wrote a job description for the position. Connie's responsibilities evolved naturally out of her responses to the parents' needs. She found herself organizing social events, showing visitors around, recruiting parents for the board of directors, doing counseling, helping parents deal with hospitals and the welfare department, advising the executive director on school policy, and doing all she could to make the centers comfortable and welcoming.

Connie drew parents in, not only to enroll their children but to serve as volunteers in classrooms, as members of school committees, and as staff members. By doing that, she literally built the schools. An example is how she got Lydia Rios involved.

Connie went frequently to 104th Street to visit her mother. There she met Lydia, who lived in the same building. Although the two developed no more than a casual acquaintanceship, Connie liked the shy, quiet young woman several years younger than herself.

After Connie began working at the 106th Street nursery, she would see Lydia, now married and living on 107th Street, pass by with her children on the way to the supermarket or the park. All three children had their mother's dark hair and big brown eyes, and they were so well scrubbed and dressed that they sparkled. Connie noticed how much Lydia seemed to enjoy being out with them.

One day, Connie stopped Lydia as she passed by, and invited her to come in. That was before the school was open for children, but Connie explained what was happening. At first, Lydia was skeptical. "An experiment where parents would be teachers? It just didn't sound right," she says, recalling her reaction. "The thing to do was to stay home with your kids."

Still, she began dropping by. "I checked it out because I knew Connie," she says. "If it had been someone I didn't know, I wouldn't have given it a second thought."

Connie's presence was also important because Lydia's husband George was "old-fashioned." Like many Puerto Rican men, he wanted to keep a tight rein on his wife and didn't approve of her "hanging out" just anywhere. Only because he knew Connie from 104th Street and trusted her, did he "allow" Lydia to start spending time at the nursery.

Lydia immediately liked being around the school. She found the people "easygoing." Their warm greetings and offers of coffee made her feel welcome. She was also influenced by what Connie said about the importance of a nursery experience in preparing children for school. Lydia's father had been an alcoholic, and her family had always been poor. Lack of money had forced her to quit high school and take a job as a clerk in a bank. Now she had three children of her own, and her husband was struggling as a handyman. Her deepest yearning was to help her children get an education so that they could "make it." As she puts it: "I wanted to give my kids the opportunity to have a middle-class life. Later, if they wanted to, they would be free to turn it down. But I wanted them to have the choice." It was not long before Lydia decided to enroll her children.

That was a big step in itself. But it did not satisfy Connie, who had an intuitive sense that Lydia would make a good assistant teacher. "I've seen you with your own children," Connie encouraged her. "You like kids, and you're good with kids. We're opening another nursery, and we need you."

At Connie's insistence, Lydia spent some time as a volunteer in the classrooms on 106th Street. She also talked it over with her husband, who liked the idea of her bringing in some money. Finally, she decided to apply for the position of assistant teacher in the Madison Avenue nursery. "I thought it would be a good thing for me and for my kids," she says. "I felt I might really enjoy that kind of work." Like the other applicants, she was screened by the director, Margaret Adams, and then interviewed by the board. During the last week in January, she began work.

The process by which Lydia became part of the Block Nurseries seems almost too easy and too natural to deserve notice. But after the nurseries became day care centers in 1968, "eligibility criteria" and "intake procedures" became major issues. When compared with the policies of New York City's Division of Day Care, Connie's approach seems extraordinary in its decency and humanity.

While Connie treated Lydia as a friend, the day care bureaucracy sent middle-class caseworkers to conduct formal interviews with parents to determine their eligibility. The caseworkers asked for detailed personal information, which went into files kept downtown; like welfare caseworkers, they made home visits to verify such things as income and marital status. In contrast, Connie asked Lydia no embarrassing personal questions. No investigation was done to see if she was poor enough. No personal information was sent downtown. Rather than being carefully screened to receive a service administered by a bureaucracy, Lydia was welcomed into a community of friends. While the Division's procedures fostered wariness, if not duplicity, Connie approached Lydia in ways that inspired confidence and trust.

Lydia's story is not unusual. Through a similar process, many parents found their ways into the school. Like Lydia, many of them had never thought of putting their children in a nursery, let alone working there. The idea of parents being teachers was strange. Even stranger was the idea of "parent control." They agreed to take the chance only because of encouragement by people they trusted from their own community.

Poor health forced Connie to resign in the fall of 1966, and the board decided to replace her with two people. In January 1967, Lydia Rios became parent coordinator of the Madison Avenue nursery, and Rose Gueits, of the 106th Street center. Their work illustrates the many facets of the job of parent coordinator.

They began by setting a distinctive tone. "When you walked into the nursery, it was like a family," says Carmen Gonzalez, a parent who would one day become a teacher in the 106th Street nursery. "They'd greet you. After you put your child in the classroom, you could come out, have a cup of coffee, and talk for a while. If you were lonely or had any problems, you could just drop by and people would be there to listen."

The welcome didn't extend only to the parents. The doors of the centers opened onto the sidewalks. Older siblings of children in the schools, friends of friends, neighborhood residents, bag ladies looking for food— all came by from time to time. The parent coordinators also entertained a steady stream of visitors from all over the country, many of whom were parents looking for advice in setting up their own schools.

To a casual observer, the daily activities of parents in the centers could hardly have looked more ordinary—"just some women hanging out." But for the women, many of whom had felt trapped and isolated through most of their adult lives, "hanging out" at the Block Nurseries was one of the first steps in a process that would change their lives. And in spite of how natural it looked, it didn't just happen.

The entire staff helped create the family feeling, but the parent coordinators did the most to create an atmosphere where parents felt welcome. Lydia and Rosie set up inviting parents' areas with couches and easy chairs. They made sure the coffee was ready every morning. They made a point of being there to greet parents as they brought their children to school and to chat with those who stayed. They thought of jobs that needed doing—volunteering in classrooms, numbering raffle tickets, making party decorations—and enlisted people's help. They organized all kinds of parent activities, from sewing groups to sessions on child-rearing with the mental health consultant. Other people might come and go, but the parent coordinators were there, orchestrating the situation, day in and day out.

But creating a warm, relaxed atmosphere in the schools required more than coffee, conversation, and things to do. "Rosie [Gueits] was a very friendly person who you could go to and talk about your problems without being turned down," recalls Carmen Gonzalez. "When you hurted, you could tell she hurted too. If I had a problem with welfare, she'd call. If I had a problem at the clinic and she had to go with me, she would. If someone was giving me the run-around, she'd find a way to get through the red tape. After a while, we started talking about our lives, about what it had been like growing up. That's when we found out we'd both lived in a home. Rosie became my friend, and she will always be my friend." More than anything else, it was the opportunity to care and to be cared about that deepened the involvement of Carmen and other women in the nurseries.

The parent coordinators provided a variety of services to parents, including counseling, referrals to other agencies, and advocacy. They went to great lengths to help troubled families.

"Elizabeth Matos was an alcoholic with a million and one problems— and I mean a million and one!" recalls Rosie. "She would call when she needed me, and then come over to the nursery and cry for hours. Some of the teachers would say, 'Why do you let her sit there and cry like that?'

"'Look,' I'd tell them. 'We started the school saying that we were going to help parents. Now that we have a school, are we going to lean back and forget what we said?'"

In addition to providing a shoulder to cry on, Rosie arranged for Elizabeth to participate in a therapy group at a local hospital—a group she attended regularly and from which she eventually graduated—and secured other resources for her family as well, including a Spanish-speaking homemaker provided by the welfare department.

Lydia also intervened in several difficult family situations. Zenalda Capaz had two children in the Madison Avenue nursery and a husband who was making life unbearable. If he wasn't home abusing her and the children, he was out with other women. Zenalda came by almost every day to hang out with other parents at the Madison Avenue nursery. A good cook, she was always eager to prepare food for bake sales and parties. She taught the other parents to crochet. She also threatened periodically to kill not only herself, but her children. The situation deteriorated to the point where it seemed likely that she would do just that. Throughout the crisis, Lydia, Millie Rabinow, and Margaret Adams talked with her constantly.

Finally she agreed to be admitted to Metropolitan Hospital, which had an excellent mental health facility at that time. While she stayed there for several weeks, Lydia took care of her children, and her friends from the school visited her frequently. "When she came back," Lydia says, "she began to get herself together. Eventually, she got away from her husband and found another man who was much better. It was finding people she could trust that made the difference. She trusted me enough, and she trusted the school."

Rosie and Lydia had the confidence and skill to take on such situations because of Millie Rabinow's support and supervision. Recalls Rosie: "Millie and I would sit down lots of times after everybody else had left, and talk about different things. She'd ask, 'How did things go?' I'd tell her, and she would say if I had done it right or not. 'Maybe you could try it this way next time,' she might say. Or 'Great. You did just right. If you keep going that way, you won't have any problem.'"

Rosie gives Millie credit for teaching her to be an effective counselor. "She made you feel that everything you did was right, that you weren't being stupid," Rosie observes. "Like me now, I had only completed high school. And yet, when I was with her, I was able to talk about all kinds of things and give her answers and even advice! She made me feel like I knew things, and gave me more confidence in myself. She wasn't a person who'd say, 'Since I'm older and more experienced than you, I'm going to deal with it.' She'd say, 'Go ahead and take care of it. If you get stuck, then come to me.' She didn't force herself on anybody.

"The main thing she taught me was how to listen to people, to listen to both sides before coming to a conclusion. She helped me to be more understanding. 'Things will work out,' she'd say, 'if you want them to work out, and you believe they're going to work out, and you have patience.' She was so natural, she was such a down-to-earth person that I could sit with her and talk about anything. Or if she talked and I just listened, I'd start to understand things I didn't think I could understand. She always took out time to explain things."

A few families were always in crisis and almost all families were sometimes in crisis, but the parent coordinators' work was usually less dramatic than their interventions with Elizabeth or Zenalda. Sometimes, it began with a problem the teachers saw in the classroom.

"Gladys Santos had three children in the school," Rosie explains. "Albert, the oldest, wouldn't be bothered with anybody. He used to just sit in a rocking chair and rock the whole damn day. We wanted to find out why he acted that way. Myrna, a year younger, seemed all right. She was bright and pretty and her mother dressed her up like a doll. But Milagros, the youngest, was thin and sickly and slightly cross-eyed. She was like

Albert—she just liked to sit. We were concerned about Albert and Milagros, and suggested to Gladys that she take them to the hospital for tests.

"But Gladys was very protective. It took me a long time to build up a relationship with her. Sometimes I'd take her kids home after school, and we'd just sit down and talk. I finally got her to build up her confidence so that she was willing to come to the school and see what was happening. Gradually, she started to talk about the problems she was having. She started opening up first about the children's health problems. And then I could say, 'Okay, would you mind if I took you to this place, or that place so that they can help you?'"

Rosie went with her a couple of times, then she started going by herself. But one day she called Rosie all upset. She'd had three appointments that day, had run from one clinic to another, waiting here and there, and hadn't seen one doctor. The next day Rosie went with her and confronted a nurse who said it just couldn't be helped. Upon returning to the school, Rosie met with Tony and some board members to decide what to do. The result was a series of meetings with that hospital (and another as well) that led to improvements in service.

In addition to recruiting and enrolling new children, making the centers welcoming, organizing activities for parents, and providing a variety of services to families, the parent coordinators were pivotal in fostering good communication among all of the people involved in their centers. They had to be scrupulous about keeping confidences, firm in discouraging gossip, and sensitive to the idiosyncrasies of parents and teachers. By having these qualities, Lydia and Rosie supplied a good part of the oil that kept the schools running smoothly.

Sometimes it was a matter of helping parents get along with other parents. "At first, Anna Rivera was extremely self-conscious about her weight," Lydia observes. "She was very uptight—just waiting for somebody to say something and then she'd be fast to say something back. I was always on the alert to make sure that nobody offended Anna. After a while, though, she started feeling more relaxed. People would say things to her, and she would take it more easily."

More often, though, the conflicts were between parents and teachers. "Natividad had just come from the Dominican Republic," Rosie recalls. "A lot of people at the school didn't care for her. One day, I'd spent the morning at the hospital with a parent. As I walked into the school at noontime, one of the teachers came up to me. 'Rosie, you've got to do something,' she said. It's Julio's mother. She's driving me bananas. Get her out of my classroom because I can't deal with her.'

"So I calmly put my coat away and walked in there. The classroom was in an uproar. '*Que pasa?*' I asked Natividad.

"'They were having lunch, and that little boy started throwing food, and I told him to stop, and he laughed at me, and the teachers didn't do anything,' she blurted out in Spanish.

"'Let's go over to my desk, and we'll talk about it,' I said. So we left the classroom, sat down at my desk, and started talking. I agreed with her that children shouldn't throw food or laugh when adults speak to them. But then I tried to explain to her that if she saw something wrong, she should not explode in the classroom, but pull one of the teachers to the side. Or if she didn't want to do that, she could wait until I came in and talk to me rather than upset the whole class."

Rosie's skills at mediation were also useful in resolving conflicts among the staff. Although tension among staff members could have many sources, that arising along race and class lines was potentially most destructive. Since Rosie had the confidence of everybody, she was able to be an effective "bridge person," and play a major role in helping people of different backgrounds understand each other.

A conflict between Toni Perez, then in her second year of teaching, and Adelaide, the professional teacher Toni was working with, provides an example. "Adelaide knew I was good with difficult children," Toni recalls. "So whenever a child gave her or Carlos a hard time, she'd call me. But I didn't like being put in that position all the time. I felt I was turning into a prison warden."

Toni's frustration built up, until one day she stalked out of the classroom and out of the school. Seeing that something was wrong, Rosie followed her out to the sidewalk. "What happened, Toni?" she asked.

"I've had it, Rosie!" she said, and started to cry. "I can't take it anymore. I'm quitting—and don't try to talk me out of it. There's no way I'm going back in there. Adelaide and Carlos let those kids get away with murder, and then I have to be the bad guy. It's not fair! I don't get any support! The kids are starting to hate me because I'm always mean to them. Before long, I'll be hating them too!"

"Have you told Adelaide how you feel?" Rosie asked.

"No," Toni admitted. "I'm afraid if I talk to her, I'll lose control of myself, and say a bunch of things I don't want to say."

They talked more, and Toni agreed to express her feelings directly to Adelaide if Rosie was present. Rosie spoke with Millie Rabinow and the educational director, and they took part in the meeting as well. Although the discussion produced no magic solution, it lessened the tension and started a process that improved the classroom greatly in the course of the year.

Partly because of her personality and partly because of the length of time she held the position (nine years), Rosie transcended any reasonable definition of the parent coordinator's role. It's hard to say where the job stopped and Rosie went on. A mother of 10 children, she also became the mother of the Block Schools. Warm, sympathetic, tough, and shrewd, she was the one to go to for help. Frustrated directors, sobbing parents, frazzled teachers, angry children—all would end up, so to speak, on Rosie's lap.

Although Rosie is undoubtedly right to give Millie Rabinow credit for helping her become a better counselor, Rosie's extraordinary empathy for other people had its roots in the hardships she experienced as she was growing up. Born in 1932, she remembers standing in bread lines, since her father, an immigrant from Mexico who was not a U.S. citizen, had trouble finding work. A member of the Communist Party, he went off to fight fascism in the Spanish Civil War. "A year later, two guys knocked at our door," Rosie recalls. "'We are sorry to inform you that your husband was killed in Spain,' they told my mother. They handed us a package with his clothes."

Rosie's mother worked doing other people's laundry, but the money she earned was barely enough to provide food for her six children. Says Rosie: "We put on plays and had singing contests to keep our minds off being hungry."

When her mother fell ill and had an extended stay in the hospital, the children were sent to Catholic orphanages on Staten Island. "They separated us—I was the only one at St. Michael's. It was the first time I had ever been away from my brothers and sisters. I cried myself to sleep every night for a month."

Rosie was eventually reunited with her brothers and sisters—they were transferred to St. Michael's—and after a year her mother began visiting them regularly on Sundays. But her mother was never able to get a real apartment, and Rosie lived in orphanages until her graduation from high school.

After high school, she lived with her aunt and supported herself with a factory job before marrying her first husband. They had three children together, but the marriage didn't last. "I was thrown out on the street because he didn't pay the rent. Do you know what it is to come home to your little room and see all your stuff and your kids' stuff out on the street and people picking through it?

"Like a fool, I went back to him when he said he'd never let it happen again. But it did, and I had to move in with my mother. That's when I said, 'This is it!'—and I never moved back."

When she and Joe began to go together, she was on welfare and living with her three children in an apartment above her mother's. After several years in which they struggled—Joe working many jobs, the family moving "from one rat trap to another"—Joe finally got into training to become a housing cop, they found a decent apartment, and Rosie settled in as a housewife: "My only goal was to see my children grow up and get married. That was it."

"But little by little," she says, "I started to become aware of the civil rights movement. I remember watching the TV news—a scene at a lunch counter. A White guy was pouring sugar over a Black guy's head, and the Black guy wasn't moving. I wondered why, and then I realized that if he moved, he'd probably be killed right there. That always stood out on my mind—that and the beatings and the dogs.

"Living in my own world with my family, I didn't think I needed to know anything else. But then I started to realize, 'Hey, there are lots of things out there I should find out about.'"

When Rosie learned that a group of friends and neighbors were starting their own school, she was eager to get involved—ready, as she put it, for a "change of pace."

As parent coordinator, Rosie seemed sedentary, relaxed, and easygoing. But she was at the center of everything that happened. And she was absolutely firm on three important principles: parent control; the schools' commitment to do everything necessary to support parents; and the schools' prohibition against adults' using physical punishment in the classroom. "We felt from the beginning that teachers should not be allowed to hit children," she explains. "When you're home, you bug your parents and you get hit enough, without having teachers hit you while you're in school too. So we said, 'Hands off!'"

Unfortunately, a volunteer from the Junior League failed to take the injunction seriously and slapped one of the children. "Did you want to see me?" the chicly dressed woman asked as she approached Rosie's desk.

"Did you hit a child in that classroom this morning?"

"Me?"

"Yes, *you.*"

"Well yes . . . I did . . . I—"

"Why? Why did you hit her?"

"She was running. I told her to stop, and she didn't. I'm sorry. I just lost my patience."

"You know you're not supposed to hit children in this school. You're going out that door now and never coming back."

Rosie and Lydia did not just advocate for the parents and their children. They acted decisively on their behalf because they had real power in the schools. They were key advisers to the educational directors and executive director; they participated in all important decisions; and they served on the board of directors. They derived their influence from the fact that the schools were parent-controlled, and they were instrumental in making parent control a reality.

*   *   *

"When I first started out," observes Toni Perez, "I was leery about parent control. I didn't know parents could really have anything to do with running a school. That was because I had my older kids in public school, where the teachers never listened to what you had to say. When Florence explained to me about parent control, I started feeling a little uppity. I said to myself, 'That means if I say something, people are really going to listen!' What Florence said turned out to be true. I started seeing it for myself in the way people treated me. I had always had trouble with my speech. But at the Block Nurseries, I wasn't afraid to talk because I knew people weren't going to laugh at me, even if I said something wrong."

Like Toni, many of the parents had ambivalent feelings about parent control. When Anna Rivera first heard that the Block Nurseries were parent-controlled, her reaction was "Bullshit!" She was certain that the slogan was merely an attempt to manipulate her into enrolling her child. Lydia Rios was shocked to hear that parents were starting their own schools.

The parents' skepticism is understandable in light of the discouraging treatment many had endured before coming to the Block Schools—experiences that had dampened their hopes and lowered their expectations.

Toni is an example. In her family, she had been "the stupid one" because she had had trouble with her speech. What could parent control mean to Toni? She thought of herself as stupid, and nothing had happened to make her question her low estimate of herself. Neither at home, nor at work, nor at her children's schools did anyone listen to her. In such circumstances, Toni was not about to assert her right to control or influence *anything*, let alone something as important as her children's education.

Fortunately, several of the founding parents believed strongly in parent control from the beginning. Florence was most adamant. "Whatever my children were into was what I wanted to be into," she says. "I didn't see why other people should determine my children's education."

Sonia also had no qualms about parents running their children's schools. "The idea appealed to me immediately," she recalls. "I knew we would have to make hard decisions, but I believed we would learn, like anybody else."

Rosie Gueits also liked the idea: "We weren't saying, 'Down with the government! Out with all White people!' We were saying, 'Give us a chance! Let us see what we can do!'"

Those energetic members of the founding group would lead the way for the other parents, encouraging them, persuading them of their rights, and modeling assertive behavior. But even they often felt uncomfortable in this unfamiliar role. Rosie Gueits, for example, may have been convinced that people from her neighborhood should have a chance to do things for themselves, but she was much less sure that *she* should be one of those people. "I had only completed high school," she says, "and I didn't think I knew anything about how to deal with people—except my own kids."

Yet, despite the inexperience of its members, the parent board had hired an executive director, found classroom space, recruited children, hired a staff, decided on an educational philosophy, selected their educational leadership, took decisive action on personnel problems, and invented the position of parent coordinator.

What explains their effectiveness?

It helped, first of all, that the members of the original founding group were young women who knew each other as friends and neighbors. All with young children, they shared a primary interest in running good schools. None had political ambitions; none were using the schools as stepping stones to "bigger and better things."

Then from the beginning, the board was a *working* board. Having spent several years at home with their young children, the women were eager to get out and do something different—to have a "change of pace," as Rosie Gueits put it. They threw themselves into such tasks as interviewing, canvassing, and searching for sites. In the process, they developed close ties, learned a tremendous amount, and increased their confidence.

Meetings with Millie Rabinow also built group solidarity. "The main purpose of the meetings was to help us work better with the children," observes Connie, "but it was a lot like group therapy. We might be discussing discipline. 'I don't believe in hitting,' I'd say.

"'Why?' someone would ask.

"'Because I know how it is! My parents used to hit me a lot.'

"Before I knew it, I'd be telling about my childhood. Then someone else would say, 'Oh yes! That reminds me of mine.' I remember a lot of tears at those meetings. And a lot of anger came out too—not at each other, but about things that had happened to us as we were growing up. We began to see that we were all pretty much the same inside."

But the key to the effectiveness of the Block Nurseries' board was the special relationship between the parents and Tony Ward. "Tony is a take-charge man, an authority figure, a father figure," observes Joe Gueits, Rosie's husband. "He has a good line of shit—he can talk. And when he's put on the spot and gets nervous, that's when he's at his best." Because of the force of his personality and the fact that the parents trusted and looked up to him, Tony had tremendous influence during the Block Nurseries' first two years.

But Tony was well aware that in addition to the usual functions of a board, the Block Nurseries' board had the aims of giving East Harlem parents real decision-making power and, by so doing, developing their leadership skills. This meant supporting parents' genuine participation, even if by helping them develop their power, he eventually would diminish his own. To do this, he had to relate to the board not only as an executive director but as a community organizer.

A fundamental task for Tony as community organizer was to counteract deeply engrained patterns that prevented the parents from seeing themselves as potential leaders and decision-makers. One of those patterns was their tendency to defer to him. "When we were hiring our first teachers," recalls Connie, "we were scared of making decisions. The first few times, we asked Tony for advice. But he wouldn't give us answers. 'It's up to you,' he'd say."

Another pattern was the parents' tendency to be overmodest about their contributions to the group. Sometimes that took the form of a willingness to skip meetings. But Tony wouldn't have it. According to Carmen: "A board meeting meant that we had to pick up people and take them home afterwards. We had to provide babysitters. We really had to set it up so that people would come." By making sure people came, Tony was giving parents the strong message: "You are an important member of this group! We need you!"

But even Herculean efforts to get people to meetings would not have sufficed, if the meetings themselves had turned people off. "Someone told me once that my major influence on the schools was that I set a tone for how people should work together," Tony says. "There was no magic to it: I listened! I was really interested in what everybody had to say." Looking back on their experience at the schools, many of the parents say that the Block Nurseries were the first places in their lives where their ideas and feelings were taken seriously.

A fourth contribution Tony made to the board's development was to help the members develop orderly processes for decision-making. "I have a very strong sense of fairness and order," Tony notes. "I'd find myself saying things like, 'You can't do that because it's spontaneous and disorderly. If you want to move in that direction, you'd better take this step, and then this step, and so on."

An example is the development of the Block Nurseries' by-laws. The by-laws were an essential part of the organization's application to become a not-for-profit organization chartered by New York State. Tony took great care in developing the by-laws and vetting them thoroughly with board members because he wanted the governance arrangements that he and the parents had developed on an *ad hoc* basis to be "writ in stone."

Two things are notable about the by-laws, which were approved by the board on May 19, 1966. First, all corporate powers were invested in the board of directors, which could comprise *only parents of children currently enrolled in the schools*. The board was to be elected by the members of the corporation (that is, the parents) at an annual meeting. (The only exceptions were founding board members Sonia Medina and Margot Maristany.)

This ruled out the possibility of a parent–teacher co-op. Attractive as the idea of a co-op might sound, Tony was convinced that it would undermine one of their major purposes. As he puts it: "I was afraid of some professional squeezing his or her way onto the board, and then driving parents out."

Since the by-laws made it clear that the parent board was the source of ultimate authority in the organization, the Block Nurseries avoided a pitfall of many alternative organizations during the 1960s, which disintegrated because no one had the power to resolve difficult issues by finally ending discussion, making a decision, and moving on.

The by-laws also gave the executive director broad powers, including "general and active control of all business affairs, general power to remove and suspend all employees subject to the approval of the Board and sole responsibility for the educational policy in the nurseries." He could be removed by a two-thirds vote of the entire board of directors, and "his determinations of policy" were to be reviewed annually by the corporation.

At a time when many young people of the New Left were trying to run organizations with rotating leadership or no leadership at all, Tony's insistence on a strong executive director set the Block Schools apart. From the beginning, Tony made a crucial distinction between control and leadership. The parents' power over hiring and firing gave them control of the schools. But the executive director had the right and the responsibility to be a strong leader: to put forth his or her ideas forcefully and to manage the daily operations of the schools.

If the danger of the "no leadership" approach is confusion and drift, the danger of Tony's approach is control by the executive director instead of by the parents. While recognizing the dangers, Tony had no ambivalence about being a strong leader. Power was a reality in human relationships. Leadership was necessary to create an effective organization. Democratic decision-making did not mean doing away with leadership and pretending that power did not exist. It meant that the locus of power in the organization was clear; that people were listened to seriously; and that the leadership, while having enough freedom to be effective, was accountable.

Early evening, June 28, 1966. The board of directors of the East Harlem Block Nurseries is meeting at the 106th Street center. A dozen people are sitting on metal folding chairs around a long Formica-top table. On the table are paper cups and three half-empty quart bottles of Pepsi. A large fan is droning in the background, muffling the sounds of children playing in the four-year-olds' classroom.

Alice Graves and Margaret Adams, the educational directors of the nurseries, have just made informal reports on their programs and shared some of their ideas for the next school year.

Joe Gueits clears his throat. "Yesterday, I picked up my son Jody at the nursery," the stocky, clean-cut man with short black hair began. "When we walked by that public school annex next door, he looked in and saw a flag. And he asked me, 'Why doesn't my school have one?' I couldn't really give him an answer. I guess it was just something we overlooked with all the headaches involved in getting the schools started and whatnot. But now it's time we get flags for the classrooms and begin teaching the kids the Pledge of Allegiance."

"A flag is meaningful for older children," said one of the parents, "but we're dealing with little kids."

"I agree," said Alice. "I don't think that saluting the flag has any meaning for three-, four-, and five-year-olds."

"Yes," said Margaret, "there are so many other important things for children to be involved in at this age."

"I don't like the idea of flags and salutes, either," said Debbie Ribb, the schools' secretary, who was sitting in on the meeting. "We have to think of the effects on the children. We don't want the kids to grow up and blindly accept—"

"Hey wait a minute!" Joe interrupted. "What are you talking about? This is a school—a public school, so to speak. We *are* getting federal money. Kids should learn about the country they live in. They should learn about the flag and what it represents. To teach them the Pledge of Allegiance— I don't think that's a cardinal sin! The flag represents their country. The government is paying for the school. A little respect for your country never hurt anybody!"

"Joe's right," added one of the parents. "In all schools, they have flags."

"But this is not 'all schools,'" said Sonia. "This is the *Block* Schools. Have some common sense! If you put up an American flag, then you have to put up a Puerto Rican flag too."

"There are plenty of Puerto Rican flags in Puerto Rico," said Joe. "You can have all you want over there."

"Even putting up a Puerto Rican flag would not be enough," said Sonia, "because we have children from a lot of different countries."

"Why not use the UN flag, then?" someone said.

"We don't need to put up *any* flag," said Sonia, "because we're a nursery school."

The discussion ended in a compromise. American flags would go up in both schools—but only in the offices, not in classrooms.

"The next day when I came in to work," recalls Sonia, "the flag was there, tacked on the bulletin board. So I measured it and went out and got a Puerto Rican flag and put it up. By the next day, someone had also put up an Italian flag. And the day after that, it was the Black Liberation flag. By the end of the week, the bulletin board was covered with flags. They stayed there for a few days, and then somebody—I don't know who—took them all down. After that, they stopped putting up flags, and the issue died."

Perhaps the battle of the flags was not the most important issue taken up by the board during its second year of existence. But it does illustrate the fact that after the approval of the by-laws and the election of new members, board meetings got more interesting. The change had a lot to do with a new member the board picked up in June.

Thirty-year-old Joe Gueits was a wise-cracking, beer-drinking, Goldwater Republican who worked as a New York City Housing cop. Of mixed-European and Mexican heritage, Joe had grown up during the 1940s on a block of East 115th Street that was predominately African-American and Puerto Rican, and became more so as the years went by.

Joe recalls fondly the "real feeling of closeness" on the block. His memories of school are good too. "For junior high," he says, "I went to Cooper, which had 2,000 students, all male, and all Black except for 12 Hispanics, one Chinese kid, and me. I was initially scared to go there, but to my surprise I found it very well controlled. When we changed periods, we had to march, and there was no talking in the hallways."

Joe dropped out of high school in his senior year to join the army. But after a three-year stint as a military police officer in Korea, he returned to East Harlem. That was where his friends were; that was home. He never seriously considered living anywhere else. He married Rosie against the objections of his father, who didn't like the idea of his son marrying a dark-skinned Puerto Rican woman with children. In 1961, he fulfilled a long-time dream by becoming a New York City Housing Authority police officer.

By then Joe could say that he was "making it." But his world was changing, and he didn't like it. The drugs that surged into East Harlem in the 1950s were destroying *his* community. The "total disrespect for authority that changed the public schools almost overnight" was affecting the education *his* children were receiving. And having grown up in the area, he knew that it didn't have to be that way. When Connie told him about the possibility of starting bilingual nurseries, he found the idea appealing because it gave him hope. A strong believer in education, he saw the schools as one way to start turning things around.

That's why he encouraged Rosie to get involved with the Block Nurseries. And as the schools became the center of her life, he was drawn in too. "Cops have crazy hours," he explains. "When I was home, Rosie would be out having a meeting. I realized that if I wanted to see my wife, I'd better get involved."

Helping to paint the classrooms, speaking to the children about what it's like to be a police officer, dropping by the centers in his spare time—those were the first steps. In June 1966, he began attending board meetings.

As a board member, Joe soon became an articulate advocate for a more conservative approach to education. "I joined the board because certain goals of the schools were not materializing," he says. "There was too much freedom. Some of those early teachers—if a kid wanted to throw food, that was all right. I didn't care for that. I fought for the basics. I felt that even at the age of three, four, and five, kids should be learning manners, cleanliness, and respect for one another."

But his first clashes with staff and other board members came over politics. Even before the flag controversy faded, the schools' bulletin boards became an issue.

"I was putting up signs like 'Demonstrate against the war in Vietnam,'" Debbie Ribb recalls. "I used to put them up all over the schools. Joe went bananas. He said he didn't want me putting them up, and the rest of the board agreed with him.

"I felt they were being reactionary. I thought it was important that they see the connections between the war and poverty in East Harlem. But nobody was interested in what I had to say, and I stopped putting my signs up. I did get support from Tony, of course. But we came to an understanding that this was not the place to make free speech an issue. Tony needed people's support, and he wasn't about to come out as some hippie radical. So we just backed off.

"Despite our differences, Joe and I liked each other. We were friendly enemies. He'd say, 'Here comes the do-gooder, the 'ban the bomb lady.' I'd say, 'Yes, and there he is, Mr. Super-patriot! Kill any kids today, policeman?' So there was a little hostility, but it was friendly."

Most of the board members felt out of their element when political issues came up. But in Sonia, Joe met his match. During the fall of 1966, a proposed Civilian Review Board became a major issue in the city. If approved by the voters, the board, composed of civilians, would review charges of police brutality. At a board meeting in October, Joe urged board members to vote "no" on the issue. "Excuse me, flatfoot," said Sonia. "If I don't have a right to impose *my* political views, you don't have the right to impose *yours*." Sonia recalls that Joe started laughing and said he understood what she was saying.

"I was the liberal of the Block Nurseries," Sonia says. "'Be careful of the pinkoes,' Joe would say. We disagreed, but we respected each other. I helped the parents bring out their political views, which they'd always been embarrassed to talk about. Lots of changes were going on at that time, and every day when we'd wake up in the morning, there'd be more. I would argue that there must be a reason so many young people were dissatisfied.

"But no matter how much Joe and I disagreed, we could always joke and laugh about it. Joe always said, 'If you ever need anything, call me.' I knew he meant it."

Other political issues came up: Would the Block Nurseries be a sponsor for a teach-in on welfare? Would the board pass a resolution of support for Adam Clayton Powell? Usually, Tony brought them to the board. But the parents followed a consistent policy of neutrality. "Lots of people couldn't deal with religion and politics," Sonia observes. "We didn't want to be disrespectful, so we said that the Block Nurseries would not take public stands on political issues. But lots of talking was going on."

Political discussion was a major aspect of life at the schools during this time. "I remember the day," recalls Dorothy Stoneman, then a teacher at the 106th Street nursery, "when Joe said, 'What's going on here? Is this a conspiracy? How come all you people think alike? How come you're all against the war and you all went to Bank Street College?'

"I understood where Joe was coming from. The men the board hired would come in clean-shaven. But within a few months, they'd grow beards, and turn out to be radicals. All the teachers who worked out were to the left politically—at least committed to the civil rights and peace movements. Yet the parents were fairly conservative. After a while, they began to wonder why the teachers they liked best seemed to think alike politically, and an interesting dialogue began to take place. Sometimes it was humorous. Ruth, the teacher of the threes, was always going to demonstrations. On one of them, she got kicked by a police officer's horse. And Joe, as board chairman, ended up having to grant her time off so that she could go down to the Civilian Review Board to file a complaint."

Despite polar differences in their points of view, though, people at the Block Nurseries managed to go about their work with a minimum of rancor. That was because everyone put the schools and the children first. As Joe put it: "I wasn't all that cracked up about parent control. But if we were going to do it, I thought we ought to do it right. We were getting money. We had a chance to help. If we messed up, we'd only give conservatives like me a chance to say, 'You can't give those spics or niggers anything.' Over the years I think we did a pretty damn good job."

Joe's initial attitudes toward parent control were almost as conservative as his political point of view. "Too many of the parents loved saying,

'We have the power to hire and fire!'" he observes. "I could never stand that. I felt it was like a sledgehammer over someone's head. As a professional in my field, I didn't want amateurs coming in and telling me what to do. I felt the same way about a teacher, a nurse, or any professional."

But although he never budged an inch politically, Joe gradually developed more enthusiasm for the idea of parents running schools for their children. His change of heart was due in part to observing some of the early teachers, whose performance made him less willing to grant unconditional respect to professionals: "On a couple of occasions, we ended up with rookie teachers—young and dumb. They had the sheepskin, but they were totally lost among the kids."

But the main reason Joe changed his attitude was that he simply enjoyed his own participation too much. While skeptical about "parent control" as a slogan, Joe warmed to the idea when he and people he knew happened to be the parents.

In June 1966, Joe became a member of the personnel committee that was reviewing the contracts of all employees. By that time, Toni Perez had overcome enough of *her* doubts about parent control to join the committee as well. She describes one of its first meetings: "When I arrived for the meeting, I remember Joe Gueits asking me how I was and making me feel at home. The parents were talking about firing a Mrs. Brown because she had slapped a child. The teacher came, and we talked with her. Then we heard what the educational director had to say about the incident. Everyone else had come to the conclusion of firing her. But I was holding out. I didn't know if I had the right to make that decision.

"Joe said, 'Look at all the facts, and make your decision. You have the right.'

"I thought about it. As a parent at the Madison nursery, I'd already been through the whole thing with Arlene. It had been *my* daughter Arlene had dragged across the room. I certainly didn't want another teacher like that in the school! So I finally agreed with the other parents. It was June. The school year was almost over. So we just decided not to renew her contract."

But although willing to take action when necessary, Joe was a consistent advocate of caution and moderation in dealing with professionals. "I felt they needed someone to protect the rights of the teachers," he notes. "I felt it was too extreme to dismiss a teacher for hitting a child. If she was a good person who just lost control, give her a reprimand and another chance. Anyone can make a mistake. I felt we should fire people only if they were repeaters—or if they were really spiteful."

On that point, at least, Joe and Tony could agree. From the beginning, Tony recognized that the success of the schools depended on good working relationships between parents and professionals. Those relationships depended, in turn, on the fairness and consistency with which the parent board dealt with staff.

Tony pushed the parents to follow through on the procedures he had helped them develop. To make the three-month probationary period more than just a sentence in the teachers' contract, he insisted that the board meet with him before the period was up to discuss each teacher. If serious questions arose about a teacher, he suggested that they meet with the teacher as well.

In June, the board reviewed every teacher's performance and made decisions about rehiring. Tony reminded the parents that they would need a preliminary meeting in April so that if they had serious doubts about a teacher, they could give the person adequate warning. Tony himself met with all the teachers individually in January to give them his evaluations of their work.

Those routines kept the parents well informed about the staff's performance, and gave staff members ongoing feedback. They helped create the climate of accountability with safety that Tony was striving for. But they were not sufficient. "I felt I was constantly having to push people into taking more stands," Tony recalls. "Joe may have felt that people were jumping up and down to fire teachers, but I didn't. I felt people were not willing enough to use their power. They were reluctant, even timid. By encouraging them to recognize their power and use it, I was preventing them from acting in more anarchistic and irresponsible ways."

The parents may have been hesitant to use their power. But by the fall of 1966, the board had come a long way. Meetings were well attended. The experienced members—Sonia, Rosie, Florence, and Lydia—were confident enough to begin educating the new parents about their rights and responsibilities. By speaking his mind openly and often disagreeing with Tony, Joe Gueits made it easier for other parents to express dissenting views.

At a board meeting in January 1967, Tony put forth a proposal for what he called "job rotation." Parents who had been working in the schools for a year should plan to move on, he suggested, and give other parents a chance.

Florence was the one board member who understood where Tony was coming from. "Tony felt that some of the assistant teachers had stopped growing," she explains. "He felt that they had done their thing—lived their dream—and that working at the school had become just a job to them. They should move on and give other parents the chance they'd had. I could understand what he was saying, because mentally at that particular time, I felt ready to step on."

But all the other board members shared Joe Gueits's reaction. "The schools had finally started to benefit kids," Joe says, "and now Tony was trying to turn it into a training ground for parents. Even thinking about it now pisses me off. It would have been idiotic to train people, and then when they were seasoned and well trained, to let them go. I told Tony and Alice they were a couple of assholes—to try to make our kids' classrooms into a training ground."

Tony was stunned. "It was one of the least friendly clashes we ever had," he says. "I got a cold blast from them at the very suggestion."

After the meeting, Carmen helped him understand what was going on. "You have to remember," she said, "that you're a White, middle-class professional. For you, a job is a means to an end, and you assume you can easily get another one. But for people here, work is really the critical issue. People will die for a shitty little factory job, because they're desperate for work. To raise the suggestion that people might voluntarily give up a job that they like very much, that has prestige and respect in the community, and that allows them to do decent work, means that you're totally unaware of what's going on."

"As soon as she said it," Tony recalls, "I realized that she was right. My suggestion had come out of a grossly insensitive misunderstanding of the class difference between us. I could be very casual about jobs. After a couple of years at the Block Nurseries, I could go on to something else. That was not true for them."

But although Tony quickly withdrew his suggestion, the cat was out of the bag. In their anger over the incident, the board realized fully for the first time the extent of Tony's influence.

"It was his personality," observes Sonia. "Tony had this magnitude of seriousness so that when he walked into a room, everybody froze. At some of our meetings, I'd look around and see everybody nodding. It used to infuriate me."

Like Sonia, other parents had been feeling that Tony controlled their meetings. But they hadn't shared their feelings with each other.

Joe changed that. Before the next meeting, he talked privately with several board members, who agreed that "the board was becoming a rubber stamp for Tony." They also agreed with Joe that the parents were strong enough to run the board themselves. When the group met again on January 30, Joe introduced a resolution that the executive director no longer attend board meetings unless specifically invited.

The meeting was hot. As Sonia put it, "Joe didn't say it in a very nice way."

But the resolution passed easily. "Everybody was glad that Joe did it," Lydia admits, "because nobody else dared to. He was the only one who had the guts."

Once Tony got over his initial surprise, he too realized that it was a good thing. "I was delighted," he says. "And I immediately perceived it as a selling point for the schools."

That night, the board also decided to elect a new chair to replace Connie Arevalo, who had been sick. On March 17, after serving as acting chair for a month and a half, Joe Gueits was formally elected to the position.

After the January 30 meeting, Tony continued to contribute items to the agenda and to lobby for his positions in private conversations with board members. But the parents were clearly in charge. As Joe put it, "The board had grown up."

But a severe test was coming—one that would call on every bit of the experience and confidence they had gained during their first two years.

The Block Nurseries Under Day Care

4

Rosie Gueits sat on the dais in the grand ballroom of Kansas City's Hotel Continental. The one thing she feared more than flying was giving speeches. But just an hour after completing her first airplane flight, she was about to address 500 people at the opening session of a conference sponsored by the federal Follow Through Program.

"I'm just a housewife," she began. "This is the first speech I've ever given, and I'm scared as hell." When she finished, she received a standing ovation.

One day later, on February 22, 1968, Tony sent a telegram to Jule Sugarman, national administrator of the Head Start Program. "East Harlem Block Nursery . . . has no funds. $39,000 in vouchers outstanding. No reimbursements whatsoever for expenses since January 1st change to Head Start. . . . Closing is imminent."

Rosie's standing ovation and Tony's telegram highlight the ironic situation that unfolded during the first half of 1968. While the Block Nurseries flourished and gained national recognition, their very survival suddenly became an open question.

National developments set the stage for this bizarre turn of events. The first major escalation of the War in Vietnam occurred during the summer of 1965. In August, Watts erupted in the worst riot to hit an American city for over 20 years. All of the 34 people who died in the riot were Blacks killed by the police. But televised images of large-scale burning and looting stirred deep-seated fears among Whites.

The Congressional elections of 1966 reflected the changes brought by war and riots. Campaigning against further governmental spending for social programs, Republicans won 47 House seats from the Democrats. When the Ninetieth Congress convened in January 1967, the House was bristling with hostility toward President Johnson's Great Society. The Republicans chose OEO as their special target. Throughout 1967 they fought to eliminate the agency, while the Administration fought just as hard to save it.

The Block Nurseries felt the direct impact of these developments in November 1967. When the government's new fiscal year started on July 1, Congress had not yet made a decision about OEO. To tide the agency over, Congress approved a continuing appropriation for four months. Late in October, with OEO legislation still bogged down, Republicans and southern Democrats managed to block passage of a bill to extend the continuing appropriation. As a result, all antipoverty programs, including the Block Nurseries, went without funds for the three weeks leading up to Thanksgiving.

This convinced Tony to take steps immediately to secure a more stable source of funding for the schools. The city's day care program appeared to offer the best hope. Unlike the War on Poverty, day care in New York City was well established. Administered by the Division of Day Care, a small agency within the Department of Social Services, the program had been running smoothly for almost 20 years. By 1967, the number of centers had reached 93, and day care advocates were anticipating additional federal money for expansion.

The drawback was the Division's conservatism and rigidity. As part of the Department of Social Services, the Division viewed day care primarily as a way to get women off welfare. Budgets for educational materials were stingy, and money for training was nonexistent. Caseworkers did detailed investigations of the "clients" to determine their eligibility. And parents were not eligible to serve on the boards of their children's centers.

While those policies ran counter to everything the Block Nurseries stood for, Tony decided that he had better find out what was possible. In November, he and several board members had an exploratory conversation with the Division's director, Muriel Katz. Although the response on both sides was lukewarm, the board decided to take the next step. On December 12, Tony wrote Muriel Katz that the Block Nurseries were interested in becoming day care centers.

Several days before adjourning on December 19, Congress finally approved an appropriation for OEO of $1.8 billion. Although President Johnson hailed passage of the legislation as a great victory, the appropriation was nearly half a billion dollars less than the President had requested. And Congress, the President, and OEO officials had already committed the agency to several major new initiatives. The only way to pay for those new programs would be out of the hide of the old.

They called it "reshuffling." Six months into the fiscal year, the Community Development Agency (CDA), established to administer the antipoverty program in New York City, had to make cuts of $2 million (or 11%) in the city's community action programs, and smaller reductions in Head Start and in legal services for the poor. On February 1, the Commissioner of CDA, George Nicolau, announced his resignation, effective March 31. "Given the recent actions of Congress and the national Administration," he said, "I no longer believe I can be useful to the City of New York in my present position."

The Block Nurseries' troubles began on January 1, 1968, when the organization lost its status as an independent community action program and was placed under Head Start. The decision seemed to make sense. Money for community action programs was being cut sharply, and the popular Head Start Program looked like the perfect place for the Block Nurseries.

But after January 1, the nurseries stopped receiving reimbursements for expenses. No explanation was given, and, despite innumerable phone calls, Tony was unable to find one. After almost two months, when he saw he would no longer be able to meet the payroll, Tony sent his telegram to Jule Sugarman.

Soon after returning from Kansas City, Tony and the parents finally learned what was going on. Administrative confusion had been partly responsible for the delay. But now that the vouchers had been processed, Head Start officials had a question: What had happened to the $40,000 revolving fund?

The answer, of course, was that it had been spent. Two years earlier, Tony and the parents had made a conscious decision to violate OEO guidelines by spending $36,000 for renovations rather than the $14,000 their budget allowed. There was another problem as well: The schools' financial records were a mess. Lots of money that had gone for perfectly valid expenses was unaccounted for. No one was sure how much this "slippage," as Tony called it, amounted to. But it was well in excess of $10,000.

Responding to Head Start officials, Tony acknowledged his responsibility to account in full for the revolving fund. But he asked that the schools get the benefit of the doubt while the issue was being resolved. He wanted a chance to argue the Block Nurseries' case for the renovations and to produce the invoices that would account for the discrepancy.

When Head Start officials reacted coldly to these suggestions, Tony knew that serious trouble lay ahead. And the deepening crisis was already affecting the schools. Once the reimbursements stopped in January, Tony had been forced to use virtually all available funds just to cover payrolls. Rent, phone, and light bills were going unpaid. Classroom materials were in short supply. Money for children's lunches was running out. The staff was worrying about whether the schools would survive. When Tony couldn't meet the February 29 payroll, the grumbling came into the open. People wondered out loud: What *had* happened to the revolving fund? Had the renovations *really* cost that much?

Early in March, the board of directors, the educational directors of the nurseries, and several of the most active parents from each center held a meeting in Tony's apartment above the office on 111th Street. Tony laid out the options as he saw them. One was closing down.

"The day I see the Block Nurseries go down the drain is the day I die," said Sonia.

"We'll put on raffles and dances and bake sales to make money," said Rosie Tirado.

"We'll get the supermarkets to donate food for the kids' lunches," said Joe Gueits.

"The parents can help cook," said Anna Rivera.

"We'll work without pay for as long as possible," said Rosie Gueits. "Then we'll get unemployment and keep working. When unemployment runs out, we'll go on welfare. But we won't close the schools."

For all the brave talk, Sonia was worried as she left the meeting. "The whole situation was depressing," she recalls. "I had the feeling that we were coming to the end of an era without any idea of what we were getting into." But she knew her next step. She went straight to Marichal-Agosto, a tropical fruit company on 111th Street. Upon hearing of the schools' troubles, the proprietor, who had known Sonia for years, gave her $10. "Whenever you need anything," he said, "just let us know." A fund-raising dance, organized by Sonia, took place five days later. The proceeds of more than $800 went for classroom materials and food for the children's lunches.

Tony moved quickly to address the problem of staff morale. Meeting with the staff in groups and individually, he explained the reasons for the crisis. While expressing confidence that funds would come through, he said there were no guarantees. According to Rosie Tirado, "He told us that if we needed to leave, he would understand. But if we stayed, we had to keep working as though we were being paid. We wouldn't be allowed to slack off."

Each nursery called a general parents' meeting. "People immediately wanted to help," says Anna Rivera, a parent active in the Madison Avenue center. "Some brought in bread and cans of soup and juice. Others went to *La Marqueta* for donations. Every day three or four parents were there preparing the food and serving the kids."

Tony and his assistant spent days going through drawers and files in search of receipts that would account for the missing funds. "In over one hundred cases," Tony wrote at the time, "we have had to seek duplicate invoices from the original vendors." By mid-March they had accounted for $10,000 of the $40,000 revolving fund.

Meanwhile, a member of the Block Schools' advisory committee was pulling some strings with city officials. A long-time activist with Citizens' Committee for Children, Ruth Feder knew many people in city government. After trying for days to reach George Nicolau by phone, she happened to sit next to him at a meeting. "He knew about the schools," she recalls. "He said he thought the project was one of the most exciting in the country. But he admitted that there was terrible confusion and frustration in the anti-poverty office."

Tony and Sonia (who was now the Block Schools' treasurer) knew that confusion firsthand. With the March 15 payroll approaching, they were spending their days downtown at the CDA office. No one said that the Block Schools would be denied the funds they needed for the missed payroll and the one coming up. But no one was authorized to sign the checks, either.

Only George Nicolau's personal intervention broke the impasse. Thanks to Ruth, Tony was able to reach him by phone and explain the situation. Nicolau's call to the fiscal office cleared the way for a temporary solution. Under the agreement, CDA officials approved the schools' payroll vouchers for January and February. They also issued a letter of credit, enabling Tony to borrow money immediately to cover the February 29 payroll.

Even as they fought with CDA for every payroll, Tony and the parents had not given up on the Division of Day Care. Since the letter to Muriel Katz in December had brought no response, Tony decided to try another tack. Late in February, he invited Nancie Stewart, president of the Day Care Council, and Marjorie Grosett, the Council's executive director, to visit the schools.

A member organization of day care center boards, the Day Care Council had been strongly committed to the expansion of day care since its founding in 1946. During the 1960s its leadership also became sympathetic to the idea of parent involvement. Marjorie Grosett, an African-American woman who had been director of a day care center, had a strong conviction, based on personal experience, that parents should help shape their children's education. Nancie Stewart, an outspoken liberal, shared Marjorie's conviction that parents ought to be allowed to serve on day care center boards.

The Council had been trying for some time to help community groups get day care funding. But so far, their efforts had met a stone wall: None of the new organizations had physical facilities adequate to meet the licensing requirements of the Division of Day Care.

That's why Nancie Stewart and Marjorie Grosett were so excited when they saw the Block Nurseries. Impressed by the quality of the educational program and by the involvement of the parents, they noted also that the facilities might just be good enough to pass muster. "We made an extensive review of the whole program," recalls Marjorie Grosett, "and came away with the conviction that this would be our test case."

When Marjorie suggested that the Block Nurseries make a formal request for funding from the Division of Day Care, the board decided to involve the entire parent body in the decision. Parents discussed the issue in class meetings, and toward the end of March, Marjorie came to a general meeting to answer questions.

"The parents gave Marjorie a hard time," recalls Dorothy Stoneman, then a teacher at the 106th Street nursery. "We got the feeling that she was putting a good face on things. The parents had lots of concerns about what the changes would do to our program. 'Will day care pay the salaries of our parent coordinators?' they asked. 'Will we still be able to decide which children to accept? Will we have to change to day care's long day (8:00 a.m. to 6 p.m.)? Will our parent board still run our schools? Will day care allow our assistant teachers to continue working?'"

But a few days later, at another general meeting, the parent body voted to go ahead. Comments Tony: "We were in real trouble with the antipoverty program. People realized that it was day care or nothing." The three-page letter Tony sent to Muriel Katz on March 27 requested that "our schools become a demonstration project funded through the Division of Day Care." It went on to state that the Block Nurseries wished to preserve such special features of their program as the parent governing board, the parent coordinators, the parent assistant teachers, and a method for determining eligibility that did not involve investigation of the families' finances.

On March 31, President Johnson announced that he would not seek another term as President. Four days later, Martin Luther King was assassinated. Within a week, riots in over 100 cities left 37 people dead. Troops had to restore order in Washington, D.C., where 12 people died. The Great Society was shattered beyond repair. And in East Harlem, people at the

Block Nurseries wondered whether they would be able to salvage the little piece of that dream they had made their own.

The prospects were bleak. The Division of Day Care wasn't answering Tony's letters or phone calls. Relations with CDA continued to deteriorate.

Early in June, Head Start officials finally summoned representatives of the Block Nurseries downtown for a meeting. The event had all the aspects of a formal hearing. The director of Head Start in New York City, members of the Head Start Parent Advisory Committee, and lawyers for Head Start sat on the dais in the large room and spoke through microphones to the small audience of Block Nurseries people.

"We are asking that Head Start approve our expenditures for the renovations, since we could not have opened our centers without them," Tony began. "We are also requesting a limited amount of time to account for the rest of the money. While we do that, we feel our schools should continue to receive the funds Head Start is obligated by contract to provide."

"You bring us the $40,000, and we'll continue to fund you," was the reply from the podium.

The communication never advanced beyond that opening exchange. When someone said that Head Start might continue to provide funding if Tony Ward resigned, Sonia rose up in defense. "We are not about to give up what we have. We have survived crises before, and we will survive this one. No matter what you do, we'll still be here alive and kicking. This will only make us stronger. It will not be the decision of Head Start to close us down."

Sonia's speech stirred her colleagues, but evoked no response from the people behind the microphones. As the hearing ended, Block Nurseries people had no doubt what would happen next. On June 19, Head Start made it official. The Block Nurseries would receive no more reimbursements for expenses. The official justification was that the schools had failed to account for the revolving funds.

But there was more to it than that. Without a doubt, Tony broke many rules and kept sloppy books. Yet, Head Start could have given the schools the benefit of the doubt. The Block Nurseries had a national reputation as an effective early childhood program. The spending for renovations had been absolutely necessary. More likely, the real source of the schools' troubles was the cutbacks that hit New York City's CDA in 1968. To protect the Block Nurseries from cuts affecting independent community action programs, George Nicolau had transferred them to Head Start. But then Head Start's budget was cut as well. With its two centers, the East Harlem Block Nursery, Inc., would have been one of the largest Head Start programs in the City. To Head Start officials, the Block Nurseries must have seemed like hungry uninvited guests at a dinner party where the host was running out of food. Under pressure to cut programs, they seized upon the schools' sloppy bookkeeping and violation of guidelines as a convenient excuse.

The Block Nurseries were also an easy target because they were isolated politically. "At the beginning of the War on Poverty, federal officials had direct relationships with many of the programs," Tony explains. "But after a couple of years, local politicians began to gain more control, and local antipoverty groups began vying for power. Control over programs came to be centralized in groups willing to play the political game. The Block Nurseries' parents had no interest whatsoever in playing political games. They were neighborhood people with no political ambitions. Their attitude was that the politicians were corrupt and did not represent the real East Harlem. That attitude, justified or not, would mean trouble eventually, as the antipoverty program became more and more important as a source of political patronage. So we were probably destined to be screwed anyway. But we left ourselves wide open by violating rules and being sloppy."

Whatever the explanations, the Block Schools' leadership was outraged. "We knew we needed to do something so that we could be heard," says Anna Rivera. That suggested a demonstration. But most of the parents had never carried a picket sign. "When I first heard the idea," says Rosie Tirado, "I thought it was crazy. Go down to City Hall with the children? March around with signs? Probably get arrested? These people have flipped their tops!"

For Rosie Gueits, the prospect of demonstrating didn't seem crazy, but it presented a dilemma nonetheless. "I wasn't worried about myself. I wasn't worried about the kids. But as a cop's wife, I just wondered what the hell I would say to my husband, Joe, if I got arrested. At first, he didn't want me to go at all. We'd seen plenty of demonstrations on television where people went bananas and started destroying things. 'We won't act that way,' I told him. 'We can't. We're taking the kids.'

"'Even with kids around, things could get wild.'

"'No, we promised the parents that it will be orderly.'

"'Well okay,' he said finally, 'but if you get arrested, make sure you give them the name you had *before* you married me!'"

Parents not so deeply involved in the schools showed even more resistance to the idea. "We really had to convince people to do it," observes Carmen Ward. "They were scared and didn't understand exactly what was going on. There's a big difference between seeing that your center is in danger and taking strong action to save it. Lots of programs have come and gone in East Harlem, and people's usual response is to sigh, and say, 'That's life.' They assume that nothing they do can make a difference.

"We had always gone out of our way to show the parents that this was *their* school. But their attitude of helplessness—especially in relation to the people downtown—remained strong. It's hard to tell people they're powerful when they've never had any power. They see themselves as followers, not leaders. And it's not even something they feel bad about. They just accept it as a fact of life. We had to convince them that they could do something to help."

The persuading worked. Early one morning, parents, children, and teachers of the Block Nurseries crowded into a Lexington Avenue subway train and took their case directly to City Hall. Parents who had been critical and unsympathetic toward the student takeover of Columbia University just a month earlier suddenly found themselves singing and parading with picket signs. Everyone went prepared to spend the day. Teachers brought paper, crayons, play-dough, puzzles, and games. The children wore name tags and carried their mats for sitting.

Sonia recalls that four-year-old Eduardo was sitting on the steps of City Hall eating his lunch when the City Comptroller and the Human Rights Commissioner walked up on their way into the building. "Do you want a peanut butter sandwich?" Eduardo asked.

"No thank you, we just had lunch. What are you doing here?"

"I'm here because my Mommy hasn't been paid," Eduardo replied, "and we're tired of eating peanut butter and jelly."

Although one of Mayor Lindsay's aides finally agreed to a short meeting, the real action took place in the afternoon. From City Hall, the entire contingent walked over to 100 Church Street, where the headquarters of the Head Start Program was located. Going right into the building and up in the elevators, they took over the Head Start offices. "We had pots and pans," says Rosie Gueits. "We figured we'd demonstrate and not let them work. We went from office to office in an orderly fashion, making a racket by banging pots and pans."

Having announced their arrival, they made themselves at home. "We spread out all over the offices," says Dorothy Stoneman. "We had the kids drawing and playing with play dough. We created a nice early childhood place. We were a good presence. We hadn't gone there with the idea of being negative or destructive."

Even the most skeptical parents got caught up in what was happening. "Going downtown to demonstrate was the last thing I thought I'd ever do," says Toni Perez. "I kept thinking, What the hell am *I* doing here? But it turned out to be a lot of fun. The women working at their typewriters were happy we came. They stopped typing and sat back and looked at us, knowing they'd have the rest of the day off. We talked with them and made friends. The whole thing was a new experience for me. It was something I never thought I'd have the damn nerve to do, but I did it!"

Finally, late in the afternoon, Head Start officials agreed to a meeting. "They had us go into a conference room," Dorothy recalls. "They wanted only a few of us, but we all packed in. The CDA Commissioner was there, along with the chair of Head Start's Parent Advisory Committee, and the director of Head Start. The meeting went on for a long time, with lots of arguing and yelling back and forth. As it began to break up, we left the conference room, and I saw that Gabe Pressman [a well-known local reporter] had arrived with television cameras. Lots of people were still arguing with the Parent Advisory chair, and I just piped up and said: 'Do you mean to say that we shouldn't have spent the money for renovations, and therefore not had a program at all, since our centers wouldn't have been legal?'

"And he yelled back at me, 'That's right!'

"As it turned out, the exchange was on the television news that evening. The cameras had caught the crux of it. They knew we were in a Catch-22 situation. They knew they were enforcing guidelines that were irrational. But they were going to do it anyway."

Dorothy remembers that as she walked down the streets near City Hall after the confrontation, she was "so mad I imagined throwing bricks through windows." But anger and frustration were not the dominant moods. After six months of tension, the day provided a catharsis and, more important, a demonstration of the strength and solidarity of the Block Schools' community. According to Dorothy: "We were delighted with ourselves that we'd done it. In fact, the whole period of trials and tribulations had a good effect in the long run. People started saying proudly, 'We are the Block Schools!' The crisis strengthened our identification with the schools and created a tradition. Years later, people would say, 'Those were the days!'"

Given the intransigence of Head Start, those good feelings were possible only because a breakthrough was near on another front. The Block Nurseries were about to become the first parent-controlled day care centers in New York City.

In March, when Muriel Katz received Tony's letter proposing that the Block Nurseries become a demonstration project sponsored by the Division of Day Care, she must have thought he had a lot of nerve. The Division had a policy that parents were ineligible to serve on the boards of their children's day care centers; Tony was asking her to accept a program whose entire board consisted of parents. The Division employed college-educated caseworkers to do "intake" and provide social services; Tony was proposing that she turn those functions over to "parent coordinators from the community." The Division required that assistant teachers have two years of college and specified that they could not be parents; most of the Block Nurseries' assistant teachers were parents who had not even graduated from high school. Tony was asking simply that the Block Nurseries continue operating as they had all along. But the points he made in his letter added up to a vision of day care very different from that of the Division.

Muriel Katz did not rush to respond to Tony's request, and her hesitation is understandable. A social worker by training, "Miss Katz" had been with the Division since the 1940s. She had helped to develop its policies, and she believed in them.

The history of day care went back to the latter part of the nineteenth century when upper-class women started "day nurseries" for immigrant children whose mothers had to work. By 1910 New York City had 85 such programs, serving more than 5,000 children daily. Staffed by "matrons" whose primary concern was the physical care of the children, the day nurseries did not provide good early childhood education by modern standards. But they were well suited to the needs of working mothers. They were open for the duration of the working day (10–12 hours). They accepted all ages, from infants to older children requiring after-school care. And they did not, by and large, project negative attitudes toward their clientele. The assumption was that, although it might not be ideal, many women had to work and needed safe places to leave their children (Steinfels, 1973).

During the 1920s, support for the day nurseries waned. Their decline reflected broad social changes, such as the death of the Progressive Movement during World War 1, the end of large-scale immigration, and a decade of economic prosperity. Large numbers of women with children continued to work outside the home, and rural Blacks migrating to northern cities needed day care as desperately as Irish and Italian immigrants had before them. But the need was invisible to more prosperous Americans.

The decade also brought professionalism to the day nurseries. Professional teachers began replacing the matrons, and social workers began to dominate discussions of day care. Reflecting the attitudes of their time, the social workers defined day care as a service necessary because of family maladjustment.

That view represented a major shift. The earlier day nursery movement had seen external circumstances as the cause of poverty. The purpose of the day nursery was to help families who were trying to help themselves. In sharp contrast, the social workers saw conditions *within* families as the cause of poverty. The need for day care, in their view, implied a pathological situation.

By the end of the 1920s, the social work point of view dominated the way most people thought about the day nursery. From a simple, broadly defined service for working mothers, the day nursery had become a marginal social welfare program for "problem families." The onset of the Depression administered the final blow to the day nursery movement, decimating the dwindling number of centers that had survived the decade.

During the 1930s and 1940s, the federal government established day care centers, first as an employment program of the Works Progress Administration, and then as part of a wartime program to mobilize women for work in defense plants. But since both programs were seen as emergency measures, all federal funds for day care were cut after the war, and centers serving a million and a half children were forced to close (Steinfels, 1973).

A well-organized coalition of liberals, social workers, and reformers led by well-to-do activist Elinor Guggenheimer managed to block the attempt to close New York City's day care program in 1947. Organized formally as the Day Care Council, the coalition pressured the city government into funding about 80 centers directly out of city tax levy funds. For the next 20 years, New York City's program and several in California were the only significant public day care programs in the country (Ward, 1979).

Lack of funding was not the only problem day care faced in the postwar period. With the "feminine mystique" shaping attitudes toward women, the conception of day care prevalent in the 1920s reasserted itself. Since women were supposed to find fulfillment in home and family, the working mother was considered "abnormal." After World War II, the number of working women grew steadily until by 1966 more than a fourth of all American women with children under the age of six were working outside the home. But day care remained a service for a small number of families willing to suffer labels like "pathological" or "deviant" (Steinfels, 1973).

Within this context, Muriel Katz was a liberal. She had joined in the successful campaign to save the city's day care program in the 1940s. She was running one of the few significant public day care programs in the country. She was, in Tony's words, "a good liberal social worker, very caring about children, genuinely concerned with helping poor families, and committed to providing a high-quality professional service."

But the prevailing conception of day care as a service for problem families had shaped her thinking and the policies of her agency. As part of the Department of Social Services, the Division was essentially an arm of the welfare system. To Muriel Katz and her colleagues, it was no more appropriate for parents to run day care centers than it was for welfare recipients to run welfare centers. Day care families needed service, not responsibility. And when it came to deciding who should receive services, what they should receive, and how, the professionals knew best.

By the mid-1960s, a convergence of forces was beginning to challenge the assumption that day care was appropriate only for a small number of families with special needs. With so many American women working outside the home, it was becoming impossible to dismiss working mothers as abnormal. Interest in early childhood education was growing as a result of research showing that the years from infancy to five are crucial in a child's cognitive development. The popularity of Head Start was reviving the federal government's interest in preschool programs. The civil rights movement was making Americans more sensitive to racism and to the needs of the poor. Noting the connection between poverty and powerlessness, neighborhood groups were demanding that poor people control the institutions that affected their lives, including their children's schools.

Muriel Katz and her Division of Day Care could not remain immune to these changes forever. As it happened, the Block Nurseries, with help from the Day Care Council, would bring them right to her door.

In December 1967, the same Congress that had wrangled so bitterly over the antipoverty program passed legislation providing substantial federal funding for day care. Seen by conservatives as a way to get women off welfare, and by liberals as an expansion of social welfare programs, the measure (Title IV-A of the Social Security Act of 1967) granted funds to the states on a three-to-one matching basis. Most remarkable, the funds were "uncapped," that is, they were limited only by the ability of the states to come up with their 25% share.

The Day Care Council quickly recognized the opportunity. "We were very excited about the possibilities of the new federal money," recalled Marjorie Grosett. "But it was clear to us that there would be a cap on that money at some point. We knew we had only limited time to bring about expansion and improvement of day care."

Standing in the way was the Division of Day Care. "We felt that with more money becoming available, the Division ought to be looking for ways to expand day care," said Marjorie Grosett. "But those ladies wouldn't hear of change. They always argued that the new centers were substandard—that the buildings were dangerous and that the staffs were poorly trained.

"Our position was that the Division needed new guidelines. We certainly didn't want to encourage bad child care programs, but we wanted the new ones that were good to have a chance. We were convinced that many of the Division's standards were not necessary for high quality."

Still, the Council was having a hard time overcoming the Division's resistance, because the first programs to ask the Council for support *were* substandard. To break down the Division's rigid licensing criteria and open the way for a desperately needed expansion of day care, the Council had to find a test case—a center that was as good as it was innovative.

That was the situation late in February 1968, when Marjorie Grosett and Nancie Stewart visited the Block Nurseries. They realized immediately that they had found what they were looking for. During the next two months, the Council's leadership gave freely of their time and knowledge to the Block Nurseries. In addition to answering the parents' questions about day care, Marjorie Grosett and Nancie Stewart helped Tony and the board develop their strategy for approaching the Division. They advised Tony and the parents to ask that their centers be allowed to keep their parent board, their parent teachers, their parent coordinators, and their "intake procedures" that did not involve investigations of parents' personal lives. At the same time, they suggested that the Block Nurseries accept the Division's policy that centers stay open from 8:00 a.m. to 6:00 p.m., since that was necessary to meet the needs of working parents.

The teachers were quite happy with their 8:30 to 2:30 schedule, and the "long day" became a major topic of discussion at the schools during March. "People kvetched and complained," Tony recalls. "We knew that it would mean working in odd shifts and that it would be harder for teachers to meet together and plan."

But nobody argued that the long day was a violation of the schools' fundamental principles. "Some people even liked it," Tony observes. "They thought that the Nurseries ought to be providing day care. And once again the driving necessity was that our funds were drying up, and here was permanent funding."

In the end the parents decided to take the stance suggested by the Day Care Council. While conceding the long day, they took a strong stand on the four "parent control" issues, which they viewed as fundamental. Incorporated into Tony's March 27 letter to Muriel Katz, that became the schools' initial bargaining position. As Joe Gueits put it: "We went for broke."

But negotiations could not take place until the two parties started talking. When two weeks went by without a response, Nancie Stewart decided to write a letter to her friend Mitchell Ginsberg, who had recently become head of the Human Resources Administration (HRA), a new super-agency established by Mayor Lindsay to coordinate and enhance all of the city's programs for the poor. People at the Day Care Council had gotten to know Ginsberg when he served briefly as Commissioner of the Department of Social Services. A liberal, he had been open to their ideas about day care. According to Marjorie Grosett: "It was clear to us from the beginning that as head of HRA Ginsberg intended to institute some innovations." A few days after Nancie Stewart's letter went out, Muriel Katz finally called Tony, and talks got underway.

Tony recalls that he and the parents had a total of about six meetings with people from the Division. The discussions focused on the four major issues raised by his letter. On the parent board, the Block Nurseries won. According to Tony: "Muriel opened by saying that the Division had a rule that parents couldn't serve on the board of a day care center because it was a conflict of interest. Our first step was to find out if that rule was a state law, or just an agency policy. We found out that it was just a policy enforced by Muriel. The Day Care Council went to people higher up—this time it was Commissioner Goldberg of the Department of Social Services. Parent control was the issue of the day. The Commissioner supported us, and the Division backed down."

The Division also agreed that the schools' parent teachers could continue to work in the classrooms. But since the parents did not meet the Division's qualifications for assistant teachers, they would have to come in under a new job category, "teacher's aide." The pay for teacher's aides was less than the pay for assistant teachers, but the amount was about what the Block Nurseries' parent teachers had been getting all along. And so Tony and the parents agreed to the arrangement. On paper the parent teachers would be "aides." At the Block Nurseries, however, they would continue to be assistant teachers.

The most difficult discussions were about the parent coordinators and the "intake procedures." In other day care centers, caseworkers were responsible for "intake." Hired and assigned by the Division, they interviewed parents who wished to enroll their children and did detailed investigations of parents to determine their eligibility for day care and their need for other services.

Tony and the parents saw no reason why their parent coordinators could not continue to interview new parents and to provide services where needed. Like the Division, the Block Nurseries had always sought to serve those families in greatest need. But personal investigations of families were completely unacceptable to the parents. As an alternative, Tony and the parents proposed what they had been doing all along: accepting families simply on a first-come, first-served basis but only from the poorest areas of East Harlem—the tenement blocks.

Unfortunately, it turned out that by state law, only people hired by and directly responsible to the central funding agency (that is, the Division) could determine eligibility for day care. That ruled out the parent coordinators since they were accountable to the board of the Block Nurseries. Even if Muriel Katz had wanted to give in on this point—which she did not—she would not have had the power to do so.

And so the parents had no choice but to accept the caseworkers. "People didn't like it one bit," Tony recalls. "We finally had to swallow it reluctantly out of pure necessity." The only bright spot was that the schools could continue to have their parent coordinators. However, they would have to be paid out of funds raised privately by the Block Nurseries.

The Nurseries' physical facilities, a major stumbling block for other centers, proved to be no problem.

The schools' finances required more finesse. When Muriel Katz asked for the schools' financial statements, Tony sent her material covering only the period through June 30, 1967. Throughout the negotiations, Tony managed to keep the Nurseries' problems with CDA from becoming an issue. "I couldn't let the Division of Day Care *or* the Day Care Council know how bad things were," Tony admits. "The total issue of how bad our records were and how much money was involved—we didn't tell them."

The final matter was the 3% agency contribution. Katz accepted Tony's assurance that he would raise it from private sources during the summer. By the end of June, the agreement was complete.

To get Division of Day Care funding for parent-controlled nursery schools was a major breakthrough. "It changed the whole day care movement," observes Marjorie Grosett. "It made possible many innovative developments, including parents on boards, parents on staff, and all-parent boards. It was our first success."

But people at the Block Nurseries were giving little thought to the larger significance of their victory. Their concern had been to save their schools, not to reform the city's day care program. And besides, they were too busy licking their wounds.

Tony had suffered most. After CDA had stopped reimbursing the schools in January 1968, it had been his responsibility to find ways to meet payrolls and pay bills. "It was a nightmare," he recalls. "I would barely manage to cover a payroll, and I'd have about 12 hours to feel good about it before the next payroll would be heading down the track toward me. We kept making it—until the middle of May—but it was awful."

At the same time, Tony was helping the parents conduct their delicate negotiations with the Division of Day Care. And on top of this, a major crisis, quite unrelated to CDA or day care, rocked the schools during the spring of 1968. The situation was all the more painful for Tony, because it had to do with his "pet project," the elementary school.

Since the days when he had run the tutoring program on 111th Street, Tony had dreamed of starting an elementary school in East Harlem. Soon after establishing their nursery schools, the parents began to wonder what would happen when their children were ready for first grade. During the winter of 1967, with Tony's encouragement, the board approved the idea of starting an independent parent-controlled elementary school. After managing to raise start-up funds and find classroom space, Tony urged the board to hire two men he'd come to know and like who were teachers at the progressive, independent Walden School. In September 1967, the East Harlem Day School opened as a first-grade storefront classroom on Madison Avenue, not far from the Madison Avenue nursery.

Although the teachers were men of integrity who cared deeply about the children, their educational methods did not appeal to the parents. "Irene started asking when she was going to read, to write, and to do math," recalls Anna Rivera. "She told me that all the kids did was play and that the teachers let the kids scream, curse, and walk on the tables. When I'd ask about reading, the teachers would say, 'The time will come.' I felt the time was already there!"

The situation deteriorated rapidly. Tony, preoccupied with CDA and the Division of Day Care, had neither the time nor the energy to deal with it. Finally, the parents took charge. With support from Dorothy Stoneman, now educational director of the 106th Street nursery, they held a series of meetings in the spring. According to Anna: "We decided that we wanted reading, math, home visits, class meetings, three report cards a year, *and* new teachers."

"That first year in the elementary school was a disaster," Tony admits. "It ended in lots of hurt feelings. The parents just didn't like what the teachers did in the classroom. And the teachers were not used to being accountable to parents. They had come to the schools because of me, and they expected my support. But it wasn't my school."

At the end of June, the schools closed for the summer, and everyone took two months off—except for Tony: "I spent the summer raising $20,000 just to pay enough bills to keep us from being evicted and to keep the phone and light from being turned off. The summer was long and hot, and I sat in the office alone, day after day, amid heaps of messy files, doing housekeeping work, paying bills, and writing letters. Mostly, I remember just feeling exhausted, and hoping I'd feel better in the fall."

Unfortunately, he didn't. In September, the nurseries opened smoothly under Day Care. The elementary school got off to a good start with its new teacher-directors, Dorothy Stoneman and me. But Tony could not shake his feelings of exhaustion. In October, he told the board that he planned to resign as executive director in June 1969, at the end of the school year. But in February, finding himself unable to do his job effectively, he resigned effective immediately. To give the board time to find his replacement, he agreed to stay on through June as the official executive director when a figurehead was required and to help negotiate any differences that arose with the Division of Day Care.

Board members felt shock and sadness. "It hit us like a bomb," recalls Sonia. "My reaction was concern for him. He was close to tears. 'I have given my time and my energy,' he said. 'I have given everything I have to give. And I just can't give anymore.' I knew we would miss him as executive director. I knew we would miss him as a person—he had always been there for us when we needed him. But I didn't feel afraid for the schools. Tony had given us the opportunity to learn. And from all we'd been through, we'd gained a lot of self-confidence."

Tony was not the only one who felt burned out in the wake of the Block Nurseries' protracted struggle for survival. "The schools in general were in disarray," Tony observes. "To some degree, everybody was in the state I was in. We all had the same feeling of exhaustion."

One symptom was the low level of activity by the board of directors. During the fall of 1968, the board met infrequently, and attendance at meetings was low. Even as he prepared to resign as executive director, Tony felt deeply concerned. From the beginning, the key members of the board had been the original founders. Their commitment and enthusiasm had carried the board along. But now, that original group was running out of steam. Florence had left. Joe, Rosie, and Sonia were tired. The board desperately needed fresh blood. And new parents were not flocking to get involved. Only a handful of parents truly understood the board's activities. Dominated by a dwindling group of "old-timers," the board had become remote and distant. It had become *the* board, not *our* board.

Tony also realized that, even when functioning at its best, the board gave only a limited number of parents the chance to have decision-making power over their children's education. There had to be ways, he decided, to involve many more than the dozen or so parents who could serve on the board.

Finally, he was aware that much of the board's time during the past year had been consumed in struggles with outside forces and agencies. That was bound to continue. And it meant that matters dealing with teachers, children, and curriculum in the schools would get short shrift. The board would have to find a way to deal effectively with the Division of Day Care and, at the same time, do justice to issues of more direct concern to parents.

What could be done? How could the board attract energetic new members? How could the board become truly representative of the parent body? How could the board and its activities become more accessible to all the parents? What would foster increased involvement of parents in decision-making, not only on the board, but throughout the schools?

In February 1969, taking the opportunity afforded by his leaving, Tony proposed "drastic reforms" in the organization and membership of the board. "I decided," he recalls, "that one last thing I could do before I left was to help the parents get the schools' structure into good order. I knew that because I was leaving, I could just push like mad without worrying about whether people liked it or not. I could shoot for everything, and get it done."

In a long memo, Tony called the board's attention to the problems, gave his view of the causes, and outlined his proposals. Some of the suggestions dealt with mechanical things. He proposed, for example, that the board set a regular time, place, and date for meetings. And he urged the board to be tougher on its members, dropping people unable to attend meetings regularly.

But the memo also contained two recommendations with far-reaching implications. One was for a new method of electing board members. Instead of electing them at a general parents' meeting, held once a year, Tony proposed that the parents of each class in the schools have a representative to the board, whom they would choose in one of their regular class meetings. Those representatives, who could not be staff members, would then elect a certain number of at-large members, who, although they had to be parents, could be on staff.

The other key recommendation was that the board establish personnel committees in each of the three schools. The committees would be empowered to deal with personnel matters, including hiring and firing of teachers, and to advise the educational director. Like board members, personnel committee members would be chosen by the parents in class meetings. The board would continue to serve as a personnel committee for the executive director, the educational directors, central office personnel, and staff working in more than one school.

The tendency to look for "structural" solutions to problems that arose in the functioning of the schools was characteristic of Tony. "I came to accept that if I really wanted the parents to have a say," he observes, "I had to create a structure for them and then push to keep that structure operating. Or if I didn't, *somebody* did. In the beginning, I believed that a good structure, in itself, was enough. As time went on, I realized that good structures don't necessarily go on working forever. There always has to be somebody there pushing. That's what leadership is all about."

On February 16, 1969, two days after Tony announced his resignation, the board adopted, with only minor changes, all the recommendations Tony had made in his memo. Tony agreed to help the parent coordinators begin implementing them immediately.

The reforms did not come a moment too soon. For by February 1969, after just five months under the Division of Day Care, it was evident that to maintain the integrity of their program, the parents would need all the strength they could muster. According to Sonia: "From the beginning, [being under the Division of] Day Care had a negative effect. When we started, we knew we would be going through a transition, but we had no idea how bad it would be."

As the teachers had anticipated, one of the problems was the long day. "We were used to the kids leaving at 2:30, and the teachers having an hour after that to plan together," says Toni Perez. "Under day care, that went out the window. Everything was rush, rush, rush. And with the shifts, it was like a revolving door, with teachers going in and out."

The Division's bureaucratic regulations were another drain on time and energy. The problem went beyond old-fashioned rules and procedures. "They just didn't understand us," Sonia observes. "They didn't understand where we were coming from, and they kept trying to change us. They thought they had better ways to do everything. The things we had taken for granted—the things that had been working for us—they questioned. We had to fight on every point."

An example was the children's lunch. According to Joe Gueits: "We'd say, 'On Fridays, we want to serve rice and beans and codfish.'"

"They'd say, 'But we don't serve rice and beans in any of our nurseries.'"

"'But this is not one of *your* nurseries. It's the East Harlem Block Nurseries!'"

"'You have to follow our guidelines. And anyway, don't you think carrot sticks and celery go better with codfish?'"

"Before we knew it, we were all staring at each other. It got to be ridiculous."

But the long day and the arguments about food were minor issues compared with problems surrounding the caseworkers.

"The caseworkers just didn't like the East Harlem Block Nurseries," observes Joe Gueits. "They were sent to discourage us, to break our balls, to get across the message, 'Get in line, or get the hell out!'"

The staff and board tried to approach the situation with openness. "We didn't want the caseworkers," Anna Rivera explains, "but we did want our centers to stay open. We wanted to work things out so that the transition to day care would be as smooth as possible."

At the same time, they had no intention of sacrificing the qualities that made their schools special. A key issue was the division of responsibilities between the caseworkers and the parent coordinators. During October, the Block Nurseries' board discussed the matter and produced a written job description for the parent coordinators. The parent coordinator would be the first person a new parent would meet on coming into the center; and she would sit in when the caseworker conducted the "intake" interview.

She also would take part in all meetings between the caseworker and the educational director of the center. The board was hoping that the nurseries would be able to conduct business as usual and that the caseworkers would be willing to provide the stamp of approval required by the people downtown.

It was not to be. The first meeting between Block Nurseries' staff and the caseworkers took place on November 1. Sitting in the parent area of the 106th Street center, the caseworkers and their supervisor listened politely while Tony explained the purpose of the schools, described how they ran, and reviewed their history. "I'm sure this is a very interesting experiment," said the caseworkers' supervisor, "but I'm concerned about the intake process. Miss Barlow and Mrs. Keener need to begin their work immediately."

"We'll begin by interviewing new parents," added Mrs. Keener, "but eventually we'll be interviewing all the parents. We can help the teachers by giving them information about the children and the families."

"We don't have any problem with you getting started with intake," said Joe Gueits, "but as Tony explained in his opening remarks, this is a parent co-op. Our board of directors has decided that the first staff person a new parent meets should be one of our parent coordinators. The parent coordinators know the school and can explain it better to a new parent."

"Don't you think it's better if a professionally qualified person interviews the parent first?" asked the supervisor.

"I've been doing it for two years," said Rosie Gueits, "and it's been working fine."

"I'm sure you have," said the supervisor, "but that's not our usual procedure in day care."

While the tone of the meeting quickly went from polite to icy, the discussion ranged over a variety of issues related to the caseworkers' role. Neither side was willing to give in, and this first skirmish ended in a standoff.

A couple of days later, Rosie Gueits managed to win one point *de facto* for the Block Nurseries. "The caseworker didn't want me to sit down with her and listen when she was interviewing the parents," Rosie recalls, "but I told her, 'I'm sitting here. I'm sitting *right* here—and I ain't budging either.'"

But Rosie could not follow the two women around all day. Almost immediately, their attitudes created friction. According to Joe Gueits: "They were very cold and matter-of-fact. You'd ask them a question, and they'd answer in four words or less. When lunchtime came, it was, 'To hell with you! You people can eat together if you want to, but I don't have to eat with you.'"

But it was not the caseworkers' personal styles—offensive as they were—that proved most infuriating to the parents. It was the questions they asked and the reports they wrote. Those questions and reports reflected their role as defined by the Department of Social Services. Despite their title of "caseworker" or "counselor," their main purpose was to determine each family's "initial and continuing social and financial eligibility for service" and to determine "the fee to be paid by the family based on the income and expenses of the family." Their role was to conduct ongoing "case investigations and evaluations"—and that's exactly how it felt.

"I see you're on welfare. Do you know where your husband is? . . . You're an attractive young woman. I can't believe you're by yourself. . . . Do you have a boyfriend? Are you sleeping with him at the present time? . . . Does he provide any support for your children? . . . Are all your children from the same father? . . . Was your mother married to your father? . . . Did your mother have children by different fathers? . . ." That was a typical sequence of questions for an intake interview. As Rosie Tirado put it, "If you wanted your kid in day care, you had to tell them the color of your underwear."

For a while, they got away with it. The first people they interviewed were new parents, who tended to be shy and quiet. But then they started calling in parents who already had children in the schools—for "recertification." Those parents were not so accommodating. "It's none of your goddamn business!" Blanche yelled. She stood up and shoved the chair she'd been sitting on into the caseworker's desk. "Would you believe this bitch?" she said, calling across the room to Rosie Tirado, who was coming out of the classroom for her break. "She wants to know how I buy such nice things for my son if my husband's dead. I told her it's none of her goddamn business!"

The staff tried a variety of ways of coping with the situation. One was hiding things from the caseworkers. "The Block Schools were known for helping parents," says Toni Perez. "We'd go with them to clinics, listen to them when they were upset, give them carfare out of our own pockets when they needed it—that sort of thing. We were there to help parents—and not to pry. But with the caseworkers there spying on us, we had to help the parents secretly so that the caseworker wouldn't find out and put it into the parent's record."

Sonia describes another tactic: "When parents heard about the questions the caseworkers were asking, they came to me and said, 'We don't want to say anything.' They were nervous—afraid the caseworker would intimidate them into answering her questions. I said, 'Don't worry. I will be your interpreter.' So when the caseworker approached a parent, the parent would say, '*No comprendo Ingles*,' and ask to have me as translator.

I'd come in and help the parents answer the questions. The caseworker never knew that those parents spoke English."

And then there was direct confrontation. "The caseworker was doing an interview," Sonia recalls. "All of a sudden, she started yelling at the parent, 'You are cheating the agency! You are cheating the agency!' Her voice was going loud and clear through the whole school, and the parent was embarrassed.

"Rosie Gueits walked over to her and said, 'You shouldn't treat parents like that.'

"'I'm just doing my job,' the woman said. 'And I'm fed up with the lack of cooperation I'm getting from this center. That woman *is* cheating the government. She's been working part-time for two months, and today is the first time I hear about it!'

"'You could have given her a chance to explain.'"

"'You don't have to tell me how to do my job. I know what I'm doing—and I refuse to discuss it any further.'

"'*Mira, niña,*' said Rosie very quietly. 'Just make sure I never hear you talking like that to a parent again.'"

The conflict moved quickly toward an impasse. While parents and staff refused to be docile, the caseworkers became all the more determined to "do their jobs." "We had very little impact on them," acknowledges Barbara Slemmer, then director of the 106th Street center. "They defended to the end what they were doing."

Finally in February came the incident that sparked the board to action. One morning Sonia noticed a commotion on the sidewalk outside the 106th Street center. "Parents were standing outside of the school in little groups," she recalls. "I went out and asked, 'What's going on?'

"'Sonia,' one of the parents said, 'that woman came to my apartment yesterday and do you know what she did? She asked me when was the last time I had sex with my husband and did I get satisfaction from it.'

"'She did the same thing to me,' said her friend.

"'Did you give her the information?' I asked.

"'No. It's none of her business.'

"'Good. You have done the right thing. But I'd like to know why you are discussing it on the sidewalk. Why don't you bring it to the board meeting? We are meeting this afternoon.'"

Following Sonia's suggestion, several parents from the 106th Street center went to the board meeting and expressed their outrage. When they were done, board members told some stories of their own. It didn't take long for a consensus to emerge: The caseworkers had to go—immediately. But board members also agreed that the decision was too important to be made by the board alone. According to Anna Rivera, then parent coordinator of the

Madison Avenue nursery: "We weren't going to fire the people who were giving us the money without having the assurance of the whole group."

The following evening, an emergency meeting for all Block Schools' parents took place at the Madison Avenue center. Despite the short notice, 50 parents crowded into the storefront classroom. They needed no encouragement to start talking.

"She asked me how many TVs I have. I'd like to know what that has to do with getting my kid into day care!"

"She asked me the same thing. And then she wanted to know how I got my TV—did a boyfriend give it to me? She's too nosy."

"What do they do with this information?"

"I'll tell you what they do with it," answered Sonia. "We have noticed a very curious thing. The caseworker talks to a parent, okay—maybe it's on a home visit, or on the sidewalk, or in the center. Afterwards, she sits right down and writes—and writes and writes! We have seen that happening for a long time. Now we have realized that all the information the parents give is going downtown—on paper."

"That's right," said Barbara Slemmer. "Our caseworker has a locked file. I'm not supposed to have access to it, but I looked through it anyway. In the file, I found insulting reports, passing judgment on the parents and their children. The report forms are in triplicate, and the copies go downtown into files that follow the child. One report said, 'This child is obstreperous . . . ' And that child is *not* obstreperous by any stretch of the imagination."

"Parents don't even drop by our classroom any more," added Rosie Tirado. "They say they don't want the caseworker to see them."

"It's the same at Madison," said Anna Rivera. "Parents don't feel welcome anymore."

For an hour, the parents poured out their stories—and got more and more angry. "I want to know how long we have to put up with this," someone said finally. "Our rights are being violated."

"Yes, but [the Division of] Day Care gives us our money."

"Look, they took away our money before, and we survived. If it was up to me, I'd say we shouldn't even allow those people through our doors again."

"The question," said Tony, "is whether you're ready for another fight."

"We have to fight—that's all there is to it. And we'll find a way to survive. We did it before, and we'll do it again."

"Right! We can't allow them to do this to us."

"Right! They're not going to take our rights away just because we live in the ghetto. We've got to take a stand."

"Right! Let's get 'em out—now!"

The decision was unanimous. "We agreed that we didn't want the caseworkers to come back to our centers," Anna recalls. "And we agreed that we didn't want others to take their places."

The parents directed Joe Gueits as chairman of the board to send a telegram to the Division of Day Care, demanding the immediate removal of the caseworkers. And they did not stop there. The real problem, the parents knew, was not with Miss Barlow and Mrs. Keener, but with their role, as defined by the Department of Social Services. To deal with that issue, they decided to press six other demands: that the Division assign no caseworkers at all to the Block Nurseries; that the schools' parent coordinators take over the caseworkers' functions; that simple statements by parents of their need for service replace the detailed investigations of their personal lives; that intake be on a first-come, first-served basis; that the fee be the same for all parents; and that all records on individual families be confidential to the schools, not filed downtown at the Department of Social Services. The parents asked Tony to write a letter to Muriel Katz containing those demands and the reasons for them.

Joe's telegram went out that evening, and Miss Barlow and Mrs. Keener never set foot inside the Block Nurseries again. Yet even in their absence, the caseworkers managed to create a stir. Anna Rivera explains what happened: "When Miss Barlow first came to our center, she gave the impression right away that she wasn't a friendly sort of person. But one day some of the parents and I were talking: 'Maybe it's *our* fault. Maybe she's standoffish because *we* haven't been friendly.' So I decided—like an ass—that I'd try to make her feel more at home. I went to her desk and started talking to her.

"Right off the bat, she started asking me all kinds of questions. Trying to make her feel comfortable, I opened up. I was naive. I thought she was asking me like a friend. We talked for an hour.

"Well, after the caseworkers left, I cleaned out Miss Barlow's desk. In a folder I found three pages stapled together with my name on them. I still remember what was written there. 'Anna Rivera is an obese Puerto Rican woman with a space between her two upper front teeth,' the report began. 'She is wearing a housedress. She is clean and well kept. Even though she is Puerto Rican and did not graduate from high school, she speaks well and seems highly intelligent . . . '

"It went on for three pages. Everything I'd told her that day—there it was. She even had my goals written down there—and an incident that had happened to me in eighth grade. The deceitful mess of it was that I had told her those things in confidence—as one person to another.

"I was outraged. If I'd seen her again, I would have kicked her fuckin' ass—I would have turned 'ghetto.' I'd been upset about what the caseworkers had been doing to other people, but now the reality hit *me* smack in the face. I wondered who was supposed to read it and what right she had to put those kinds of things on that form. Had she written down every conversation parents had had with her? If she could write three pages after an hour's conversation, what else might be in my file downtown? What else might be in the files of the other parents? We said lots of personal things around that office. And if you're a person with a title, people feel obligated to answer your questions. So I could imagine how much information she had on us."

The news of Anna's discovery spread quickly throughout the schools and strengthened the parents' determination to maintain a tough stand. Meanwhile, Tony was working on his letter to Muriel Katz, which finally went out on March 3. "I did it under extreme pressure from the board and the parents," he admits. "I was following everybody else on it. My feeling was, 'Let this cup pass from me . . . ' But I knew I had to do it."

Despite his reluctance, Tony managed to write a masterful letter, which would become a key position paper in the citywide day care reform campaign. "We regret that we must request removal of the caseworkers," the letter began. It noted that although the caseworkers themselves had brought on some of their problems, the real difficulty lay in the nature of the caseworkers' position. "We are convinced," Tony wrote, "that we can define their role and responsibility in a way which will satisfy parent and community groups, and at the same time fulfill all the essential requirements of State law and of the Department of Social Services." The heart of the letter was a new definition of the caseworker's role, which incorporated the parents' six demands. It closed with a request for a meeting with people from the Division "at the earliest possible moment."

That meeting took place on March 10, 1969, in Muriel Katz's office. Joe, Rosie, Sonia, and Anna were among the board members who accompanied Tony. "We entered the room and sat down around the table," Joe recalls. "Miss Katz came in with a couple of other people. 'Good morning, good morning,' they said, smiling and frowning at the same time. (I could never understand how they did it, but they had that knack: smile, frown, and tongue-in-cheek—all at the same time.) We started off discussing Tony's letter. For a while, everything went nice and smooth. Miss Katz was very soft-spoken, very matter-of-fact, but I could tell right away that she wasn't an easy person to bully. She was from the old school. She was like one of those mean old teachers you had when you were a kid. Without raising her voice, she could intimidate you. She could upset you very much, just with her attitude."

"Basic to the contractual agreement you signed is the assignment of a Department of Social Services caseworker," Muriel Katz said, in Sonia's recollection of the meeting. "That responsibility is spelled out in Day Care Bulletin Number 27—"

"I don't want to hear anything more about this regulation or that regulation," replied Sonia. "Do you know what age this is? This is the age of *space*! We are soon going to send a man to the moon, and you are talking about memos written in the 1940s. Please deal with us from the year we are in."

"You can read the regulation for yourself. It's part of the contractual agreement."

"I don't want to read some old regulation. I want precise information from 1969. I don't see why you can't treat us with respect, instead of dealing with us through memos. I don't see why you can't deal with us according to who we are. We are the first group in day care that is different, and you knew ahead of time what the Block Schools were all about. So why can't you accept us the way we are?"

"We are prepared to be as flexible as possible within the framework of our legal mandate."

"Fine. Since you have respect for us and we have respect for you, let it continue that way. But in the future, make sure you relate to us in the era that we are in."

"I want you to know that I am prepared to assign a Spanish-speaking caseworker to your center."

"Because somebody speaks Spanish does not necessarily mean that they know East Harlem."

"I'm afraid that's the best I can do at this point. Now on the matter of the fees—"

"Just a minute," Joe interrupted. "The thing Sonia is trying to get at is that we have parent coordinators. True, they don't have degrees. They aren't so-called 'professionals.' But the school has trained them and they're doing the job. They know how to deal with parents. Those caseworkers you sent—it's ridiculous. I'm a police officer, and your people ask more goddamn questions than I do when I investigate a rape or burglary."

The meeting went on for two hours. In the course of the discussion, Muriel Katz expressed support for a number of points in Tony's letter. She acknowledged that the questions about personal history that the parents found offensive did not have to be asked. She agreed that the existing fee rates were unrealistically high. To ensure confidentiality, she said, case records would not be made available to anyone other than day care caseworkers and Block Schools personnel, without the written permission of the parent; and the caseworkers would not examine any other records about the family, such as a welfare case record, without the written permission of the parent. But the income investigation and the sliding fees were state requirements, beyond her power to change. And the Block Nurseries had to accept caseworkers hired, assigned, and supervised by the Division of Day Care.

Tony and the parents returned from the meeting and talked it over. A letter went out to Muriel Katz on March 21 outlining the board's decisions. In the letter Tony noted the areas of agreement that had emerged in the March 10 meeting. He said the board had agreed to accept her suggestion for ensuring confidentiality of records. Acknowledging that the income investigation and the sliding fee scale were state requirements, Tony noted that the schools would continue to press for a flat fee and income affidavit—on the state level, if necessary—and expressed the hope that the Division would support the schools' effort. "However," he wrote, "a counselor assigned to us by the Division of Day Care without the approval of our board, and not subject to direct supervision by our staff, is not acceptable. We will continue to insist that the counselor be a Spanish-speaking person, hired from our community by our board, and subject to our supervision."

Muriel Katz held firm. "I am prepared . . . to assign a Spanish-speaking caseworker, . . . " she wrote in her letter dated April 11. "I must know from you, however, that the caseworker will be accepted and permitted to function. . . . The continuation of our funding agreement is of necessity contingent upon this cooperation."

At its April 23 meeting, the board finally gave in. It voted to accept the new caseworkers provisionally, but to suggest that before starting work, they visit the schools and meet with the board. As Anna admits, "We didn't have much choice. It was either accept them—or no money."

In May, two new caseworkers—one African-American and one Puerto Rican—showed up at the schools and began work. The Block Nurseries were now, once again, in compliance with the Division's regulations. But the principled stand taken by the parents was already beginning to reverberate throughout New York's day care community. The days of the caseworkers were numbered—not only at the Block Nurseries, but at every day care center in the city.

5

Battling the System, Part I

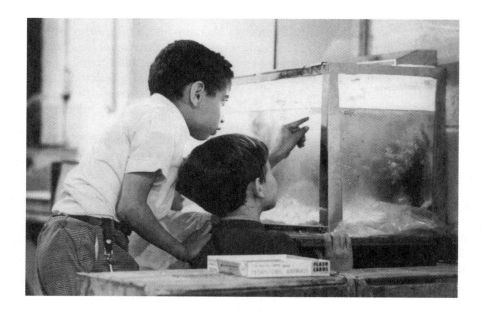

On May 7, 1969, two weeks after agreeing to the compromise on the case-workers, the board asked Dorothy Stoneman to become executive director. The 28-year-old woman accepted the position immediately, and the period of limbo that had begun in February with Tony's resignation came to an end.

Dorothy had no illusions about the enormity of the task that lay before her. But meeting challenges was nothing new for Dorothy Stoneman. As a senior at Radcliffe, she had resolved to "go as far out onto the frontiers of fighting injustice as my temperament would allow me." When her plans to go to the Congo to set up schools for Angolan refugees fell through, she came to New York City, enrolled in a master's program at Bank Street College, and immediately set to work organizing a summer program for African-American preschool children. Needing help, she thought of Lois Goldfrank, an old friend who recently had graduated from Bryn Mawr. "Come to Harlem," Dorothy urged. And Lois did. During the summer of

1964, when many of their peers went south for the "Mississippi Summer Project," the two young White women, who had grown up together in an upper-middle-class suburb of Boston, ran a program for 120 five-year-olds in Central Harlem.

During the next two years, Lois found her way to the Block Nurseries, and Dorothy became a second-grade teacher at Public School 92 in Central Harlem. Lois enjoyed her teaching at the 106th Street nursery, while Dorothy found her work as a second-grade teacher ever more frustrating. This time, it was Lois's turn to do the persuading. When a teaching position opened up at 106th Street in November 1966, she convinced her friend to apply.

If it had been up to Tony, Dorothy wouldn't have gotten her first job at the Block Nurseries as teacher of the three-year-olds. He preferred the other candidate, who seemed "softer and gentler." But the board, impressed by Dorothy's energy and sense of humor, hired her enthusiastically over Tony's recommendation.

Tony would never regret being overruled. After a successful year in the classroom, Dorothy became director of the 106th Street nursery. During the spring of 1968, she not only steered her center through the funding crisis with Head Start, but intervened effectively in the elementary school, helping the parents act on their dissatisfaction with their new first grade. In September 1968, she became first-grade teacher and co-director of the elementary school.

On the surface, the dynamic young woman who would lead the Block Schools for two years could hardly have been more different from Tony. In contrast to Tony's reserve and wry humor, Dorothy was warm, earthy, open with her feelings, and overwhelming in her enthusiasms.

But the board had no doubts that she was the best person to take Tony's place. "We didn't interview anybody else," recalls Joe Gueits. "We knew her. We'd worked with her as a teacher and as a director. She was very active and full of energy—always ready to go someplace to fight or argue. We knew she was totally committed to the philosophy of the school."

The first challenge for the new executive director was to deal with the schools' desperate financial situation. Dorothy had never done fund raising before. "It was all new to me," she admits. "Every time I picked up the phone, my heart would beat faster. I wouldn't know what to say, and I'd have to force something out."

One of the first people she called was Saul Wallen, executive director of the Urban Coalition, an organization created by business leaders and using the slogan "Give a Damn!" "My father had an old business relationship with Saul," Dorothy recalls. "He invited me to his office. I told him about the Block Schools, and he said we should submit a proposal."

Jan Douglas, staff member for the Coalition, made a site visit, liked what she saw, and recommended funding. "I was at 1712 Madison [site of the first- and second-grade classrooms] when I got the call," says Dorothy. "Jan Douglas told me that we would get all of the $19,000 we'd asked for. I got off the phone, and jumped up and down screaming and yelling 'Hooray!' I let loose—all the way—and the children thought it was the most amazing thing for an adult to act like that."

The victory was short-lived. At home in the evening several days later, Dorothy got a phone call from Tony. "They can't do that!" she yelled. "They just can't do that to us!"

"Yes they can," said Tony, "and they just did!"

"They" was Manufacturers Hanover Trust, where the Block Schools had their bank accounts. Tony informed Dorothy that the bank had just seized $11,000 of the new grant as repayment plus interest for a $10,000 loan it had made a year earlier when Head Start had cut off funds for the nurseries. "We were left," recalls Tony, "with nothing but feelings of totally helpless rage."

But once Dorothy recovered from the shock, she saw an opportunity to turn the setback to the Block Schools' advantage. For by grabbing $11,000 of the grant money, the bank had stung not only the parents and staff of the Block Schools but influential people at the Coalition, who had intended their money to support a school, not a bank. When Dorothy told Saul Wallen and Jan Douglas what had happened, they were outraged. And when she filled them in on the background—the cutoff of funds by Head Start and the dispute with CDA over the revolving funds—they agreed to help.

Saul and Jan got on the phone to CDA officials and to their higher-ups in the Human Resources Administration. They instructed their lawyer, who happened to be Robert Egan, an old friend of the Block Schools, to write a letter threatening a lawsuit. Ruth Feder, a member of the schools' Advisory Committee, also used her influence with HRA's Commissioner Mitchell Ginsberg. The result was a meeting, held in July at the Coalition's offices, in which Dorothy and Robert Egan won a written agreement that if the schools could prove their case, the city would cooperate in arriving at a fair settlement.

Despite the bank's action, the Coalition's grant also marked a turning point in bringing private money to the Block Schools. Money attracts money: Potential funders were impressed by the Coalition's generosity. Before the summer was out, grants from foundations came in, providing much-needed cash for back salaries and bills. Then in August the Block Schools received a $30,000 grant from Follow Through, a new federal program to extend the advantages of Head Start into the early elementary grades.

With September approaching, the Block Schools' financial prospects looked better than they had for a long time. Like everyone else, Dorothy wondered what the coming year would bring for the nurseries. Would staff and parents be able to live with the new caseworkers? Would Muriel Katz object if the centers closed for a week for staff training?

During their first year under Day Care, the Block Nurseries had fought hard to change policies that were undermining the integrity of their program. Muriel Katz had resisted with equal determination. But time was running against "Miss Katz" and her colleagues at the Division of Day Care. A powerful grassroots day care reform campaign was coalescing. The Block Schools would no longer have to fight their battles alone.

Dorothy Stoneman and Tony Ward attended the first meeting of the Committee for Community-Controlled Day Care, which took place on Saturday, February 1, 1969. Organized by Dorothy Pitman, director of the West 80th Street Center, and Bob Gangi, a community organizer who was helping her with fund raising, the gathering brought together a dozen representatives of struggling grassroots child care programs from around the city.

The agenda was survival. All of the programs except the Block Nurseries received their funding from the Office of Economic Opportunity. With the poverty agency suffering severe cutbacks, they faced an uncertain future. People from these centers were interested to learn that the Block Nurseries had already lost their antipoverty funding and were the first parent-controlled day care centers in the city.

Within two weeks, fears and rumors had become reality: The city informed five small child care centers on the Lower East Side that funding for their programs would end in two months.

The Committee discussed having a demonstration, but Elinor Guggenheimer, the well-to-do veteran of day care struggles and a friend of Dorothy Pitman, told the group: "You don't really want to have this demonstration. Public officials are much more scared of demonstrations *before* they happen than after they happen. You want to get them to give in before the date you've set so that you can call it off."

Taking that advice, the Committee staged a well-orchestrated campaign that involved newspaper publicity and meetings with public officials. "We went right to Mitchell Ginsberg, head of the Human Resources Administration," recalls Micaela Hickey, a recent graduate of Wellsley College working as a volunteer for the Committee. "We called him up and to our amazement he called us back! There was the head of the HRA calling this handful of little people and begging us: 'Please, *please* call off the demonstration.'"

On March 24, three days before the date set for the demonstration, an agreement was signed. The Community Development Agency agreed to continue funding the five centers while the centers, with the city's help, looked for ways to finance the major renovations required for compliance with the Health Code, the major hurdle that stood in the way of the centers' getting funding from the Division of Day Care.

Buoyed by their success, Dorothy Pitman, Bob Gangi, and Micaela Hickey plunged into the work of the Committee. They were a powerful trio: Pitman, a militant African-American woman with an enormous Afro whose knack for intimidating "my strait-laced ladies at the Division of Day Care" was matched only by her ability to impress the rich and famous (Isaac and Vera Stern were helping to furnish the kitchen of the West 80th Street Center); Gangi, six feet three inches tall, brash, driven, a native New Yorker of Italian working-class background, a recent graduate of Columbia University, and a New Left radical; and Hickey, willing to do the nitty-gritty work behind the scenes.

Describing their vision, Gangi says: "We felt the torch had been passed to us. The struggle for community control in the public schools had met serious defeat. We felt we'd have a better chance to achieve community control of day care because the union and the bureaucracy in day care were less powerful."

During the spring the Committee developed solid position papers on three major issues: facilities, eligibility and intake, and staff qualifications. The paper on eligibility and intake was essentially Tony's letter to Muriel Katz explaining the reasons for the dismissal of the caseworkers.

Armed with these documents, railing against bureaucracy and calling for community control, the "handful of little people" who made up the Committee for Community-Controlled Day Care soon established a presence in the city far beyond their actual numbers.

A former teacher at the Bank Street Children's School would find a way to provide invaluable support for the Committee and ultimately for the Block Nurseries as well. Peter Sauer recently had become director of "Bank Street on Morningside," an office established to create good will for the institution in order to pave the way for its move from Greenwich Village to the Upper West Side. Peter discovered immediately that lots of groups in the neighborhood wanted to start day care centers, or had already done so but needed help. After he met Dorothy Pitman and Bob Gangi and saw the Committee getting underway, he conceived of a day care consultation service, independently funded but part of Bank Street College. "I saw it as providing staff support for the Committee, technical assistance for community groups, and resources in early childhood education." Since day care was a natural idea for the College, Peter had no trouble selling the idea to President John Niemeyer. Staffed by Peter Sauer and Micaela Hickey, Bank Street's Day Care Consultation Service went into operation by the summer of 1969.

During that summer, day care reformers got another boost, when President Nixon appeared to pick up the day care banner. As part of a proposal to overhaul the welfare system, he asked Congress for $386 million for day care. Although his welfare reform plan ultimately died in committee, Nixon's apparent endorsement of day care helped turn what had always been a tidy liberal cause into "the issue of the day."

While the country was split over the Vietnam War, the civil rights movement, and the fate of the antipoverty program, day care seemed, for the moment, to be something Left and Right could agree on. Suddenly everyone was talking about day care. Local politicians were quick to recognize the possibilities. By becoming advocates for day care, they could garner support among African-Americans, Latinos, working women, antipoverty activists, and liberals, while making a case to conservatives that they were saving money by getting people off welfare. Best of all, the federal government would pay for it! Since Title IV-A provided federal funds on a three-to-one matching basis, New York City's day care program could be tripled at relatively modest cost to the city and the state.

On September 4, the city announced that it would finance 40 new day care centers within 12 months. The timing of the announcement was no accident. Mayor John Lindsay, having lost the Republican primary, was battling for a second term (and his political life) as the candidate of New York's Liberal Party. Since day care was the issue of the day, all of the candidates were trying to outdo each other in advocating day care expansion and reform. No matter who won, it seemed that there would be strong political support for expansion and reform of day care, and that was good news for the Block Schools.

The new caseworkers assigned to the Block Nurseries in April 1969 had worked out better than anyone had dared hope. "Everybody hit it off with Monica and Fatima right from the beginning," recalls Joe Gueits. "The first thing you noticed about Monica was her Afro. She was a young, tall, lanky, attractive, Black chick. She had a great personality; she was radical; and she spoke Spanish. Fatima was also Black. She was conservative in attire—neat, proper, hair always just in the right place.

"Fatima was the more conservative of the two: She would follow Day Care's guidelines but bend them for the Block Nurseries. Monica would follow the schools' guidelines, but bend a little for Day Care. Both Fatima and Monica gave their allegiance to the Block Schools. So it worked very well."

It did indeed! Thanks to Monica and Fatima, the Block Nurseries could operate much as they had before becoming day care centers.

Then on December 5, Dorothy Stoneman, Monica, Fatima, the educational directors of both nurseries, and parent coordinators Anna Rivera and Rosie Gueits had a routine meeting with several people from the Division to discuss what kinds of case records would be mutually acceptable. At issue was the "family history," defined by the Division as a "diagnostic study of the family." The requirement that caseworkers do family histories had been a major cause of the conflict over the first pair of caseworkers.

The negotiations with Muriel Katz following the removal of the first set of caseworkers had resolved one aspect of the problem: confidentiality. The Block Schools had accepted Muriel's promise that case records would not be made available to anyone other than Division of Day Care caseworkers and Block Schools personnel, without written permission of the parent. But what should go into the records had not been settled. To address that issue was the purpose of the December 5 meeting.

The discussion seemed constructive enough. The people from downtown listened while Anna and Rosie explained their position. Anna and Fatima agreed to write a sample record—one that would include only information that Anna found acceptable—as a first step toward creating a form for case records that everyone could agree on.

But in the course of the meeting Monica and Fatima let it slip that they had not done any family histories since beginning work with the Block Schools. Upon returning to headquarters, the Division's people passed that little piece of information on to Muriel Katz.

"I am shocked to realize that the caseworkers at the Block Nurseries have not been writing family histories," she told Dorothy Stoneman over the phone on December 9. "They must do them, and they must begin immediately!"

As soon as Muriel Katz hung up, Dorothy got on the phone to Anna and Rosie and told them what had happened. With their help, she drafted a response. "Parents feel that these records invade their privacy and represent an attitude of disrespect and paternalism," she wrote in the letter, which went out on December 12. To make her point, Dorothy quoted at length from a case record she had obtained from another center. Single-spaced and two and a half pages long, it began: "She is an emotionally inept woman—that is, she is very namby-pamby in her attitudes towards herself and towards other people. She impresses you as being a person with little or no personality of her own. She has strong Roman Catholic beliefs. . . . It becomes evident that this woman has deep seeded [sic] emotional problems. . . . She is, I believe, trying to punish her husband with this last pregnancy knowing that he could not afford to take care of another child."

"I am sure you will agree," wrote Dorothy, "that this kind of record serves no useful purpose. We not only question the usefulness of these records, but we question the larger social attitudes which give one group of people the idea that they have the right—even the responsibility—to record the personal lives of other people, and pass them on to be read by whoever may share the professional privilege of reading the intimate details of another person's life.

"We would like to sit down with you immediately to discuss this issue and to present the format for case records which we believe would be useful."

The meeting was set for January 7. The Block Schools' board of directors met in emergency session on December 18 and agreed on an acceptable format for case records: the reason for the meeting with the parent; health information; social service resources used by the family; assistance requested; action taken; and follow-up. On December 29, Dorothy sent Muriel Katz an outline of the board's proposed format, along with several case records from other centers rewritten according to the board's guidelines.

On January 7, a dozen representatives of the Block Schools' board and staff went down to the offices of the Division of Day Care and filed into a drab conference room for the meeting. The Division's director made it clear from the beginning that she hadn't been swayed by Dorothy's letters. Nor was she in the mood for compromise.

She began by flatly rejecting the Block Schools' proposed format for case records since it provided "too little information." "You can keep whatever records you want," she said, "but the Division will keep the same kinds of records we have always kept down here." She said she understood that at the board's request Monica and Fatima were putting off making home visits to families until after their children had been admitted to the program. That had to stop. Since the purpose of the home visits was to verify the families' eligibility, they must be done *prior to* admission.

She admitted that the family histories Dorothy had enclosed with her December 29 letter were unfortunate. The caseworkers who wrote them certainly had shown bad judgment. But those case records were not typical. And the solution was not to change the format but to provide better training and supervision for the workers.

Rosie Gueits was first to respond. "Why should a caseworker go into a whole thing about a parent when it doesn't have anything to do with the child coming into day care?" she protested. "Why do you need to know what the parent looks like or whether it was a rainy day or a cloudy day?"

"The description of the parent is part of the diagnostic study of the family we expect the caseworkers to do at intake," Muriel Katz replied.

"I know that. I'm asking what difference it makes what the parent looks like? What difference does it make whether the parent is fat or thin or has blue eyes or brown eyes? It's the child who needs the service, right?"

"It gives a picture of the family, that's all. And I don't see how it does any harm."

"Well I do!" Rosie was angry. "It's offensive—the way they describe people."

"Can you give me an example of what you mean?"

"Yes. When they describe someone as an obese Black woman, that's offensive. When they put down that someone is a fat Puerto Rican, that's offensive."

"Why? I don't see what's offensive. How would you describe the person?"

"Maybe I can explain what Rosie's getting at," Joe Gueits said. "How would *you* like to read a case record of *yourself* described as . . . er, a 'horseface'?"

When Joe said the word "horseface," Rosie recalls that Muriel Katz's back stiffened and everyone else's jaw dropped. "For a moment," says Dorothy, "we weren't sure whether Joe was actually calling her a horseface—but he was! Miss Katz had a long face for her height and that's how Joe saw her, as a horseface. He and Rosie were both very angry. But when the rest of us realized what had happened, it was all we could do to keep from laughing."

Seeing Muriel Katz flinch when Joe called her a horseface made the whole meeting worthwhile as far as Rosie Gueits was concerned. According to Rosie: "We made her know how parents feel when they're described in the case records."

The Block Schools also got an important piece of information. When pressed on the question of whether the Division's intake procedures were dictated by state law or by city policy, Muriel Katz admitted that they were a matter of city policy. State law laid down the criteria, but it was up to the city to submit a plan to the state describing the exact process by which it would determine eligibility. Acknowledging that those matters were "under review," the Division's director said that until a new plan was submitted by the city, she felt bound to follow the old one.

And so it had come down to the same thing it always came down to with Muriel Katz: policy—policy that for one reason or another couldn't be changed.

As usual Sonia had the last word. "We will go above you," she said as the meeting broke up. "We'll go to the one above you and to the next one and to the next one; and if we need to go to Ginsberg, we'll go to Ginsberg.

We will go right to the people who have more power and demand that these case records be changed!"

Unknown to Sonia or to Muriel Katz, the higher-ups had already gotten the Block Schools' message. A few days after the January 7 meeting, an inside source told Dorothy confidentially that the State Commissioner of Social Services had already decided to change the intake procedures for day care without informing the Division's director. The format for case records would be changed to include only a simple statement of the family's need for day care. "We deserve much of the credit for pushing the state to make changes," Dorothy told the Block Schools' board. "We have been the loudest voice of protest with the most concrete, factual objections."

Pressing their advantage, the Block Schools and the Committee for Community-Controlled Day Care immediately began calling for the removal of caseworkers from day care centers altogether and their replacement by "parent coordinators," hired by and responsible to each center.

The matter of the caseworkers was part of a broader issue of staff qualifications that dominated discussions among day care reformers during the winter of 1970. Dorothy Pitman wanted her entire staff to be people from the community "because they were more concerned about what's happening with people's lives." As far as she was concerned, formal credentials were not a requirement—or even an asset. "What does a credential or a degree tell you about how good a teacher is?" she told a *New York Times* reporter at the time. "All they ever teach children is White middle-class values that tell Black children they are second-class and that stifle curiosity." But Marjorie Grosett of the Day Care Council attacked as racist the suggestion that centers be allowed to choose uncertified people to be group teachers. "That would lower standards and impose inferior education on Black children," she charged.

The Block Schools had several parents whose talent and experience qualified them to be group teachers. But the parent board had shown a marked lack of enthusiasm for making them group teachers on a permanent basis since they lacked the appropriate credentials. They needed the chance to fill in gaps in their education, in some cases to earn their high school equivalency diplomas, and to get college degrees. Then they would be ready. Accordingly, the Block Schools emphasized staff training. Greater flexibility in hiring was necessary, but it had to be accompanied by effective training or standards would indeed be lowered.

In March, the Carnegie Corporation awarded a substantial grant to the Bank Street Day Care Consultation Service. During the spring and summer of 1970, Peter and Micaela hired a staff (including Tony Ward), expanded from aiding only West Side organizations to helping groups all over the city, and began putting together a thick manual for neighborhood people on "how to organize and finance your own day care center."

On March 9, Mayor Lindsay announced the appointment of a Task Force "to examine early childhood services in New York City, to assess their effectiveness . . . and to recommend changes in the quantity and quality of the programs as well as to explore the feasibility of establishing an office for early childhood services."

Dorothy Stoneman was one of the people invited to serve on the Mayor's Task Force, whose 21 members also included Elinor Guggenheimer, Muriel Katz, Nancie Stewart of the Day Care Council, Dorothy Pitman, Peter Sauer, and representatives from the union, Head Start, and other city agencies concerned with early childhood education. The chair was Trude Lash, executive director of Citizens Committee for Children, a prestigious child advocacy organization.

Supporting the Task Force's work was a staff of 11 people, directed by Georgia McMurray, an African-American woman in her mid-thirties who was director of social services planning for HRA.

The Mayor's Task Force was the reformers' dream come true. After years of struggling on the outside, the veterans of day care reform efforts and a new generation of activists were coming together with people from the relevant city agencies to hammer out a program for major change in New York City day care.

A positive outcome was far from guaranteed, however. "The biggest challenge I faced as chair," recalls Trude Lash, "was to get people with such violently opposed opinions and beliefs first to talk to each other and then to agree on recommendations that were meaningful, that would benefit children, that would lead us out of the situation where people were fighting each other so much."

A particularly contentious issue was whether day care center boards must include parents. Recalls Dorothy Stoneman: "Day care directors from the old-line centers were saying they couldn't run their centers if parents were on their boards—that parents would just come around to complain and wouldn't make the sacrifices necessary to make a real contribution. Dorothy Pitman and Peter Sauer backed off, but I held out. I said, 'All centers should have *a majority* of parents on their boards, whether they're old-line or new.' I wouldn't budge, and I pushed and pushed and pushed, and Dorothy Pitman and Peter Sauer came back on, and Nancie Stewart [of the Day Care Council] was freaking out. In the end Nancie Stewart lost and my position on parents went into the final report. The Day Care Council was very upset."

Surprisingly, the idea of establishing an umbrella agency for the city's programs for young children provoked little controversy. A long-time goal of Elinor Guggenheimer, a comprehensive agency for early childhood services fit in with the Lindsay administration's overall plan for reforming the city's bureaucracy by creating super-agencies.

Community control advocates might have questioned whether a super-agency eventually would pose a threat to local autonomy. They might have pointed out the contradiction between parent control and a powerful city agency. But no one did. As Trude Lash observed shrewdly, "Everyone was comfortable with an overall agency, but many secretly hoped they would run it."

The Task Force met from March through June, at least once a week and sometimes twice, with subcommittee meetings as well. The staff often prepared minutes and memoranda overnight. "For a while, I thought there were going to be two reports," Trude Lash admits. "It looked as though there might be one report that stressed standards and another that stressed community control. But in the end we came through it together—there was no minority report."

In June, as their work was nearing its end, the Mayor's Task Force went upstate for a weekend retreat. "That was when I burst into tears when Trude didn't call on me," Dorothy Stoneman admits. "I was so embarrassed. I was the youngest member of the Task Force, but I wasn't that young. I shouldn't have been bursting into tears!"

A high point of the retreat was an exchange Dorothy Stoneman had with Muriel Katz. "One evening on the porch, she told me that she really knew that I had the best interests of children at heart, that she had no doubt whatever about my motives, and that she trusted me. 'You people at the Block Nurseries really truly do stand for something you believe in. You really do have integrity and you're not out for power or glory or to do something awful—and I respect you.'"

Despite Dorothy's tearful scene, Trude remembers her as an extremely useful member of the Task Force: "She was very, very helpful most of the time. She was also very stubborn. She came out of working with children, and couldn't be easily deceived. I think she probably had little patience with bureaucrats. I had visited the Block Schools and been very impressed. I talked with a lot of Block Schools mothers. I was impressed with how different it was from other schools. There was a freedom about the place—an inviting atmosphere. You could see the effect on the people who were there."

The Task Force's report was presented to the Mayor in July at a press conference. The first recommendation was to create a new Department of Early Childhood Services. The other recommendations bore the strong stamp of community control advocates. On the issue of eligibility, the Block Schools' position carried the day. The Task Force recommended that a family's eligibility for day care be determined by residence in a target area and that the staff of individual centers be responsible for implementing eligibility guidelines. The clear implication of this recommendation was that caseworkers from downtown would no longer be necessary.

The Task Force recommended that one-third of the board members of existing agencies be parents, and that parents be a majority of board members of future sponsor agencies.

On staffing qualifications, the Task Force recommended: more flexible routes for becoming group teachers, released time for training, exploring ways to help staff get college degrees, and creating the position of family worker in each center.

Anticipating a major expansion of early childhood programs, the Task Force acknowledged the need to eliminate the "Kafkaesque maze of red tape" that was making it so difficult for community groups to open new centers. The report argued that the city should fund the operation of programs in temporary facilities and make the direct lease program more responsive to community needs.

The work of the Mayor's Early Childhood Development Task Force was a high point for the Lindsay administration and for the day care reform campaign. A serious effort to address a critical societal need, the Task Force, in both its process and its recommendations, represented 1960s liberalism at its best. Trude Lash and the members of the Mayor's Task Force were justified in savoring this moment and congratulating themselves for their hard work. Only later would New York City's day care reformers become painfully aware that there were serious contradictions in the plans they had hammered out together and that their campaign was all too vulnerable to forces beyond their control.

On July 1, three weeks before the Task Force presented its report to the Mayor, Dorothy had the pleasure of sending out a letter to friends and supporters of the Block Schools. "I want to share our joy with you because I think you will remember the agony that preceded it," the letter began. "WE HAVE ONCE AND FOR ALL COMPLETELY SETTLED OUR OLD ACCOUNT WITH THE CITY. WE HAVE JUST RECEIVED A CHECK FOR $33,878.33 FROM THE CITY TO PAY OUR STAFF AND TO PAY OUR BACK DEBTS. . . . We have learned a lesson in persistence and have again demonstrated our staying power."

They had indeed. It had taken a year of indescribably tedious work, but Dorothy and her assistant, Peggy Fahnestock, had researched and redone all of the financial records of the Block Nurseries' first two years, and had produced a document that convinced officials at the Community Development Agency that the city owed the Block Schools money rather than the other way around.

In response to the good news, the Block Schools received lots of congratulatory letters, including one from Nancie Stewart. "You've done the impossible," she wrote. "You have gotten money out of New York City, which is like squeezing milk out of a rock."

The favorable settlement with the city capped a year of impressive achievement. The Urban Coalition and Follow Through grants, the elimination of the family histories, Dorothy's strong presence on the Mayor's Task Force—these victories had burnished the schools' reputation and demonstrated their growing influence in the outside world.

But within the nurseries, it was a different story. On January 4, 1970, just three days before the meeting with Muriel Katz about case records, Dorothy received a letter signed by all five of the professional teachers in the nurseries. (One professional teaching position was open at the time.) "The purpose of this letter is to bring to the attention of the administration and the board of directors some of the foremost thoughts and feelings of the 'head teachers' within the preschool of the East Harlem Block Schools. Our positions are extremely demanding. . . . We have come to the conclusion that unless certain steps are taken . . . we will be unable . . . to be the kind of teachers we want to be. Furthermore, there are some of us who will be unwilling to compromise our programs or ourselves if such steps cannot be taken."

Dorothy was stunned. What is going on? she asked herself. What do they mean by "the administration"? We're a community—of friends. Why did they write a letter anyway? They could have just told me.

Their demands were reasonable enough. They wanted half a day a week for teachers to meet; staff meetings to discuss the schools' philosophy; their rooms painted; staff hired for 3:00 to 6:00 p.m.; and no enrollment to take place without consultation with the head teacher. Dorothy saw no problem with most of those things. They were asking for a meeting on January 14. That was fine too. But what did they mean about being unwilling to compromise their programs? That sounded like a threat.

While distressed by the way they had chosen to express their concerns, Dorothy knew where the teachers were coming from. Under OEO, the nurseries had been able to run optimally. Teachers were with the children only from 9:00 to 2:00, and then had an hour for planning daily. With Day Care's 8:00 to 6:00 day, teachers had to work different shifts, and it was difficult for classroom teams to find time to meet.

Looking back, Dorothy could understand that the teachers also might be feeling neglected by the schools' leadership. Battling day care and chasing private dollars for the elementary school, she had had little attention for the teachers in the nurseries during the past year.

The absence of the executive director might not have been a problem if the educational directors of the nurseries had been strong. But in June 1969, Barbara Slemmer, director of the 106th Street nursery, had left, drained by the paperwork and tension of the nursery's first year under Day Care. The board had not been able to find a replacement until October, and that person had left after two unpleasant months. The situation was not much better at the Madison Avenue nursery. There, the director, a veteran early childhood educator and Bank Street graduate, was well intentioned and conscientious, but she had lost the respect of her teachers, who found her patronizing.

In these circumstances, the teachers, a gifted lot who set high standards for themselves and others, had grown increasingly dissatisfied with the conditions surrounding their work. At 106th Street Susan Kosoff, teacher of the fives, and David Collins, teacher of the fours, decided to combine their classes to create an open situation where the children would have free access to both classrooms. "Our styles were different—David was much more permissive than I was," explains Susan, a Wheelock College graduate whose commitment to the civil rights movement had brought her to the Block Schools. "So we really needed support to make it happen. But no one was available to help us."

While Susan and David wanted more support, Michael Hunter, teacher at the Madison Avenue Nursery, wanted only for his director to get off his back. A tightly coiled young man, Michael was a dedicated and effective teacher, much loved by children and parents alike. He had been David Collins's student teacher and greatly admired David and his approach to education. But he didn't like anybody telling him what to do, especially his director, an older woman whom he viewed as a busybody with nothing to offer.

While Dorothy's response to the teachers' letter was surprise, followed by concern and soul-searching, board members were just plain angry. In the week before the January 14 meeting, the schools buzzed with conversation; rumors flew about; people walked around with attitudes, refusing to speak with each other. Dorothy spent lots of time talking with people and listening, letting them vent their feelings, trying to calm things down.

But when the long-awaited January 14 meeting finally came, people let each other have it. "This is our school, not your school," an angry Sonia Medina told the staff. "The Block Schools belong to the parents."

"You say you'll quit if things aren't changed," joined in Rosie Tirado. "Go ahead! This is our school. If you want your own school, go and start one. But don't try to mess up what we're doing here."

"You have no business meeting without inviting your assistant teachers," said Rosie Gueits. "They are in the classroom with you every day, and you're supposed to be working together. They have a right to know what's going on and put in their two cents."

"The parent teachers are upset because you met separately without inviting them," Dorothy explained. "It's the first time we've ever had a separate meeting of professionals at the Block Schools. I was shocked when I found out you'd done that. It's a terribly divisive thing to do. It threatens everything we've been trying to build here."

Michael Hunter, the leading spokesperson for the professional teachers, defended their action and gave an impassioned speech in which he said that he shared the parents' commitment to helping their kids "make it" in a society that stacked the odds against them. We have the same goals, he asserted. "Help us improve our working conditions so that we can do our best by your kids."

David Collins attacked Dorothy. "We seldom see you," he charged. "We don't know what you do with your time. But the burden of making the school work for kids is falling on us."

Looking back on the January 14 meeting, Susan Kosoff says, "I hated it. I felt manipulated. Those meetings were excuses for people to emote all over the place."

Despite her discomfort with the "emoting," Susan acknowledged that Dorothy and the board members had a point. She believed in parent control. She had always liked Dorothy and knew how hard she was working. But the meeting only made David and Michael feel more angry and isolated. Observes Susan: "They were reinforced, being told by the parents that this is *our* school, not yours. That's exactly what they had been feeling."

After the meeting, Dorothy and the board attempted to respond to the teachers' demands. They appointed Susan acting director at the 106th Street center; granted the teachers half a day for planning every two weeks and recruited volunteers to make that possible; scheduled a series of meetings to discuss the schools' philosophy; created a rules committee to clarify school policies and job descriptions; and began seeking funding for additional staff for 3:00 to 6:00.

To the teachers' demand that "no enrollment take place without consultation with the head teacher," Dorothy and the board said no. "Our position was that the teachers should never have the power to accept or reject a child," Dorothy explains. "That was a power teachers would tend to misuse, because they would see it as in their interest to accept only 'nice' children. If you allowed that, no difficult children would ever find a school to go to."

Despite these efforts to respond to the teachers' concerns, tension remained high throughout the winter and spring of 1970. In March, the board made another move it hoped would strengthen the schools. Acting on Dorothy's recommendation, it hired Judi Macaulay, parent of a child in the elementary school, to become assistant executive director. Dorothy had no trouble convincing the board of the need for the new position. Looking to the future, she also wanted to begin grooming someone to take her place. "I thought that the work I was doing should not be so mysterious, that there needed to be a parent who was really learning the same skills I was developing." Fortunately, the Carnegie Corporation agreed and made a grant of $15,000 to underwrite the salary for one year.

Judi was the only candidate the board interviewed for the job. Thirty years old, African-American, a single parent with three children, she had served on the personnel committee of the elementary school where she had impressed everyone as highly intelligent, articulate, fair, and a good listener. Low-key, easy to be with, Judi got along well with Puerto Ricans as well as African-Americans, professionals as well as parents, parents new to the school as well as the founding board members. As a result, she had quickly won people's trust. Although she had attended college, she did not have a college degree. But facile with language, she could speak in a hip Black style to make a point in a parent meeting uptown, or use White folks' language to impress a foundation executive or city bureaucrat downtown.

In April, Dorothy went to Puerto Rico for a brief vacation and made an important decision: "I decided that I would leave the Block Schools after spending a year grooming Judi. I made a plan on the beach in Puerto Rico after Judi had been my assistant for a month and was obviously smart and good."

When she returned, she was more grateful than ever to have Judi at her side. For Michael, David, and another of the professional teachers now joined in demanding that teachers be represented on the board of directors. The board had no sympathy for this demand, which challenged the principle of parent control on which the schools were based.

Another round of meetings and discussions ensued. The issue was finally laid to rest at an all-school staff meeting when all of the elementary school teachers and half of the nursery school teachers said that they saw no reason for teachers to be on the board, and that board membership for professional teachers was not a useful role in the context of the Block Schools.

Abruptly, Michael, David, and the other teacher resigned. And Michael did not go quietly. As his parting shot, he called a parents' meeting in which he explained that he was leaving because working conditions were intolerable and the administration intimidating. The schools were not parent-controlled in a way that was helpful for the children, he charged. What they had was parent control from the top down—administrative parent control rather than a mutual process of parents and professionals developing a good educational program for children.

"Teachers who came out of the civil rights movement tended to be sympathetic to parent control," says Dorothy, reflecting on these events. "But teachers who came of age a few years later, during the student movements on college campuses, had difficulty understanding where the parents were coming from. Their orientation was toward overcoming their own oppression by affirming their own right to govern, not toward playing an historical role in someone else's struggle. There seemed to be a change in consciousness over just a few years between graduates of the civil rights movement and graduates of the campus struggles. I found it discouraging that these good teachers—politically aware, eager to participate in important social change—couldn't understand what the Block Schools were all about."

Michael's action was all the more disturbing because most of the parents of children in his class happened to be African-American. Recalls Joe Gueits: "At this time, in School Two [the Madison Avenue Nursery], you started to get a different kind of parent. They were more radical. We started getting like a race thing. The Black parents were criticizing, saying that there were too many Puerto Ricans on the board. Michael was feeding fuel to the fire."

No one was surprised when, soon after Michael's resignation, the director of the Madison Avenue nursery resigned as well. As a prime target of Michael's attacks, she saw that her situation was untenable.

Now the Block Schools faced what would turn out to be a fateful decision: the selection of a director for the Madison Avenue Nursery. The choice ultimately came down to two candidates: Susan Kosoff and Ros Wiener. As teacher and acting director at 106th Street, Susan was known and widely respected. Ros was very different from anyone who had ever occupied a professional position at the Block Schools. An imposing White woman with a mop of curly black hair, careless in her dress, a chain smoker, constantly in motion, Ros was a militant advocate of Black power and freedom for young children.

"The old board would have hired Susan," Dorothy explains. "But several Black parents had recently come onto the board—parents of children in Michael's class. They said, 'We don't want the old regime. We want to try something new.' There was a certain amount of health in that attitude; and several of the older board members and I were trying to be conciliatory. So we were influenced by a new point of view that said, 'We'll never really be great unless we're willing to take risks. Let's take this risk.' I told them it was clearly a risk because her references were mixed. But they hired Ros—over the vehement objections of several of the older board members."

By June, Ros Wiener was director of the Madison Avenue Nursery, all of the professional teachers had left, and the directorship of the 106th Street nursery was open as well. Once again the parent staff was providing continuity for the children.

Drained by all of the internal strife but buoyed by the revolving fund victory and the success of the Mayor's Task Force, Dorothy, Judi, and the board spent the summer of 1970 putting together a new professional team.

Mayor Lindsay did not waste any time acting on the major recommendation of his Early Childhood Development Task Force. On July 31, he announced that the new Commissioner of the Human Resources Administration, Jule Sugarman, would move immediately to create a department of early childhood services within HRA.

With Mitchell Ginsberg as HRA Commissioner, day care reformers had had a sympathetic ear. In Jule Sugarman, they had a strong advocate. The first national administrator of the Head Start Program, Sugarman had a special commitment to early childhood education and his vision included parent control.

Sugarman appointed Georgia McMurray, the African-American woman who had directed the staff of the Mayor's Task Force, as interim acting head of the new Agency for Child Development. Her job was to get the agency up and running. He also hired Bob Gangi to be part of the HRA team charged with implementing the recommendations of the Mayor's Task Force.

Sugarman welcomed demonstrations because they provided the leverage he needed for his goal of expanding day care. According to Peter Sauer: "We'd give Gangi a list of day care centers that would be demonstrating. He'd tell Sugarman which ones. Sugarman would prepare letters. They'd sit in. By the end of the day, they'd have their letters."

During the fall of 1970, such "demonstrations" secured interim funding for an additional 50 community-controlled day care centers. Interim funding meant that although the centers were not yet licensable, the city would take them on and work with them to bring their programs up to standard. Sugarman's embrace of interim funding was a major breakthrough for the campaign. Says Gangi: "It was a case of people's victory. After the second demonstration [in the fall of 1970], interim funding was institutionalized."

Meanwhile, Bank Street College's Day Care Consultation Service (DCCS) took on the issue of staff training. Training was clearly necessary

since most of the interim-funded centers had staff without traditional qualifications. But who would pay for it? The Consultation Service found out
that federal and state guidelines *required* that the Department of Social
Services provide funds for training day care employees. Informed and led
by DCCS, day care advocates waged a successful year-long campaign to
get the city to make training funds available.

With new centers opening every day and nothing being taken for
granted, these were exciting times for day care. People were rethinking the
curriculum, governance, and even what day care ought to be. New ideas
included interage grouping, drop-in care, 24–hour care, integrating African-
American and Puerto Rican culture into the curriculum, and serving foods
that reflected the ethnic background of the children. Observes Micaela:
"Apart from community control, the overriding philosophy was to explore,
experiment, knock out all the old rules and see what the new ones ought
to be. We were trying for something much more integrated into the community. That's not to say we approved of everything that went on in the
name of experimentation. There was a militant Black power center in Brooklyn where the kids did a lot of military-type stuff and White people weren't
allowed to visit. On the Lower East Side, you had a hippy center where
the kids often went without clothes. There were centers with the kids in
rows and the teacher lecturing.

"Sometimes we confronted people. But mostly our approach was to
try to enable groups to see good educational practice. We did workshops
and set up visits so that people could see each other's centers. The Block
Schools were always one of the places we had them visit because there
was a large non-White teaching staff. They could see that open education was not just a scam White people were trying to pull on Black people's
children."

The Block Nurseries were happy to be a model for other parent-
controlled centers. But the priority during 1970–71, Dorothy Stoneman's
second year as executive director, was to strengthen the schools internally.
Among other things, that meant pressing for implementation of those recommendations of the Mayor's Task Force that had the most direct bearing
on the Block Nurseries. These were: getting the city to reimburse the Block
Schools for high school equivalency classes for parent staff; getting the city
to pay the salaries of the family workers (parent coordinators); and eliminating the 3% agency share. (The 3% agency share was the requirement
that nonprofits running city-funded day care centers take responsibility
for 3% of their center's budget. Although appropriate for day care centers
run by boards of wealthy do-gooders, this imposed a crippling financial
burden on the new community-controlled centers.)

   Immediate implementation of these Task Force recommendations would be a serious test of the Lindsay administration's commitment to community control. They were also bread-and-butter issues for the Block Nurseries, costing a total of $37,000 that the schools were forced to cover with hard-to-raise private money.

   On September 8, the Block Schools and the day care reform campaign won an important victory when, in an emergency meeting with Dorothy and Block Schools board members, Muriel Katz announced that the Division of Day Care had agreed to eliminate the 3% agency share.

   Progress on high school equivalency and the family workers would not come so easily. But the Block Schools' greatest challenge during 1970–71 was dealing with conflicts surrounding the new director of the Madison Avenue nursery, Ros Wiener.

   In a few short weeks, Ros had infused the demoralized center with fresh thinking and enthusiasm. Her innovations included a huge sandbox, a loft, and a playroom in the basement—an elaborate apparatus for crawling, sliding, and swinging, constructed of wooden beams, old tires, and barrels—built by one of the teachers with Ros's support.

   Celeste Macias, a parent in the Madison Avenue nursery for several years, became parent coordinator. She and Ros became very close and often worked together in the center until 11:00 or 12:00 at night.

   Ros shared the Block Schools' vision of schools closely tied in with the neighborhood, and she enjoyed working in a storefront. "I loved the way people passing by were always poking their heads in," says Ros. "The Young Lords were nearby at 111th and Madison. They'd drop by; we'd visit them. After six months, I had the feeling that everyone in the community knew me, whether I knew them or not."

   Ros didn't hestitate to offer help whenever it was needed. Curtis was a tough street kid about 11 years old. He didn't go to school, and he didn't spend much time at home either. Ros took him under her wing, let him hang out at the school, gave him food, and got him involved in working with the nursery school children.

   From early in the morning until late at night there was always something exciting going on at the Madison Avenue nursery. After two years of doldrums at the center, the change was refreshing. Ros was imaginative and released tremendous creative energy among children and adults. She wasn't afraid to go against the grain, to create conflict, to challenge.

   But some parents felt Ros was going beyond the boundaries of what was appropriate in her efforts to reach out to the community. Joe Gueits called an emergency board meeting when he heard that Ros had taken a group of young children to the headquarters of the Young Lords—a group Joe considered too radical. Others expressed concern about Curtis. He obviously needed help, and he was often charming. But when he got miffed about something, he could turn destructive—in anger, he had once spray-painted the classrooms, for example. Parents also questioned whether the Block Nurseries should be supporting Curtis's decision not to go to school.

Parents also raised questions about the loft: "Shouldn't it have railings? Won't the children fall off?"

Ros responded by saying that the children wouldn't fall off, that adults tend to underestimate children, and that she was not going to be guilty of that. She may have swayed some of the parents, but she didn't convince Paul, one of the fathers, who got so infuriated that Ros wouldn't put up the railings that he went in one night and tore the whole loft down.

Then there was the sandbox. Lots of early childhood classrooms have sand tables, but this was a sand swimming pool! The children could get in—about seven at a time. They could climb ladders in and out of it, and the loft was overhead. They absolutely loved it. But they often went home with their hair filled with sand. Parents started complaining. Finally there was a big open meeting about whether to keep the sandbox. Thirty people came to debate whether the sandbox should stay or go. The parents said, "Look, the time we have to spend brushing sand out of our children's hair is really phenomenal—and we won't do it."

Ros described how much the children were enjoying it, what wonderful play went on there, and how much they were learning, and said, "What's a little sand in the hair compared with all that?"

The parents asked, "What does playing in sand have to do with teaching the children to read and preparing them for first grade?"

Ros said, "It's the best possible preparation they could get." It went around and around. There were eloquent arguments on both sides. A minority of the parents supported Ros. But when the issue finally came to a vote, the sandbox lost. So the sandbox had to go, and Ros was heartbroken.

Even the wonderful playroom in the basement did not bring cheers from all the parents. "The playroom was a work of genius," recalls Dorothy. "But the parents' attitude was, 'It's nice—except for the splinters—but we'd like our children to be spending more time learning to read.' Ros would say, 'This is teaching them how to read! Better than any other thing.' Most of the parents didn't buy that, and I was always on their side."

With all of her gifts, Ros had a strong streak of paranoia. In order to survive in a situation she viewed as increasingly hostile, she developed her personnel committee as her base of power. Before long, she was talking about "my personnel committee" and "Dorothy's board." She got into an argument with board member Rosie Tirado that turned personal and insulting. And she spoke derogatorily about the 106th Street nursery.

Dorothy met privately with her and told her bluntly that such things couldn't happen in the Block Schools. She seemed to hear, but as soon as one controversy died down, another would erupt. In May she and her bookkeeper charged each other with irregularities. In June, her maintenance man, incensed by the lack of cleanliness at Madison Avenue and feeling that Ros was ignoring his complaints, called the Health Department and wrote a letter to the board demanding that Ros be fired. After lengthy and heated discussion, the board decided not to fire Ros but to give her a probationary period of two months.

While struggles with Ros marred Dorothy's last four months as executive director, there were some bright spots. In April Georgia McMurray went beyond a commitment she had made in January to reimburse the schools for high school equivalency classes and agreed to provide the Block Nurseries with substantial funds ($23,000) for training, of which high school equivalency could be a part. The city was making good on its promise to transform day care into a quality educational program with professional development for staff.

Also in April, Jule Sugarman sent out a memo to all publicly funded day care centers in New York City announcing the "authorization of a new staff position called Family Counselor, to assume the responsibilities of the Division of Day Care Caseworkers now assigned to your group day care center. . . ." The result of two and a half years of struggle, this was a sweet victory for the Block Schools and for the day care reform campaign. Observes Marjorie Grosett: "The model for the position of Family Counselor was provided by the Block Schools. That was one of the most important impacts the Block Schools had citywide."

Finally, Dorothy's plans for grooming and installing her successor came to fruition when the board hired Judi Macaulay as executive director, effective May 5. Dorothy agreed to stay on until June 30 as Judi's assistant. In one of her last official acts, Dorothy talked with Tony Ward, who was then working for Peter Sauer at the Day Care Consultation Service, and convinced him to apply for the position of director of the 106th Street nursery.

Battling the System, Part II

6

In June 1971, Tony returned to the Block Nurseries as director of the 106th Street center. During the two years since his resignation as executive director, Tony had done some consulting, worked for the Day Care Consultation Service, and stayed in touch with the schools through his wife Carmen and through Dorothy Stoneman, who had called him "whenever things got interesting or difficult."

Although the Block Schools welcomed Tony back into the fold, the Day Care people downtown questioned his credentials as an early childhood educator. According to Judi: "We had to send letters downtown and go through a whole series of meetings. Finally they agreed to accept him."

Meanwhile, Ros survived her two-month probationary period, and the school year got off to a smooth start.

On July 1, 1971, a year after Mayor Lindsay had asked Jule Sugarman to create an umbrella agency for early childhood services, the Agency for Child Development (ACD) officially went into operation with Georgia McMurray as its head. The hope was that the Agency would serve as a powerful advocate for children.

Day care in New York City needed a powerful advocate. For despite their recent victories, day care reformers faced two major challenges. One was the rapid expansion of the city's day care program. In July 1970, when the Mayor's Task Force originally issued its report, the city had 8,000 children in 119 publicly funded day care centers. By August 1971, the number of children in day care had nearly doubled to 15,000 children in 220 centers, and that didn't begin to address the need. In families on public assistance alone, there were 62,500 eligible children.

The other challenge was the struggle with New York State over eligibility. The conflict had arisen over a new fee schedule announced by the state in the fall of 1970. The new fees and eligibility requirements tied day care to reducing the welfare rolls, effectively restricting the service to women on welfare making the transition to paid work. And the schedule was not designed to reward a parent's efforts to improve her situation: As soon as the family's income rose above a very low cutoff point, the child was no longer eligible for free day care.

The city's Human Resources Administration, the Day Care Council, the Committee for Community-Controlled Day Care, and most of the city's day care centers, including the Block Nurseries, immediately joined together to protest. The new state plan, they argued, would impose a hardship on upwardly mobile low-income parents. Shuffling in and out of day care according to their parents' financial status, children would suffer from the disruption of relationships with teachers and friends. The turnstile effect would undermine efforts to improve the education offered to children in day care centers. And day care centers would no longer serve an integrated mix of children from diverse socioeconomic backgrounds.

New York City day care advocates also questioned the right of the state to impose these rules on the city. Here, they were on shaky ground. Before the passage of Title IV-A of the Social Security Act in 1967—the law that provided uncapped federal money for day care on a three-to-one matching basis—the city had set its own rules for eligibility, and the state had a limited role. But although the 25% that was the responsibility of the local governments came half from the state and half from the city, the law clearly required the *state* to come up with a plan in order to draw down the 75% federal reimbursement.

With its new eligibility rules, the state was trying to limit the amount of money it had to contribute. Although 12½% is a relatively small percentage, the dollar amount was substantial because New York City had been aggressive in drawing down Title IV-A funding for day care, and the city accounted for 90% of New York State's program.

While officials of the Lindsay administration and day care advocates argued with the state's Department of Social Services, the city's day care centers simply refused to follow the new rules. Finally the state agreed to a "grandfather clause" that exempted from the new fee schedule any family enrolled in day care programs as of July 21, 1971. However, families who came in after that date would have to meet the new eligibility requirements.

Everyone recognized this as a cynical attempt to buy off the opposition. Unfortunately, it worked. After the announcement of the "grandfather clause," the majority of day care centers decided to comply. But 50 centers associated with the community-control campaign, including the Block Nurseries, refused on principle to go along.

Georgia McMurray, as head of ACD, was caught in the middle. In a memo to ACD-funded day care centers, dated August 31, 1971, she reaffirmed her opposition to the state's new regulations but reminded the centers that the city's day care program depended on federal money. "Lack of compliance," she wrote, "can only serve to dry up the very lifeblood of our plans for expansion." So despite her opposition to the new rules, she proceeded to see that they were implemented.

The Committee for Community-Controlled Day Care and the noncomplying centers were aware of the political and financial realities Georgia was struggling with. But they were adamantly opposed to compromise. They saw the new rules as challenging everything they'd been fighting for: day care as a genuine educational program for children; day care as an opportunity for community-building in neighborhoods; day care as an opportunity for democratic participation.

For parents at the Block Nurseries, these were not theoretical issues. The schools had improved their lives and the lives of their children. But they probably would not have enrolled their children if rules such as those the state planned to impose had been in effect. They were not about to go through a humiliating process of proving their eligibility. They were not about to be forced into alienating, low-paying jobs that would separate them from their children. They were not looking for a place to "dump the kids" but a school where their children could begin their education. Like the caseworkers, the state's new rules undermined those aspects of the schools that had made them so attractive to parents.

The battle lines were drawn.

The one development that provided some basis for optimism during the summer and fall of 1971 was the passage by Congress of the Comprehensive Child Development Act, originally introduced by Senator Walter Mondale. Based on the idea that quality day care was critical for the healthy development of children, the law would have provided $2 billion a year in federal funds to expand day care services.

However, on December 9, 1971, President Nixon vetoed the bill and explained his action with a stinging attack on the whole idea of day care. In contrast to the support he had voiced for day care two and a half years earlier, Nixon charged that the bill's laudable purpose was "overshadowed by the fiscal irresponsibility, administrative unworkability, and family-weakening implications of the system it envisions." Signing the bill would "commit the vast moral authority of the national government to . . . communal approaches to child rearing over against the family-centered approach."

New York City advocates reacted with outrage to Nixon's veto and his attack on day care. But Nixon wasn't listening, and supporters of the bill were unable to find the two-thirds majority needed to override the veto. By December 10, the Comprehensive Child Development Act was dead.

Looking back on this sudden turnabout in Nixon's attitude toward day care, Tony says: "It was an antifeminist backlash. Nixon was always a bellwether of conservative sentiment. The other reason, of course, is money. Day care is an expensive program—and optional. True, women need to work outside the home to make ends meet, and the country needs them in the workforce. But women will make do. They'll find ways to work—by putting keys around their children's necks, leaving them with relatives or older siblings, hiring babysitters, and so on. Day care has never been a 'hard' service in the sense that without it there'll be an immediate drastic change affecting the economy. As far as conservatives in Congress are concerned, poor people's children are expendable."

The bad news continued for the Block Nurseries and the 50 other noncomplying centers, as Georgia McMurray informed them that they had to begin following the new state rules by February 1 or lose their funding. The leadership of the Committee for Community-Controlled Day Care agreed that the situation called for dramatic action."We had a big meeting," recalls Bob Gangi, who had ended his brief tenure with HRA and was now back with the Committee. "We discussed taking over HRA's offices.

We knew this was a last ditch effort. If this demonstration failed, as I expected it would, we'd be done for."

Tony and Sonia were at the meeting representing the Block Nurseries. A call to the Madison Avenue center confirmed that parents and staff there were enthusiastic about participating in a demonstration, but the 106th Street center was another story. When Sonia called Rosie Gueits, who was conducting an emergency parent meeting about the threatened cutoff of funds, Rosie told her that parents there didn't want to take part.

"Can I know the reasons?" Sonia asked.

"They're afraid there's going to be chaos."

So Tony and Sonia immediately left the meeting and took a taxi to 106th Street. "We talked to the parents," recalls Sonia. "Tony got nowhere. I said, 'Tony, let me try now.' I told them: 'We have a school, not because it was served to us on a silver platter, but because a lot of people worked very hard. This school was not made on the notion that it will be only for a certain group of children. We are for all the children that still are not born, and they will be born and someday they will come here.' I got angry and Tony got angry and reinforced what I'd said. We hit them back and forth, right to the belt. And it worked, because by the end of the meeting, the parents decided to take the day off and go with their kids."

Later that evening, Sonia got a call from Bob Gangi. "Peter Sauer and I had a phone conversation after the meeting," he told her. "And we realized that taking over HRA is flat and unimaginative. We've decided instead to take over Lindsay's Presidential campaign headquarters!" Sonia agreed that it was a great idea and said she'd be there with the Block Schools' contingent.

The demonstration, which took place on January 19, 1972, was a great success. "HRA, expecting a demonstration, made elaborate security arrangements—they chained typewriters to desks," Gangi recalls. "But somehow, nobody at Lindsay's headquarters heard about it. The press did! They were there in force!"

Sonia describes the Block Nurseries' participation: "We met in the subway station [at 103rd and Lexington] and went downtown to the building—parents, staff, and children. We carried very big shopping bags with every game possible. We arrived at 8:15, before lots of people came into the building. Before they realized, we were already in the office. I put papers up on the wall: '[East Harlem] Block [Nursery] 1' and '[East Harlem] Block [Nursery] 2.' When Block 2 arrived, everything was ready. They went inside—the kids had breakfast and we had juice for snack and sandwiches for lunch."

Within the next hour, hundreds of other protesters arrived, representing 25 day care centers. While children drew pictures, played games, and listened to stories, some of the adults wrote slogans on the walls calling for free, universal day care and nullification of the state's eligibility standards.

Meanwhile, Bob Gangi and Dorothy Pitman got on the phone to friendly legislators like Bella Abzug, asking them to put pressure on the Mayor's office. "With Lindsay running for President," says Gangi, "Deputy Mayor Hamilton was in charge. He was supposedly about to make a decision to send in the police, which would have been a disaster. But [Richard] Aurelio [Lindsay's campaign manager] appeared on the scene. He was the kind of person you could deal with—a gentleman politician. He saw that we had them, and he persuaded Hamilton to agree that the city would defy the state and continue funding these centers. As a result, the state might cut off the city's funds, but the city was willing to take that chance. It was one of the rare instances where the city was willing to become an advocate for community groups."

The demonstration had saved the defiant centers, at least for the moment.

The Block Nurseries were extremely grateful for the reprieve, for they were having more than their share of trouble dealing with Ros Wiener. Once again the Madison Avenue center was swirling with conflict, rumor, frenetic activity, and sparks of brilliance. At her best, Ros was a bold and powerful ally for the oppressed, especially children. Learning of an 18-month-old boy whose parents could not hear or speak, she took him into the center so that he could learn to talk—in defiance of Day Care policy that barred day care centers from accepting children under three—and waged a successful campaign against Day Care bureaucrats to keep him.

But what a headache she was at her worst! "The rhetoric about children was great," says Judi Macaulay, who as executive director was now her supervisor. "But she was always pushing the limits—and lots went on that had nothing to do with education. She began hiring men recently released from prison as substitute teachers. They would hang out at the center. There were charges of drinking in the center after hours, of partying on the playground, of food, money, and materials disappearing. There were rumors that some of the staff were into voodoo. We were looking into the situation, trying to see if there were grounds for firing, trying to separate fact from rumor. But we didn't have anything concrete because the staff were afraid to talk—and they were the ones who knew most about what was going on."

Fed up with the situation, Rosie Tirado and another board member spearheaded a move to fire Ros, but it backfired when their intense personal hostility toward her, coupled with their lack of documentation, turned off several key board members.

Upon learning of Rosie's failed attempt to get Ros out, Tony intervened. Never sympathetic toward Ros, he was now convinced that she was splitting the schools, stirring up racial antagonisms, and draining precious energy. "Tony made a presentation to the board in March," Judi recalls. "He said that the board should consider firing Ros, but he also insisted that they set up a process." Accepting Tony's suggestion, the board decided to appoint three people to monitor the situation and document what was happening: Sonia Medina, Judi Macaulay, and Peggy Walton, who was African-American and a parent teacher in the elementary school.

The board's decision made Ros all the more insecure. To her, the issue was power. "The kind of education I brought to the schools was excellent, but I was taking Madison in a direction the schools were not going. They said I was splitting the schools, but the real source of the conflict was this: Since neither Dorothy nor Tony could control me, I wasn't going to stay there."

In Ros's analysis, racism was involved. "East Harlem Block was a plantation," she charges. "All the group teachers were White; all the parents were on the aide line. The schools had become nationally famous. Tony and Dorothy had built their careers on East Harlem Block. To them and to the board, parent control meant their being in charge. They in no way created an educational program committed to helping people. East Harlem Block was anti-Black because it accepted the dominant ideology of America and was trying to help people find their place in American society. There was no view toward changing that society. East Harlem Block accepted the ideology of compensatory education. Tony, Dorothy, and the board saw the schools as a path to Harvard, not to liberation—as if the path to Harvard was whether you could read by seven, not whether your father was rich (and your mother good looking)."

But despite Ros's feelings, the monitoring process continued, with Sonia, Peggy, and Judi keeping an eye on the books, visiting the center regularly, and attending staff meetings. "I was open for a really long time," Judi recalls. "The real turning point for me was a tirade Ros went into against Peggy. The incident was so vivid, so concrete, that I could see how she could create factions and turn people against each other.

"We had a meeting at the Madison nursery, and Peggy came in a little late. We were all sitting around a table. Celeste [parent coordinator at the Madison Avenue center] stood up to give Peggy her seat, because she knows Peggy has bad feet. (They had lived up in the same building since 1962—right next door to each other. They had taken care of each other's kids, gone shopping for each other—all that kind of stuff.)

"Ros turned to Celeste and said, 'Why are you giving up your seat? You don't have to give up your seat to her just because she's in power. You're afraid of her because she's a board member. Sit back down there.'

"Celeste shrugged and said, 'I want to stand now.'

"But Peggy was afraid to sit down then. She said, 'I'll get another chair and pull it up.'"

"Celeste said, 'I'll stand up.'

"I knew that it didn't have anything to do with Celeste being afraid of Peggy's power as a board member. Celeste simply knew that Peggy had bad feet—they had been friends for ages. I saw clearly how Ros manipulated things to turn them from one thing into another."

On May 12, Ros and her staff failed to attend an important Block Schools' staff meeting scheduled weeks earlier. That evening, the board met to decide what to do. By this time, the monitoring had been done, the documentation was thorough, and Ros had directly defied—and either encouraged or permitted her staff to defy—a direct order of the executive director. The board decided to remove Ros as director of the Madison Avenue nursery, effective immediately.

That wasn't the end of it. On the evening of Friday, May 19, the board was holding a meeting at the 106th Street center. They had just made the decision to appoint Sonia Medina interim director of the Madison Avenue nursery when 30 people marched in through the unlocked door that opened onto the sidewalk and presented a petition requesting that Ros be reinstated! The group consisted of staff and parents from the Madison Avenue nursery and of folks from another day care center as well, headed by Judith Prior, a militant Black power advocate and friend of Ros.

One after another, a dozen parents spoke: "My daughter is asthmatic, and Ros took her to the emergency room and stayed with her for an hour and a half." "Ros has helped me as a mother—she's a beautiful person." "Why wasn't she given the opportunity to answer the charges against her?"

Board members began defending their decision, and the discussion got heated. "Judith Prior really thought she could intimidate us, because that's how she operates," charges Judi. "She manipulates and intimidates and she comes across with this strong voice and you're supposed to melt away. But I didn't melt away. Nobody did! She started asking me where I grew up, and did I know this person and that person. She was trying to say that I didn't really grow up here, that I'm not really Black. I said, 'I was born in East Harlem. You haven't proved anything because you're of a different generation—I'm much younger than you are.' She turned and walked out. That cut it. There was nothing she could say behind that."

At one point a parent giving a speech in support of Ros climbed up on a table. "We must keep Rosalind because Rosalind is a saint!" she cried.

"I was watching this," Sonia recalls, "and I said, 'This is it for me. People, I've been with you for years but this is one time that I'm leaving'—and I just left.

"But as soon as I had gone a few steps down the street, I remembered Bill Stewart [Judi's husband], I remembered Rosie Tirado, I remembered Rosie Gueits. I remembered Anna Rivera. 'Oh my God!' I said. And I had to come back and be a policeman.

"Anna wanted to hit somebody and I said, 'Anna, please don't. Anna, no matter what happens, if we all lose our tempers, it's going to be nasty and ugly.'

"Rosie Tirado said, 'I'm going to hit her now.' And I said, 'Rosie, you're not going to do that because you are not going to give a reason to those people that they came here, that we don't know how to control ourselves.'

"Besides Rosie, there was her husband Willie, and I said, 'Willie, you are not going to do that for the simple reason that Rosie's not going to do that.'

"Then Bill Stewart said to Bill Henry [teacher in the Madison Avenue nursery], 'You're not going to talk that way to my wife,' and he was going to punch Bill Henry, but I said, 'Bill, you are not going to do it.'

So I was there in the middle, running back and forth between Rosie Gueits and Rosie Tirado and Willie and Bill—and I knew where my head was at—and I said, 'The last thing we need right now is to punch anybody, in or out.' Finally, when everybody left, it was such a relief, because it was really ugly."

Relief indeed! The board stood firm in its decision, and in June asked Sonia to drop "interim" from her title and become the director of the Madison Avenue nursery. After taking the weekend to think it over, Sonia accepted, and a tumultuous period for the Block Schools came to an end.

Looking back, Judi feels good about the way she and the board handled the situation. "The structure of the school worked," she asserts, "because even if some people got so emotionally involved that they went off the Block Schools' mind in terms of doing it by process, there were always people to pull it back into line and to say, 'No, this is the process, we have to be fair and do it the way we outlined. We have to document it so that we have a strong position.' Even though it went on until May, it still happened and it happened right. I think the Block Schools came out of it strengthened."

Firing Ros was not the only major event at the Block Nurseries that spring. In the midst of all the turmoil, the Block Schools laid the groundwork for one of its crowning achievements: a college program that eventually would lead to more than 35 parents earning bachelor's degrees.

The college program was a natural extension of the adult learning that had been a hallmark of the Block Schools from their inception. The founding parents had gained more from a few months of working together than from years of formal schooling. Visiting schools, canvassing the neighborhood for space, knocking on doors to recruit children, interviewing teachers, creating a board of directors, making decisions—activities such as these brought the parents into contact with the world beyond their families and blocks, and showed them that they could be actors on a wider stage.

Formal training—the sessions with Millie Rabinow, for example—contributed to parents' learning about the topic that interested them most: the development and well-being of their children. Those who worked as teachers also learned a great deal from their daily interactions with college-educated professionals, and the professionals learned a lot from them as well. While the Block Schools' efforts to overcome class and racial distinctions were not entirely successful, the walls became porous enough for a real exchange of skill and insight to take place.

This learning had special meaning because it was not an individual matter, but part of a group effort to create excellent schools for children. People were gaining understandings and learning skills that they could use immediately at home and in the classroom. As each individual grew stronger and more competent, the whole school community became more effective in educating children and serving families.

Although appreciative of this informal learning, the parents soon realized that it would take them only so far. Many had not completed high school and were painfully aware of gaps in their academic skills. They knew also that no matter how competent they became as teachers, they would be stuck at the level of assistant or aide unless they had teaching credentials, including a college degree.

During the 1970–71 school year (Dorothy Stoneman's second year as executive director), the Block Schools had taken the first step in this direction by setting up high school equivalency classes. Although Dorothy had to pester Jule Sugarman and Georgia McMurray, they finally came through with reimbursement for the classes and agreed to fund them for the following year as well.

Anna Rivera has fond memories of the program and of Carmen Banton, the instructor from Bronx Community College who came to the Block Schools to teach the classes. "I had always wanted to be a teacher—always, as far back as I could remember," she says. "When I was in eighth grade, I had a teacher I liked and looked up to a lot. But when I told her *I* wanted to be a teacher, she said, 'Anna, you can't be a teacher. You don't have the patience. Try something else.' I felt completely disillusioned. The only other thing they were offering was to be a beautician. I hated it. I quit high school after three years. That little thing my teacher said took away my confidence.

"Carmen Banton was the total opposite. She was very understanding. If you haven't graduated from high school and they ask you to write a paper or something, you're always afraid the teacher will red-mark it. But she would sit down with you and explain what she wanted you to change rather than just give you the paper and you figure it out. She prepared me well because when I took the test, I passed it the first time. I was very weak in math. I had run a candy store, and I can deal with math when it comes to money, but when it comes to fractions! And I had never had algebra in my life! She made the formulas so that I could understand them. When I took the test in math and passed it, I was shocked—I was sure I was going to fail—and I was so happy. I had always wanted to graduate."

Toni Perez had a harder time of it: "I went to get the GED [General Equivalency Diploma]. When my results came back, I started to cry, and I said, 'Oh my God, I failed it!' I had to have 225 and I had 223. By two points I missed!

"Carmen Banton said, 'Okay. Your literature was high.' Literature! Of all things my literature was high! She said, 'Concentrate on the literature part so you can bring it up.' And I did, and the next time I took it, I couldn't believe it, when I got the news that I had passed, I swear I started screaming all over the house, 'I got it! I got it! I got my GED! Oh God! Finally, finally, finally I got it!'

"When my mother used to help me with homework, she'd say, 'You're so stupid!' and hit me in the head, and say, 'Didn't I tell you how to do this?'

"But Carmen was the best because she gave me individual help when I needed it. She even gave me her phone number. 'Call me if you ever get stuck with anything,' she'd say. She gave me confidence. She was a teacher that cared."

By the spring of 1972 most of the parents in Carmen Banton's classes had received their GEDs and were ready to go on. Judi Macaulay, a parent, was executive director of the Block Schools; Sonia Medina was now director of the Madison Avenue nursery; and Donna Williams (later Benton), a parent, was a group teacher in the elementary school. Although eminently qualified for the positions they took on, none of them had a college degree.

Meanwhile, Tony Ward learned that the Day Care Consultation Service had interested the Carnegie Corporation in funding a college program for day care center staff. The Block Schools were a top choice to be one of the participating agencies. Accordingly, Tony opened up discussion within the schools about a college program. During April and May, the board of directors and the staffs of the 106th Street nursery and the elementary school (the Madison Avenue center being otherwise occupied) discussed the idea thoroughly and expressed enthusiasm.

On May 23, 1972, Tony gave the board a formal proposal. "[We] will have no courses, credits, or grades in the usual sense," he explained. "Instead, the staff, as a group, will define their own learning goals and plan activities to help them reach those goals. When, after three or four years, we and Bank Street, and the degree-granting institution, all feel that we have reached those goals, we will all receive the degrees."

The program would be synonymous with the Block Schools' inservice training program: Starting in September all inservice training would count toward degrees and everyone would participate in the college program. It would have four major themes: basic academic skills; social and cultural studies; human development and psychology; and classroom skills.

His proposal having been approved by the Block Schools' board and the Day Care Consultation Service, Tony went after the best person he could think of to direct the program: Dorothy Stoneman. After nine months in California, she had returned to the city with the dream of working as Donna Williams's assistant teacher "so that I could teach children to read and write, which is something I'd be great at—and I wouldn't have to worry for a second!"

But Tony had other plans for Dorothy. "He told me I had no right to do that," Dorothy recalls, "that I had a moral obligation to return and be the director of the training program—and I believed him."

Moral obligation aside, Dorothy liked the idea because she saw the college program as a way to strengthen the Block Schools and bring them closer to her vision of an ideal community, free from racial and class distinctions. "With people from outside the neighborhood holding the professional positions, you had a caste system," she observes. "The staffing patterns reflected, rather than changed, the patterns of racial and class discrimination of the society at large. To eliminate class distinctions, the Block Schools needed to have stable teachers who came from the community rather than a two-tiered setup of mostly White professionals from outside and Black and Puerto Rican nonprofessionals from the community."

Dorothy also believed that the college program could provide a much-needed boost for a community battle weary from three hard years of internal and external conflict. "I saw it as a way to get people moving in the same direction again, with enthusiasm and real sensitivity to the children."

Hired by the board in June, Dorothy got to work immediately. "The first step was to get the training committee going—and that was fun," she recalls. "We had representatives from each part of the Block Schools. It was composed of staff and maybe one or two nonstaff parents. We met every week.

"One issue that came up immediately was the policy that participation was required. There was some resistance from people who didn't want to load themselves down with classes during their lunch and rest periods. But we felt strongly about this. The main point was to improve the Block Schools, not only to provide career ladders for individuals.

"A second thing that came up right away was the desire on the part of the staff and the training committee for a competency-based program. They said we don't want anybody to be certified as a teacher unless we think they're a good teacher. We discussed what makes a good teacher. And naturally people started saying, 'Well, it isn't just a degree because we've seen lots of teachers with degrees who aren't very good.' And that led to: 'Well, what is it then?' So we decided to make a list of competencies which defined a good teacher."

During the summer, while beginning to schedule some courses for the fall, Dorothy met individually with the entire staff, guiding people through a process of assessing what they wanted to learn and how they wanted to grow.

As the 1972–73 school year began, the Block Schools had never been stronger. They had fended off attacks from inside and out, and had landed on their feet. With Judi as executive director, Tony and Sonia firmly in charge of the nurseries, and the college program generating renewed excitement about learning, the schools were poised for a most productive year.

Productive it was. Calm and free of conflict it was not!

On September 21, 1972, 350 people sat down in the middle of Madison Avenue and took over President Nixon's campaign headquarters at 53rd and Madison to protest impending cuts in federal funds for day care.

Unlike Mayor Lindsay, Nixon had nothing to lose by ignoring the protest. By 1972, social services under Title IV-A were due to cost the federal government $4.8 billion compared with only $500 million in 1965. Calling this increase "a raid on the federal treasury," Nixon and his supporters in Congress pushed through in October a cap of $2.5 billion on Title IV-A.

With this, the federal government's generous support for day care, inaugurated in 1967 with the passage of Title IV-A, came to an untimely end. In truth, Congressional support for the day care provisions of Title IV-A had never been strong, based as it was on the supposed efficacy of day care in reducing federal welfare costs. With the funding uncapped and oversight loose, Title IV-A had led to rapid expansion of day care, especially in New York City, and inadvertently had fueled a grassroots day care campaign aimed at empowering poor and working-class people and addressing the real needs of low-income parents and children. Nixon had no interest in supporting that agenda.

After day care protesters took over Mayor Lindsay's Presidential Campaign headquarters in January 1972, the City had agreed to join forces with day care activists in defying the State on fees and eligibility. As a result Rockefeller backed down, suspending the state's proposed new fee scale and promising to come up with a new one. In November 1972 Rockefeller kept his promise. But in the wake of the cap on Title IV-A and Nixon's re-election by a landslide, the new fee and eligibility rules now announced by the State were worse than those it had tried to impose a year before. Sugarman protested the new rules. State Commissioner of Social Services Abe Lavine shot back that "New York City's failure to enforce" day care eligibility and fee standards already put into effect upstate the previous spring had been "a primary factor" in the rise of statewide day care costs from $53 million in the 1971–72 fiscal year to nearly $90 million in 1972–73.

With the stakes high on both sides, a bitter tug of war ensued between city and state officials against a backdrop of grassroots protest: On December 11, 500 parents and day care staff rallied in Brooklyn to protest the new day care fees. On January 6, hundreds of parents went up to Albany to meet with Commissioner Lavine and lobby their legislators.

Finally, the state agreed to let the city postpone the implementation of the new fee and eligibility rules for 18 months and to share the cost of carrying those children. In exchange for this concession, Georgia McMurray made what Bob Gangi referred to as her "devil's agreement" with the state: While the city would maintain its eligibility *policies* (for the next 18 months), it would begin immediately to implement the state's *procedures* for determining eligibility. This meant that although the city would continue for 18 months to maintain its eligibility requirements, which were more liberal than those of the rest of the state, day care centers would have to begin gathering the information the state decided was necessary for determining eligibility and entering that information on forms the state provided.

Georgia McMurray had barely finished working out these arrangements with the state when Caspar Weinberger, Nixon's Secretary of Health, Education, and Welfare, proposed new federal guidelines for Title IV-A. Issued on February 16, the new rules stirred immediate outrage across the country. "The ACD is extremely concerned about these proposals," wrote Georgia McMurray in a memo to day care centers. "It is clear that the intent is to put a halt to program enrichment and expansion. They are also designed to limit services to the very poor—and to them only long enough to enable them to get off public assistance, after which services will be terminated."

Georgia immediately helped launch a national campaign that forced Weinberger to withdraw his draconian regulations. Says Georgia: "The city administration was prepared to accept the inevitability of the new regulations. I wasn't. I had a national network I could use. The federal government received a quarter of a million letters, and Weinberger withdrew his amendments altogether. What happened was that in 1974 Congress passed new legislation, Title XX, which gave states and local agencies discretion on eligibility and fee scales for social services."

It was while waging her effective campaign against Weinberger's oppressive regulations that Georgia, keeping her promise to the state, sent out on March 1 a memo to all group day care centers: "We have revised certain forms pertaining to eligibility and reporting . . . we need to collect information in order to claim reimbursement from the Federal and State government. . . . By March 23, 1973, all families . . . must have a completed 'Day Care Application and Eligibility Report, Form DSS-2105' . . . it must be understood that Day Care Centers who fail to submit complete records place their funding in jeopardy." Georgia claimed that "these new procedures do *not* constitute any change in the procedure to be used for determining financial eligibility and fees," but she failed to convince the Committee for Community-Controlled Day Care.

"In the middle of everyone's concerns about the federal regulations," the Committee informed its network, "ACD has tried to slip by a new set of eligibility procedures that are repressive and dangerous. These new procedures will increase government control over the centers and their parents. . . . The city is collecting information that can easily be used by federal and state administrations—under Nixon and Rockefeller—to harass parents, to take control of centers, to limit centers to serving welfare people only. . . . Parents seeking admission will have to sign a form stating: 'I understand that my application may be investigated and I agree to cooperate in any such investigation. I further understand that the law provides for fine or imprisonment or both, for a person hiding facts or not telling the truth.' The only way to defeat these regulations is for many centers to unite in a position of defiance."

The leadership of the Block Schools agreed with the Committee that it had to draw the line here and refuse to comply with the new eligibility procedures—specifically the new state Form DSS-2105, which came to symbolize the state's attempt to absorb day care into welfare. "It was the logical step to take after the position we had taken on the caseworkers," observes Judi Macaulay. "There was the whole issue of confidentiality. We were concerned about gathering all of this information and putting it on a form that would be available to all of New York State."

On the evening of March 19, 1973, the Block Schools held an open board meeting to discuss whether the nurseries should comply with the new registration procedures. "We are entering a period of severe crisis," Tony told the 150 parents and staff in attendance, "not just for day care, not just for welfare, but for all low-income people—everyone in this room, whether teacher or parent, on welfare or working."

He went on to describe new state and federal policies and asserted that they would reduce day care to little more than a babysitting service for welfare families. No funds would be available for staff training; health services would be abolished; and new staff ratios would eliminate two or three of the Block Nurseries' teaching positions.

"What can we do?" he asked. "We can fight! We can write letters. We can sign petitions. We can go on demonstrations. We can stay firm and united. We can be prepared to chip in, lend support, volunteer. The final decision is up to the board.

"I know people are tired, but there are only two choices: join with others to fight these things—the Block Schools can play a key role. Or give up, and suffer anyway—there is no escape."

Unanimously, they decided to fight.

On March 22, several hundred people filled the auditorium and lobby of Bank Street College of Education on West 112th Street for an emergency meeting organized by the Committee for Community-Controlled Day Care. The mood was grim, angry, and defiant. Speakers railed against Form 2105, charging that data would be fed into a massive state data bank and "Big Brother" would become a reality. In light of Watergate and the Nixon administration's attempt to steal the psychiatric records of Daniel Elsberg, one speaker asked, "How can anyone expect us to trust the government with the personal and financial information requested on the 2105s?" To cheers and applause from the group, Tony and Sonia described the open board meeting on March 19 at which the Block Schools had decided not to comply and explained their reasons for drawing the line on the issue of Form 2105. The main outcome of the meeting was the decision to have a demonstration—on Monday, March 26.

Dorothy Stoneman described what happened on Monday as "the wildest demonstration in day care." It began conventionally enough with a picket line of about 1,000 people outside 26 Federal Plaza where a House Subcommittee was holding a public hearing on the phase-out of the Office of Economic Opportunity. At 11 a.m., about 600 demonstrators marched over to 240 Church Street, the offices of the Agency for Child Development.

Sonia, her husband, Willie, and Shirley Johnson of the Committee for Community-Controlled Day Care were already inside the building, having arranged an appointment with an ACD consultant supposedly to discuss a problem Sonia was having in preparing a proposal for staff training. At a prearranged time, Sonia and Willie excused themselves from the meeting, went downstairs, and opened half a dozen emergency exits on the ground floor. Outside each exit, Sonia had posted a Block Schools staff member to hold the door open. While a hundred demonstrators stayed behind to maintain a picket line on the street, 500 protestors—mainly women and children—streamed through the open doors, took over all four floors of the Agency for Child Development, and demanded a mass meeting with Georgia McMurray. Recalls Sonia: "Everybody was going into different places at ACD. It was hysterical. ACD never had so many visitors."

Georgia McMurray, locked in her office, said she would meet only with a delegation. The demonstrators said there would be no meeting except with the whole group and that they would not leave until three demands were met: "(1) No funds would be withheld from centers for noncompliance; (2) day care must be considered an educational program, not custodial care; (3) day care centers [would] maintain control over their own programs: who is eligible for services, staff hiring, purchasing equipment, etc."

The demonstrators made themselves at home, singing, "liberating" documents, and throwing records out the windows. Someone came up to Judi and Sonia, waving a file in her hand, and said, "Look, East Harlem Block is a demonstration program. You're the best in New York City! It says so right here in this file." As the stand-off continued, demonstrators used ropes to hoist food up from the street. Children sat on the floor, eating peanut butter and jelly sandwiches and drinking juice.

Dorothy Stoneman tried to get through to Georgia. "I had a different relationship with Georgia and Jule because I knew them from the [Mayor's] Task Force," she explains. "I liked them and respected them and didn't see them as enemies. So while Georgia was locked in her room, I was writing notes to her, saying, 'We don't want to fight with you. However, we need to know when you will say no. Until you tell us when you will stand up against these things coming down, you can expect that people are going to be on your case.'"

Georgia didn't respond to Dorothy's pleas, but she did finally agree to address the whole group. Suffering from a degenerative neurological disease, Georgia could walk only with braces and crutches. Under police guard she made her way to a crowded open area on the third floor where she spoke to the demonstrators. When she announced that starting in April funds would be withheld from centers that failed to comply, some of the more militant demonstrators announced that they would hold her captive until she relented. That sparked a prolonged and rancorous discussion as the demonstrators, using bullhorns, argued with each other about whether to permit her to leave. They finally decided that Georgia could return to her office, but that they would stay.

At 8:15 p.m. Deputy Administrator Howard Stein of the Human Resources Administration read a statement saying that if the demonstrators left the premises, no charges would be filed against them.

At 8:25, 20 tactical police officers entered the occupied offices, escorted out the protestors who remained, and took them to nearby police stations where they were served with summonses for criminal trespass (Perlmutter, 1973).

The demonstration left Dorothy feeling embarrassed and ashamed: "People said they were 'liberating' documents, but they were really stealing them. Georgia took it as a personal affront, as a deep hurt from the day care community. She thought that her offices had been ransacked and that people had treated her with profound disrespect—and they had."

It also stirred Dorothy's worries about the future of the Block Schools. For Georgia hadn't budged an inch. It was comply or lose your funding. Several days after the demonstration, Dorothy took second and third graders from the elementary school to the circus. "Sitting there and looking at this group of kids that had come through the Block Schools," she recalls, "I was overwhelmed with the feeling that they couldn't destroy the Block Schools, they just couldn't do this to us. It tore my heart out that powerful forces were trying to destroy us, either by stopping our funds or by forcing us to do things that we didn't believe in. Either way they were destroying what we had built. There at the circus I made a decision to do everything in my power to prevent that."

As for Georgia, the demonstration served only to harden her stance toward the Committee. "As someone in the civil rights movement, I was used to direct action," she observes. "Demonstrations, to be effective, have to be orchestrated. As time went on and more anarchists jointed the Committee, they would try to force confrontations and violence. I was not intimidated."

On the substantive issues, she simply disagreed, believing that she was making the best of a bad situation. "The state was under pressure from the federal government," she explains. "The Nixon administration was concerned about the growth of day care in New York City. They weren't dumb. They saw that if it continued, it would mean a great increase in government spending. Nixon and Rockefeller joined forces. If there had been a higher degree of trust between the Committee and me, I could have helped them understand the political climate. The sixties were over."

Angered by Georgia McMurray's "rigidity," the Committee decided to stage another demonstration on Friday, March 30, with the objective this time of tying up traffic on the Triborough Bridge. Shirley Johnson tried to involve the Block Schools, but Sonia and Judi demurred. "I don't need that kind of antagonism," Sonia told Shirley. "People are going to be very angry getting stuck on the bridge in the morning at rush hour."

Friday morning 200 protestors tied up traffic for two and a half hours by parking rental cars to block the roadway and forming a human chain. To break it up, police beat people with clubs and arrested five, including Bob Gangi.

According to *The New York Times* (Metropolitan Briefs, 1973): "Jule Sugarman deplored what he called 'the use of children in a manner which is dangerous and exposes them to physical harm.' He also attacked as a 'cruel hoax' what he said was 'the purposeful spreading of rumors that certain day care centers will be closed down.'"

What a difference from two years before, when he had encouraged Gangi to stage demonstrations! Reflects Gangi: "We isolated ourselves by our militancy. It was a serious mistake to have the bridge demonstration when we did. After doing that, it was hard to top it. The strategy should be to escalate—to build and build and build. To demonstrate was always our response. But the climate had changed. Our best course would have been to maintain a militant posture but to be patient and mature—qualities which I and many people on the Committee didn't possess."

On Saturday, March 31, 70 people representing 27 noncomplying day care centers gathered at the Block Schools' Madison Avenue center. The purpose was to work out a definition of noncompliance that would unify as many centers as possible. Dorothy and Tony ran the meeting, which produced agreement on the following position: "We are concerned about the city's need to be reimbursed by the state for day care services. We are willing to cooperate with the city and provide some information about families to help the city get state reimbursement. BUT we are not willing to expose parents to harm by revealing their names, social security numbers, and signatures to the city."

People acknowledged that their centers might have to survive for a while without funds. A meeting was set for the following Saturday to discuss ways to help each other.

On April 2, the Block Schools' board officially adopted the position hammered out by all the noncomplying centers at the Saturday meeting.

On April 3, Tony and Sonia received letters from the Agency for Child Development, informing them that because of their "failure to complete and submit the required eligibility forms, the ACD could no longer expend public funds for purchase of day care services from your organization." Eleven other centers received similar letters, including The Twig Is Bent, Dorothy Pitman's West 80th Street Day Care Center, and others with such names as Children's Mansion, Children's Storefront, and Kissing Monster.

On April 4, representatives of noncomplying centers met with law-yers to begin preparing a legal challenge to Form 2105.

Later that day, a group met with Georgia McMurray. Six spokespeople, including Tony Ward and Bob Gangi, explained the position the centers were taking and presented proposals for establishing parents' eligibility that did not involve revealing parents' names, signatures, or social secu-rity numbers to the city. Commissioner McMurray reiterated her position, but agreed to review the proposals.

On April 5, Judi, Sonia, Dorothy, and Tony went down to ACD to hand-deliver a letter expressing the official position of the Block Schools. Jule wasn't in his office, but Georgia was, and an impromptu meeting took place at around 5 p.m. "We hope you'll give serious consideration to the points we make in the letter," said Judi.

"I most certainly will," Georgia assured them, "but the regulations coming down from the state are very strict, and I have to act now or put New York City's entire day care program in jeopardy."

"People feel you're selling out," said Tony.

"You know I wouldn't do that. As I'm sure you're aware, Jule and I did everything we could to fight the state on this."

"Georgia, we just can't do what you're asking us to do," said Dorothy. "It would be violating the trust of our parents to provide personal infor-mation with no guarantees that it wouldn't be used against them."

"Frankly, I don't see how providing social security numbers is such a big deal," replied Georgia. "We all put our social security number on every-thing all the time. I'm not saying this is true of the Block Schools because I know you serve low-income people, but I suspect that for some centers the resistance to the form is just a smokescreen to cover up the fact that they have ineligible families."

"The form contradicts the principles the Block Schools have always stood for," insisted Sonia. "We won't ask our parents to fill it out."

"In that case, we will have to defund you."

"Then we will fight you with everything we've got!" said Tony.

The letter they gave to Georgia that day pinpointed the central ques-tion: "Can we agree on a form of information sharing which will serve the needs of the city for claiming state and federal reimbursement, and which will serve the need of the Block Schools to protect its families?" It reminded her that this was not a new issue for the Block Schools. In 1968 and 1969, they had sought to protect families from "a voyeuristic and paternalistic caseworker mentality." Now they were concerned about protecting fami-lies from something they viewed as even more oppressive. The information the state proposed to collect, fed into the welfare system's new computers, would, they argued, "facilitate . . . the imposition of . . . eligibility requirements so that families with working-class incomes will be forced out of day care in favor of families who are either on public assistance or earning sweatshop wages." Parents on welfare would have to enter "new forced-work programs" in order to keep their children in day care.

"These new day care measures, together with other broad cuts in social services, with rampant inflation, with wage controls without adequate price controls, are having a tragic effect on people's lives here," the letter continued. "The East Harlem Block Schools will not cooperate in the process. We will neither allow our working parents to be ejected from our centers, nor our welfare parents to be forced into a cheap welfare labor force."

The letter suggested three ways the Block Schools might cooperate—by providing eligibility information about individual families without names and social security numbers; by showing, but not giving, an ACD representative the proof of eligibility forms; or by giving statistical summaries of sworn statements by parents that the information they'd given was true.

"We look forward to negotiating with you," the letter concluded. "We are not eager to close our centers. We hope it is not your purpose to close our centers. We hope it is your goal, as it is ours, to serve families without submitting them to oppressive and punitive registration procedures."

On April 7, the second of what ultimately would be six Saturday meetings of representatives from the noncomplying centers took place at the Block Schools' Madison Avenue center. This time, the purpose was to organize a citywide campaign to generate support for the noncomplying centers and their position on the new registration procedures. Again, Dorothy and Tony played a strong role, organizing people into work sections to plan various aspects of the campaign.

On April 12, Tony and Sonia received letters from ACD detailing procedures "to assure the orderly termination of our relationship."

On April 17, Georgia McMurray responded to the Block Schools' April 5 letter. Dismissing their concerns about the new registration procedures as unfounded, she wrote that the state in Administrative Letter 72 PWD 194 had laid down conditions for day care reimbursement. "If you choose not to adhere to the conditions, we can only assume you do not wish public funds."

On April 18, the cutoff of funds officially went into effect. The Block Nurseries remained fully open, as teachers decided to go on unemployment but continue working. The directors and parent coordinators organized mandatory parent meetings to enlist parents' support.

"Such high stress!" recalls Tony. "No money was coming in, and that meant brown bag lunches and no substitutes. We couldn't pay the rent or the phone bill. Everybody had to pitch in, which meant that parent coordi-

nators and directors were in classrooms a lot. Then there were all the meetings within the schools—at least one or two meetings a week of the board
or parents from one center or the other to make sure that everybody knew
what was happening, because we were asking for agreement and support.
Hardest of all, we weren't winning!"

The tension got the better of Tony at one point. "We were trying to set
up a meeting and Sonia was being uncooperative, as she often is," he recalls with a smile. "No matter what time I suggested, Sonia was 'too busy.'
'Do you want me to beg you to come to this meeting?' I asked. 'Shall I kiss
your feet?' I got down on my knees. 'Okay, I'll kiss them.' And I did!"

"Do what you want!" Sonia said firmly, looking down at Tony. "But
I'm not going to one more meeting. I've been attending meetings seven days
a week. I already know the people—every Tom, Dick, and Harry—I know
before they open their mouths what they are going to say."

But true to character, the Block Schools community pulled together to
deal with the crisis. "I was impressed by our unity in the 2105 struggle,"
observes Judi Macaulay. "And not just the staff. Of course, it was fantastic
that they kept working. But lots of the parents came in to help. They canvassed the stalls in *La Marqueta*, and brought in food and milk and all kinds
of things to keep the schools going."

"What I liked the best," says Tony, "was the series of meetings where
everyone in the schools had these long discussions. First the staff, then the
personnel committees, then the board, then the parent group as a whole.
The attendance at those meetings was extraordinary—we got all but one
or two of the parents. And we had long discussions and really explained
the issues and got a unanimous decision to do what we did, which was
part of the reason we could do it. By the time we moved, everybody had
really thought about it and agreed. Nobody's disagreements were run over
or ignored—they were fully discussed."

On May 16, the Block Schools submitted *coded* 2105 forms to ACD
from parents in both centers. The cover letter reminded Commissioner
McMurray that the Block Schools had always determined the eligibility of
their families and collected fees. "We are unwilling to believe that . . . your
apparent desire to have us either close down or compromise our principles
is really intended. We are therefore taking this initiative to show you that
our proposal has been made in good faith from the beginning."

On May 24, a U.S. District Court made a decision on the legal challenge to the 2105 form. Judge Kevin Duffy ruled that "ACD may no longer
require day care parents to complete Form 2105 and must re-fund all of
the non-complying centers retroactively." Although the Block Schools and
the other noncomplying centers were delighted with the ruling, their joy
was tempered by the realization that the judge was not questioning the

state's right to collect the information, but only pointing out legal problems with this particular form.

While city officials moved immediately to appeal the judge's ruling, ACD found one excuse after another to delay re-funding the centers. Five weeks without funds became six and then seven and then eight. Finally, the Block Nurseries got their reimbursement. But then, on June 29, a higher court reversed Judge Duffy's decision.

A "Dear Friend" letter from the Committee for Community-Controlled Day Care had an uncharacteristic tone of resignation. "Most of the non-complying centers whose funds were cut will probably comply with the new forms in order to get their money," the letter predicted. "They have struggled for months without public funding. They simply cannot carry on. . . . Although we seem to have lost our specific struggle against the new punitive eligibility policies, we did some good in the process. By some of our centers holding out for three months, we educated lots of day care people about what the government is trying to do."

But the Block Schools were not ready to give in. Through July, they continued to refuse to comply—and as a result received no funds. Judi Macaulay took part in meetings with the lawyers, who saw hope in eventually reversing the decision of the appeals court. "But then," says Judi, "we found out that the other centers had already started to comply. They had sent their forms downtown, but had kept a low profile about it. We could continue to hold out, but it would mean going for three or four more months without money. The outcome was uncertain, and we were all alone."

On August 16, 1973, a letter went out to Georgia McMurray: "The parents at East Harlem Block Nursery have decided to comply with the regulations regarding the submission of Form DSS 2105. The issues we have raised over the past several months are not resolved. . . . However, since . . . the government . . . is relentless in its demand for the 2105s, the parents have weighed the alternatives and made their decision based on the belief that preserving day care service for the children is the first, immediate priority."

7

Political Setbacks, Personal Victories

In the aftermath of their defeat in the "2105 struggle," the Block Schools carried on. After all, as Sonia never tired of reminding them, they *were* the Block Schools. But Georgia McMurray was right: The 1960s were over. Gone was the sense of ever-expanding possibility. Gone was the heady feeling of being at the forefront of a campaign that was achieving significant reforms and keeping the spirit of the civil rights movement alive in New York City.

The Block Schools and their allies in the campaign for community-controlled day care had been faithful to their trust. They had fought hard and won significant victories. But now, a counterattack was underway, and they would have to dig in and try to hold as much ground as they could.

Complying with ACD regulations, Sonia Medina (director of the Madison Avenue center), Vivienne Dyce (newly hired as director at 106th Street), and Rosie Gueits (parent coordinator a.k.a. "family worker") implemented the new intake procedures. Parents had to fill out the DSS-2105 forms—until the courts again declared them illegal early in 1974.

The cap on Title IV-A led to the elimination of training money from ACD's budget. During the 1973–74 school year, Dorothy Stoneman ran the college training program on virtually nothing until January, when Peter Sauer came through with funds from the Day Care Consultation Service. Despite the funding problems, 45 staff members and 10 other parents participated. The training committee met regularly. Courses took place at the Block Schools. In the spring, Bank Street College's curriculum committee, which the previous year had approved up to 15 credits for competencies people had already achieved, okayed a Block Schools' plan for up to 30 credits from a variety of "learning experiences," including courses, projects, and mastery of advanced competencies.

Dorothy left in June 1974, and the board hired Jim Meier, former Peace Corps volunteer and doctoral candidate in educational administration at Columbia University's Teachers College, as her replacement. Seeing that future funding from ACD and the Day Care Consultation Service was unlikely, Jim submitted an application to the federal Fund for the Improvement of Post-Secondary Education (FIPSE). Although the Block Schools were going up against colleges and universities from around the country and the grants were extremely competitive, FIPSE approved the proposal, enabling the college program to continue.

Then, in the fall of 1975, came New York City's fiscal crisis. The impact on day care included the elimination of 70 of the city's 420 day care centers, the reduction of the teacher aide position (the third person in the classroom after the head teacher and the assistant teacher) to part-time, and bare bones budgets for supplies and educational materials.

Georgia McMurray was a casualty of the fiscal crisis as well. "[Mayor] Beame called me in," she recalls, "and said that the state was refusing to reimburse the city for millions of dollars in expenses for day care. When they finally arrived at a settlement, one condition was that I resign. I had become a thorn in their side."

Worst of all, from the Block Schools' perspective, was the elimination of the family worker position. Both Georgia McMurray and Marjorie Grosett agree that the state wanted to eliminate the family workers anyway and used the fiscal crisis as a convenient excuse. Marjorie says that although the Day Care Council worked with ACD to develop a new form to replace Form DSS-2105, family workers still resisted requiring parents to fill it out. Soon after Georgia left, the state put the screws on the city to force ACD to take direct responsibility for determining eligibility. Says Georgia: "The state assumed that as long as day care centers controlled intake, they would manipulate it to allow ineligible people. The protests about the forms were counterproductive because they led the state to eliminate the family workers and impose its own procedures."

After ACD stopped paying Rosie Gueits's salary, the Block Schools kept her on the payroll for several months with private funds. When the private money ran out, she continued working for several months as a volunteer. Finally, she retired in 1976.

During the summer of 1973, with the 2105 struggle entering its end-game, Tony Ward had left for Germany, where he spent two and a half years doing research on Germany's "guest workers" for his doctorate in anthropology from the New School for Social Research. In December 1975, he returned to New York City, just as ACD was announcing severe cuts in the city's day care program.

By then, the Committee for Community-Controlled Day Care had faded, and the day care community was in disarray. Tony got right to work. Joining the staff of the Day Care Consultation Service, he plunged into day care advocacy, focusing first on documenting and exposing "the direct lease scandal," with the help of *Village Voice* writer Wayne Barrett. During the years when day care was rapidly expanding, the city had entered into dozens of long-term leases for day care sites. The idea was good in theory: With the guarantee of a long-term lease with the city, a landlord could get bank financing for the major renovations required. But as Tony discovered, the rents the city had agreed to were exorbitant, the renovations often shoddy, and the landlords politically connected. If the city needs to save money, Tony argued in his *Action Bulletin*, which he began to send out twice a month to day care centers and advocates throughout the city, why not renegotiate the leases instead of cutting programs?

In December 1976, Governor Hugh Carey proposed a state budget with $30 million in additional day care cuts. "A year earlier, when day care had been cut 25%, the day care community had not managed an effective protest," says Tony. "This time, we decided we'd try to do better."

They did. Activists mapped out a strategy of local protests culminating in a day of hearings, demonstrations, and lobbying in Albany. As the protests gathered momentum, Tony hammered away in the *Action Bulletin* against the direct leases and another instance of waste he'd uncovered: dramatic increases in ACD's central administrative costs even as programs were being cut.

On February 7, 1977, 2,500 day care advocates streamed into Albany to confront state officials and legislators. Governor Carey got the message. His revised budget contained no cuts for day care, and he never tried to cut day care after that.

To carry on their work, leaders of this successful campaign established the Day Care Forum. Tony became the Forum's co-director with Velmanette Montgomery, a former day care center director from Brooklyn who would later become a state senator. By 1977, the Forum was ready to go beyond reacting to crises and help day care advocates set their own agenda. Choosing eligibility as its focus, the Forum organized a coalition of 13 day care organizations in New York City. Working with that coalition and with a statewide coalition already in existence, the Forum coordinated a three-year drive that achieved substantial liberalization of eligibility rules.

January 28, 1978. An intimate auditorium at Goddard College in Plainfield, Vermont, is packed with Latinos and African-Americans from New York City—friends and family of women from the East Harlem Block Schools and two other day care centers who are receiving their bachelor's degrees from the college.

The stage is decorated with flowers. The 10 graduates, dressed in their Sunday best, sit on the stage on folding chairs. John Eurich (now Eyrrich), Dean of the Goddard Experimental Program for Education, is presenting the women with their degrees. "Antonia Perez," he calls out. Beaming, Toni stands and walks up to John, who hands her the diploma and gives her a big hug. Now it's time for Toni to give a brief speech. Turning to the audience, she cries: "The stupid one got it! The stupid one got it." The audience bursts into laughter and cheering.

"It was the happiest day of my life when I received my B.A. degree," Toni says. "My husband didn't go because he didn't want no part of the program, but my children went. My kids were so happy and I was just ecstatic. I just couldn't believe that I accomplished that. There's no way I can tell you the feeling I had. I said, 'I've got a B.A. degree!' I kept looking at it and saying, 'Oh my God! I can't believe that I have received this.' I said, 'Look at this! I have a B.A. degree!' I told my daughter Sandy, 'Look! Look what mommy did!' and she hugged me and kissed me."

Anna Rivera graduated that day as well and says that getting her B.A. was one of the high points of her life: "Two days before [we were supposed to go up to Vermont], I broke my toe. Everybody wanted me to go, but I couldn't walk and I couldn't put shoes on. Finally, my husband found these old boots—brown leather boots that came up to the ankle. I shined them and put them on and put my pants over them—you could only see the tip.

"I took my daughter Irene with me because I felt she had been the biggest support I had had. [The morning of the graduation] the college sent a car [to the dorm where we were staying] to pick me up.

"John [Eyrrich] was very eloquent. He talked about how much work people had put in. He spoke with respect for the women that were there—working women with families—who still did this because they wanted it so badly. For each of us, when he called us up, he had something to say—he made it personal.

"Well, when he called my name, I'm telling you, I *walked*! He had his arms open. We hugged. I cried—everybody up there cried. And then I had a chance to say something. You could say whatever you wanted. I choked up so much that all I could say was, 'I owe this to my family. This diploma belongs to me and my family because of their support. Because without them I couldn't have done it.'

"We partied all night. We were screaming in the hallways. We danced. We played music. We poked fun at each other. We scared each other and threw blankets over ourselves and ran into the woods. We were like teenagers!"

Goddard College had not figured in the original plans for the Block Schools' college program. The program needed a relationship with an undergraduate college because, although Bank Street could give college credits, it was a graduate school and could not award B.A. degrees. Peter Sauer had tried first to involve Pratt Institute and then Empire State College, but neither had worked out. Of Empire State, Anna Rivera says: "It was too open. You were too much on your own. You met with a mentor, but people didn't feel supported by their mentors. We wanted something more structured."

Finally, Peter entered into discussions with Goddard College, or, more specifically, the Goddard Experimental Program for Education (GEPFE).

Founded in 1938 and based on the philosophy of John Dewey, Goddard College had been an innovator in higher education since its inception. By the 1960s, the College had undergraduate and adult degree programs, but both catered primarily to the upper middle class. Goddard faculty members John Eyrrich and Mary Jane Carlson decided to change that. Says John: "We had the idea that the blessings of progressive education should be available to the poor."

Launching GEPFE in 1965 with a modest grant from the Office of Economic Opportunity, they focused on women whose education had been interrupted. By 1971, four low-income women from Vermont had completed their credits and received a Goddard B.A. With inservice training funds from Head Start and day care, and later with federal Basic Education Opportunity Grants and Pell Grants, GEPFE expanded beyond Vermont, eventually establishing programs also in five other sites.

By 1976, Peter Sauer had completed an agreement with Goddard to establish a GEPFE site in New York City, serving the Block Schools and the two other day care centers involved in the college program being sponsored by the Day Care Consultation Service and Bank Street College. GEPFE operated on a shoestring, and critical to the agreement was Bank Street College's willingness to provide space free of charge for the classes.

GEPFE proved to be a perfect match for the Block Schools. "Our focus was doing something with what you learned—especially for other people," explains Brooke Bushong, faculty member with New York GEPFE and college adviser to many Block Schools' parents. "The motivation was: change the world; the model was: do what Freire did."

Paolo Freire was a Brazilian educator who became internationally known for his "pedagogy of the oppressed." In his work with peasants in Central and South America, Freire combined literacy instruction with a process of dialogue aimed at "conscientization"—in which people analyzed their current reality and came to see it not as something they simply had to accept, but as the starting place for creating a more just and democratic social world (Freire, 1970). John Eyrrich knew Freire, who told him that "for North American conditions, GEPFE was exactly the right concept for adult Freirean education."

Every student in GEPFE had an adviser who visited her regularly at her work site. (Almost all of the GEPFE students in New York City were women.) Brooke, for example, often came to the Block Schools to meet with her advisees during the children's rest time. All of the students had individual contracts worked out with their advisers at the beginning of the semester. At the end of the semester, students had to write an evaluation of what they'd learned and how they planned to use it. The faculty set up "group studies" (courses) based on needs students identified.

The major focus of the semester was a "core project" in which the student explored a question and wrote a paper documenting the learning and its applications.

Classes took place on Friday evening and Saturday two weekends a month. Once a semester, the students would board chartered buses and go up to Plainfield, Vermont, for a weekend on the Goddard campus.

By the early 1980s, more than 35 Block Schools' parents had earned their bachelor's degrees through GEPFE. Like Toni Perez and Anna Rivera, they had all but given up on the idea of college before getting involved in the Block Schools' college program. Most were high school dropouts who had bad memories of the classroom and low estimates of their abilities. In addition, they were burdened with jobs, family responsibilities, and, in many cases, husbands who felt threatened by their efforts to improve themselves. Yet, 35 of them succeeded in getting college degrees because they worked hard and received a tremendous amount of support—from the Block Schools, from Bank Street College, and from the GEPFE faculty, who provided a program uniquely suited to their needs and strengths.

Labeled a failure at home and at school, Toni was so afraid of failing again that without a strong push from a Block Schools colleague, she wouldn't have participated at all. "I never thought of college," she admits. "But I was working with Eva [a professional teacher at the 106th Street nursery]. She said, 'Toni, go!'

"'No, I don't want to go. I'm too busy.'

"'Go!'

"'I can't. I have kids.'

"For more than a month I kept telling her, 'You can tell me to go till you're blue in the face—I'm not going!'

"Finally she said, 'Yes, you are. You're going to go whether you like it or not, and I'm going to take you.' She did. I went with her over to Bank Street on a Saturday and I loved it. I didn't want to go because I didn't think I was going to make it. I didn't have confidence in myself. But once I got there, the teachers gave me self-confidence. They told me that it wouldn't be so hard because of all the experience I already had working with children—I already knew a lot."

Once she started going, she had conflicts with her husband. "I had a husband who was a son of a gun. He would say this was red and I saw it was black but I'd have to say it was red because that was the kind of machismo man he was. He didn't want me to join the college program. I said, 'You're not stopping me from going to the college program, oh no! I'm staying in this college program.' I was determined.

"He said, 'Ever since you started working for the Block Schools, you have changed.' He was right. The Block Schools opened my eyes, and he didn't want that. He wanted it to be the way it was before, but I had already seen that it didn't have to be that way."

For Anna Rivera, the biggest challenge was finding the time. "I was working full-time, I had three children, and I had a husband; and I had to be thinking about their needs. I enjoyed doing the college work. And I knew that if I had problems—in math, for example—there would always be somebody I could go to. But managing the time at home was the hardest."

While Toni never got support from her husband, Anna's family eventually came around. "I have a gorgeous daughter who began to take care of my responsibilities," Anna says. "Irene was already 12. She would do the shopping. She and Michael [age 10] would do the laundry. And my husband started pitching in because I told him, 'I want this *so* bad.' Once my husband and Irene and Michael started to pitch in, it became a little easier. That's why I said, when I got my diploma, that all my family got it with me, because without them I wouldn't have been able to do it."

Whether support from family was available or not, participation was viable only because the schedule suited the needs of working parents. All of the courses took place on two weekends a month at Bank Street College. As a result, all of the Block Schools folks could go over as a group—and that made all the difference. Given the obstacles that stood in the way of their getting college degrees, few would have stuck with it if they'd had to go it alone. Reflects Anna: "The Block Schools had always had a philosophy of being one and helping each other. The college program just extended that and took it to another level. It built on the sense of family and community that was already here. Everyone who went for those weekends came back fulfilled. For a few hours we got away from home, spent time with people who cared, and did things that were different. Being able to go with the people we were working with made us even closer."

In light of their fears and the pulls on their time and energy, support provided by the advisers was critical. Recalls Anna: "Brooke met with me every week at the Block Schools. She gave me lots of support and guidance. And she wouldn't let me slide. She'd ask, 'How's it going? How can I help you? How are the courses? What can we do to improve them?'"

People at the Block Schools were used to taking part in decision-making. In GEPFE as well, their ideas and suggestions were taken seriously. "We would meet—all the students in a group—and talk about the semester," recalls Anna. "We knew certain things were required, but we also had choices. We could say, 'This is what we're interested in,' rather than people just telling us, 'You have to take this and you have to take that.'" Recognizing the talents of their students and wishing to maintain a favorable adviser–student ratio as the program expanded, GEPFE tapped Anna Rivera, Judi Macaulay, and others to become advisers after they'd had a year or two in the program.

The trip to Vermont each semester is on everyone's list of high points for the college program. Workshops and discussion groups took place during the day, with entertainment in the evening. But the informal activities made the biggest impression. Says Anna: "Going to Vermont was a treat because it gave you three days of no children. When we went up there, we went back to when we were younger and didn't have responsibility for children and cooking and all that. The meals were done for us. It was like when you go to college and you're 20 or 21 and you're away from home and you have that feeling of camaraderie. We would joke around, and in the winter we'd have snow fights. Thirty-five-year-old women throwing snowballs! It was like a birthday party every six months."

Toni echoes Anna's sentiments: "I loved going up to Goddard College because for me it was, 'I'm away from this man. I'm in peace over here. It's beautiful here. I'm with my friends. I can be myself the way I really want to be.' And that's why I say that there's nothing like the Block Schools. I'll die for the Block Schools. I have grown to be the person I am today because of the Block Schools. I would never have received a GED if it wasn't for the Block Schools. I would never have received my bachelor's degree. I would never have done the work I've been doing with the kids and the adults—who I care about and who care about me."

Thirty-six years after their founding in 1965, the Block Schools endure. In May 2000 they hired a new executive director, a young woman named Dianne Morales, who has made the journey from Bedford-Stuyvesant to Harvard Graduate School of Education where she is now a doctoral candidate with only her dissertation to complete. In between she earned a master's degree from Columbia School of Social Work and was a founding member and chief operating officer of Jumpstart for Young Children, a national organization.

Dianne's office is in 94 East 111th Street between Park and Madison Avenues, the brownstone that has housed the central office of the Block Schools since the 1960s. Trains still rumble by on their tracks above Park Avenue. But the enclosed space beneath the tracks from 111th to 113th Streets, once crowded with vendors selling their wares from wooden stalls, is now dark and cavernous, *La Marqueta* having shrunk to a single block between 114th and 115th Streets. And the buildings where Sonia and other Block Schools founders lived are gone. Across the street from the Block Schools' office, a grassy baseball field for the Harlem Little League and two elaborate community gardens have replaced the tenement buildings that in the 1960s housed thousands of people.

When I asked Dianne what drew her to the Block Schools, her answer was reminiscent of that of Alice Graves, the first teacher candidate interviewed by the parents in 1965. Alice was struck by the genuineness of the people. Says Dianne: "I spent a full day visiting the schools, going from program to program. The faces of the organization are the faces of the community we serve—and that's hard to find these days. The organization is genuinely community-based. If you have that, running good programs is easy."

At the same time, she feels she has much to offer. "A link seems to be missing," she explains. "The Block Schools should be bigger and better known, given how authentic they are. I feel I may be able to make that happen because of my versatility—my ability to go back and forth between East Harlem and Wall Street."

It's a credit to the leadership of the Block Schools that during a 25-year period of relentless hostility to the poor—a time in which many similar organizations died—the Block Schools have not only survived but have stayed faithful to their founding principles."

It hasn't been easy. Judi Macaulay served as executive director for 10 years—from 1971 until 1981. Besides dealing with Ros, helping the nurseries adjust to oppressive new regulations imposed by ACD, and overseeing the college program as it led to college degrees for dozens of Block Schools parents, Judi guided the elementary school through its painful transition into the public system. Reserved, stoical, always kind, fair, and generous with her colleagues, she stood at the helm as the Block Schools weathered New York City's fiscal crisis, which in addition to its negative consequences for day care led to the layoffs of 10,000 public school teachers, including the entire professional staff of the elementary school (since they didn't have Board of Education tenure).

Also during Judi's watch, Dorothy Stoneman in 1978 started the Youth Action Program (YAP) under the auspices of the Block Schools. A conscious effort to apply to young people what she'd learned from her work with parents at the Block Schools, YAP involved high school dropouts in rehabilitating housing in the neighborhood, while earning their high school diplomas, learning construction skills, and participating in the governance of the program.

During her 10 years, Judi got strong support from Jim Meier, whose FIPSE grants sustained the schools through lean times; from Anna Rivera, who directed the college program when Jim began disseminating it to other community groups; from Peggy Walton and Donna [Williams] Benton, who as parent teachers in the elementary school survived the fiscal crisis, then got their degrees, became licensed Board of Education teachers, and continue to teach in the public East Harlem Block elementary school; from Tony Ward, Dorothy Stoneman, and me; and from Ethel Velez, a parent who chaired the board of directors from 1975 to about 1985.

By the late 1970s, however, Judi was exhausted and depressed. A private person, she was suffering from personal woes her colleagues could only glimpse and from the accumulation of years of stress as executive director. She had never been one to take initiative—her style was responsive and low-key—but as deadlines were missed and bills went unpaid, Ethel grew increasingly concerned. Finally in 1981, the board asked Judi for her resignation. She died several years later of cancer.

By the time of Judi's resignation, the Block Schools were in serious financial trouble. Jim had left, the FIPSE grants had run out, and the schools had been drifting for several years. Ethel called Tony Ward and asked if he would return to put them back on their feet. By then Tony was executive director of the Day Care Forum and a leading figure in day care politics, not only in the city but in the state. Unable to say no to Ethel but fully committed to his day care advocacy work, Tony from 1981 to 1985 served as executive director of both organizations!

Fully appreciative of the importance of good financial management as a result of his bitter experience the first time he served as executive director, Tony did what the schools needed most: He straightened out the books, instituted sound financial procedures, raised money, and paid outstanding bills. He also got the directors of the various programs meeting together again; re-established a positive image for the schools in the funding community; and, after several years of persistence, managed to convince Gardenia White to apply to be his replacement.

African-American, a native of South Carolina, Gardenia had come to New York City in the 1950s as a young mother. Swept up by the civil rights movement, she convinced her husband and aunt to look after her children while she spent the summer of 1964 in Mississippi. Upon her return, she plunged into the city's civil rights struggle: the campaign for community control of the public schools. Working for Two Bridges Community Organization on the Lower East Side of Manhattan, she organized parents and promoted parent participation in the public schools. In the course of her work, she brought a group of parents to visit the Block Schools. "We were just in awe at the quality of the program and the depth of parent participation," she says. Gardenia went on to become a member of the school board in her Lower East Side district and to do parent organizing throughout the city. Then, in 1972, she began working for Peter Sauer and the Day Care Consultation Service as coordinator of the college program in which the Block Schools and two other centers were participating. In 1976, she returned to the South where she started her own organization focused on organizing and educating parents.

"At least once a year, Tony would call me," says Gardenia. "'Aren't you ready to come back to New York? I have a job for you,' he'd say. Finally I said, 'Okay.' In 1986 I interviewed for the position and got it."

For the next five years, she ran a growing organization with a million dollar budget and seven programs, including the two nurseries and the elementary school. Under Dorothy Stoneman's leadership, the Youth Action Program had thrived. By 1988, it had achieved such visibility that Dorothy launched a national replication effort, which began as part of YAP but in 1990 became a separate organization, YouthBuild USA, run by Dorothy from its headquarters near Boston.

Not surprisingly, given her passionate commitment to parent organizing and education, Gardenia focused on working with the nurseries and the elementary school to make parent control and participation a reality day in and day out. "Most organizations just pay lip service to parent involvement," she explains. "This is one organization that truly respects and supports parents—all parents. You hear people from other schools saying they can't get parents involved. You don't ever hear us saying that because they are involved here. When we call a parent meeting—whether it's the nursery school or the elementary school—the place is filled. The reason is that we truly respect parents, we don't put them down, and we feel they have a right to be involved in their kids' education."

By 1991, Gardenia was "just totally burned out." Deciding she needed a break, she left; and for several years the organization drifted without an executive director.

In 1995 the Madison Avenue nursery became a casualty of this period without an executive director. The issue was not the quality of the educational program, but a missed deadline. Under Mayor Rudolph Giuliani, the city had changed the contract renewal process, making the application more complicated. And unlike in the past, the deadline was absolutely firm. The Children's Aid Society, a large nonprofit social service agency, now operates its Taft Nursery at the former site of the Block Schools' Madison Avenue center.

Gardenia returned to the Block Schools in 1995, and served as executive director until May 2000. By the time of her return, the Youth Action Program had spun off, incorporating as a separate organization, and there were only three programs: the remaining nursery, the elementary school, and a small after-school program.

Gardenia considers that one of the main accomplishments of her second term as executive director was the sale of a building at 109th Street and Fifth Avenue, which the Block Schools had acquired in 1974 as a gift from the Schubert Foundation. Over the years, the structure—a windowless building formerly used as a studio for shooting television commercials—had first housed elementary school classes and then YAP. But, says Gardenia, "it was going to be an elephant on us, needing money we didn't have." After looking for a year, she found a buyer and sold it in 1997 for $1.7 million. The money allowed the Block Schools to pay off debts, provide some cash for each of its programs, renovate 94 East 111th Street, and establish a modest cash reserve fund.

Through all of the ups and downs of the past 36 years, the 106th Street nursery has maintained its identity as a parent-controlled school with strong parent participation and a solid educational program for young children. Toni Perez served as group teacher of the five-year-olds from 1978, when she received her bachelor's degree, to 1994, when she left for Florida to care for her eldest daughter, who was dying of cancer. "That's the only thing that could have made me leave the Block Schools," she says. Anna Rivera was the group teacher of the three-year-olds from 1981 until complications from diabetes and asthma forced her to retire in 1998. And Vivienne Dyce, hired when Tony Ward left in 1973, is now in her twenty-eighth year as director.

Vivienne grew up in Jamaica, came to New York City as a teenager, and got her early childhood training at Fordham University and Hunter

College. She says she has stayed with the Block Schools all these years because of the support people give each other. "Judi [Macaulay] and Sonia [Medina] were my teachers," she says. Grateful to them for the ways they supported her when she came to the school as a young professional, she carries on the tradition, going out of her way to help her staff succeed and bearing with them during hard times in their lives.

To be eligible for day care, parents must be either working, looking for work, involved in job training, or certified by a doctor to have a special need for day care. "It's not like years ago when you could get day care simply because you wanted your child to have an education," Vivienne observes. "The result is that parents are too busy to volunteer in the classrooms, help answer the phones, or just hang out the way they used to." But parent meetings are well attended, and an active parent personnel committee still makes hiring decisions after an initial screening by Vivienne.

ACD provides scant resources for creating an exciting educational program. The budget for educational equipment and materials is small, and virtually no money or time is available for staff training. "If you want to do more than babysitting," says Vivienne, "you have to make your own center that way." She is proud of the staff workshops she organizes with private funds raised by the Block Schools, the lesson plans she requires the teachers to submit regularly, and the amount of time she spends in classrooms supporting teachers (which means spending evenings attending to paperwork).

The hardest part is dealing with the bureaucracy. In a major reorganization, Mayor Giuliani moved the Agency for Child Development from the Department of Social Services to his new Agency for Children's Services. Says Vivienne: "What used to take six months now takes about 18 months because we have to wait for our turn with a bunch of other social agencies. We waited a year and a half for a new refrigerator."

And that's not the worst of it. Gardenia and Vivienne agree that under the Giuliani administration, the city has favored large agencies over small community-based groups like the Block Schools. In addition to the Block Schools' loss of the Madison Avenue center to the Children's Aid Society, they cite ACD's recent closing of another day care center in the neighborhood. Like the Block Schools, the center had started in the 1960s and was run by a small community group. "They just closed it," says Gardenia. "We joined in the fight to keep that center open, but they closed it— and they did it in a really nasty way. They told the parents right up till the last minute that they were going to keep it open, and then overnight they just closed it.

"When people from ACD come to visit the 106th Street nursery," she says, "I get the feeling that they aren't there to help or support but to find something wrong so that they can close you down. They're punitive in every way. The Board of Education is much easier to deal with than ACD."

The 106th Street nursery faced a threat in 1995, when Franklin Plaza tried to oust the center from its storefront location, saying that improvements made on the windows (by ACD) were a violation of its lease. "Instead of trying to help the center," remarks Vivienne, "ACD sat on its hands. I think they thought this was a way they could get rid of us. But we resisted—in a very determined, organized way. Flyers, phone calls, meetings, lawyers—we did all of it. Our parents and our staff are fantastic. Everybody just pulled together and said, 'No!' And when we were finished, ACD saw that they couldn't mess with us, that they couldn't intimidate us. We have a good relationship with ACD, and we keep it that way by being strong, by doing the things that will give us a quality program."

Ultimately, the strength lies in the deep roots the school has in the community. Explains Vivienne: "I've seen the children that we had, have their own children. The little one who's coming into the center now, we had his mother, or his father, or his uncle. That's our survival. Parents whose kids went through the nursery come back to us all the time. We had a kid who attended the nursery and the elementary school, got her B.A., and then returned to direct the after-school program. She's just one of many. They come back and want to see how they can help—they say things like, 'You all made it so great for me, what do you need?'"

The Block Schools' new executive director, Dianne Morales, expects to build on that strength. She has already seized one opportunity. Advocates for early childhood education waged a successful campaign to get the state to allocate significant new money for prekindergarten programs— and to restore the funds when Governor Pataki, after announcing the new allocation with great fanfare in 1998, proposed to eliminate it from the budget the following year. Leading the fight were Child Care Inc., founded by Tony Ward as a merger of the Day Care Forum and PAWS (a child care referral agency), and Citizens Committee for Children. The Block Schools strongly supported the campaign. Says Gardenia: "We really fought. I hadn't written so many letters since the 1960s."

This new initiative, which aims ultimately to make prekindergarten programs "universal," is primarily a Board of Education program, far from the original Block Schools' vision of early childhood programs provided by hundreds of centers rooted in neighborhoods and run by parents. But ACD is getting some of the money. And since public schools are strapped for space, they are partnering with nonprofit agencies in some cases. As a result of these developments, ACD has decided to expand day care, providing funding for additional centers for the first time in many years.

Dianne submitted an application in response to ACD's request for proposals, and the Agency has approved it. "Creating a second nursery school will give us the chance to help fill the real need this community has for child care, while giving more parents a chance to get involved and learn new skills," says Dianne.

"I want to take the Block Schools back to their roots. At their best, the schools have exemplified the philosophy of Paolo Freire: helping people learn to question, analyze, and think critically about their lot in life and see places where they can take back some control, be more in the driver's seat. We've moved away from this over the years as we've focused on survival. I want to put it at the center of our work once again."

In Dianne's vision, the Block Schools are also a place where neighborhood activists and leaders will come together to look at the factors that affect life in East Harlem and support each other in bringing about positive change. "I'm exploring how we might develop the Block Schools as an 'urban Highlander,'" she explains, referring to the popular education center in Tennessee that has been a gathering place for social activists since the 1930s (Horton, 1998). "The idea is to get people who are at different stages talking to each other, to connect leaders so that there's less a sense of helplessness."

Dianne Morales seems poised to lead a new generation in adding powerful new chapters to the Block Schools' story.

8

Lessons from the Block Schools

"I have no doubt that for a lot of people, being part of the Block Schools was really a transforming experience," reflects Tony Ward, "and that the transformation came in part from the sense of community and group effort across racial and class lines that took place there. What has always stayed with me is the possibility of that. The Block Schools weren't *the* spark for the movement, but early on they caught the flame and made other places flame up too. For a time, people experienced a sense of purpose and control over their lives—a direction toward something really worthwhile for themselves and other people, of service and sacrifice. The Block Schools were among many places where that happened in the sixties."

A School of Our Own focuses on events that began more than 35 years ago. But the story is not primarily about the past; it's about possibility. It's not so much about what happened then as about what people can do now—if they have the vision, the know-how, and the will.

The story speaks for itself. I hope it has spoken to you. Below are my reflections on three aspects of the Block Schools' experience.

Changing Lives

Drawing on many years of research, Lisbeth Schorr, director of the Harvard University Project on Effective Interventions, argues in her book *Common Purpose* (1997) that the key ingredient of successful programs is "strong relationships based on mutual trust and respect" (p. 10). Block Schools folks certainly would agree. As Schorr also points out, "Life-transforming relationships don't happen in a vacuum—they must be sustained by supportive institutions" (p. 10). What explains the schools' effectiveness in sustaining life-transforming relationships?

At the Block Schools, parents and professionals made a serious, sustained, and at least partially successful effort to work together as equals. More than anything else, that's what changed people's lives. The organization challenged prevailing attitudes about status in our class society and insisted on a different set of assumptions based on high expectations and mutual respect. As a result, the Block Schools became a "free social space," relatively free of class and racial prejudice, in which both low-income and middle-class people could flourish.

Supporting the process were a number of factors, including liberating work, adequate resources, the Block Schools' approach to education, parent control, and strong leadership.

At the Block Schools, parents moved from volunteering to subbing to assistant teaching to teaching. Since the jobs were in the neighborhood at their children's schools, they could stay close to their families. On a daily basis they learned skills that made them better parents and teachers. Through their work, they also could pursue their dream of a college education. And the context for all of this was a community of friends, neighbors, and professional colleagues who cared about each other. Work like this really does set people free.

Running a good school takes resources—not so much fancy space or expensive equipment, but people, training, and time. Daily meetings of each classroom team, classroom coaching by the educational director, professional development for staff through the college program—these were essential in making the Block Schools good learning places for children and adults. They cost money, take time, and, unfortunately, cannot be taken for granted.

Time is critical in another way as well. Lives don't change overnight; the process takes years. And so it was essential that the Block Schools were not a revolving door, but a community people could be part of for many years. Aside from the possibility of getting a job in the organization, parents could participate for three years as a child went through the nursery and then for another six if the child went on to the elementary school.

The approach to education developed by the Block Schools was another factor that supported life-changing relationships. A hybrid of Bank Street's progressive learner-centered philosophy and a community development model that stressed parent participation, the approach aimed to provide the best possible education for the children. But infused with warm support, high expectations, and the idea that learning can be fun, it also nurtured the parents' confidence in themselves as learners and awakened their interest in continuing their education. Once they started on the path to their college degrees, they had a network of friends close at hand to support them. The Block Schools provided many parents with a second chance for an education—and one that proved immeasurably more pleasant and fruitful than their previous schooling.

As the founding principle of the schools, parent control is essential in explaining their impact. In our society, so the founders' reasoning went, the cleavages along class and racial lines go so deep that to set the stage for parents and professionals to relate to each other on a basis of equality, the usual power relationships have to be flipped upside down. Tony and the parents designed the organization so that at all levels it reflected that assumption. Making up the board of directors and the personnel committees, the parents had ultimate control in setting policy and hiring and firing. Since the parent coordinators worked closely with the educational directors, parents were involved in all significant management decisions. And every classroom had parent assistant teachers as well as a professional. The primary aim was to benefit the children by ensuring that both parents and professionals would contribute their wisdom to shaping the educational program. At the same time, parents got opportunities for democratic participation that few had enjoyed before joining the Block Schools.

But if building parent participation into the structure of the schools at every level was necessary in establishing liberating relationships between parents and professionals, it was not sufficient. Even in their parent-controlled organization, the Block Schools discovered that societal patterns of middle-class dominance over low-income people reasserted themselves and had to be challenged on a daily basis. Alice Graves had to push Rosie Tirado to break out of her comfort zone, try new classroom activities, and insist on a role in planning. Alice also had to confront the professional teacher with whom Rosie was working and insist that she stop doing all of the planning while leaving the clean-up to Rosie.

The process required a delicate blend of challenge and support. When Rosie Gueits encouraged Toni Perez to ask Millie Rabinow what the word "masturbation" meant, Toni was terribly embarrassed. But when Millie told her what it meant and nobody made fun of her, it freed her to ask questions in the future and begin to fill in some of the gaps in her education. Several years later, Eva had to push Toni to get her to attend the college program because Toni was so afraid she was going to fail. But when Toni finally went, she loved it because the teachers gave her the message that they believed in her.

For many schools started by educational reformers in the 1960s, the watchword was freedom. At the Block Schools, the core value was respect. In his "I Have a Dream" speech, Martin Luther King envisioned a world in which people would be judged by the strength of their character, not by the color of their skin. Inspired by King's vision, people at the Block Schools tried to create an institution in which people would be judged by their contribution to the schools, not by the color of their skin *or by their class status.* The Block Schools' story is studded with instances in which the parents parted company with people who assumed that they deserved special treatment because of their college degree or professional training.

Sometimes class bias was internalized, as in Rosie Tirado's reluctance to take part in planning. Sometimes, it was interpersonal, as in the professional teacher's habit of leaving the cleaning to Rosie. And sometimes oppression was institutional, as in the Division of Day Care's sending caseworkers to investigate the parents' personal lives and then write "family histories." The Block Schools challenged class prejudice in all of these forms and made a concerted effort to resist it.

The lessons for practitioners and policy-makers are clear.

- Organizations providing services in low-income neighborhoods are most effective when neighborhood people participate substantially in governing the organization and carrying out its work. Relating on a basis of "mutual respect" goes way beyond "being nice." It's about people truly listening to each other and respecting each other enough to share power. At the Block Schools, that meant parent control. In YouthBuild, it means that there's a "policy committee" comprising young people who help set policy and take part in hiring and firing of staff. Although the form may vary, the idea is to build into the organization participation by the people being served. And, as we know from the Block Schools' story, that's only the first step. Constant vigilance is required to prevent class bias from creeping back in.
- Public policy aimed at eliminating poverty must begin by acknowledging that the so-called economic boom of the 1990s left many people out.

According to the most recent data from the National Center for Children in Poverty, 17% of all children in the United States (and 18% of children under the age of six) live in poverty—that is, in families with incomes below the federal poverty line. The child poverty rate for African Americans is 33% and for Latinos, 30%. And contrary to widespread negative stereotypes, most poor children have at least one employed parent (Child Poverty Fact Sheet, June 2001, *www.cpmcnet.columbia.edu/dept/ nccp/*). The market alone cannot begin to address this situation. Government must assume its responsibility. President Clinton had included government funding for training, job creation, and child care in his original welfare reform proposal. From my point of view, the most serious lapse of his presidency was that he launched the welfare reform juggernaut, then lost control of it, and ended up signing the Republican version of the bill, which included virtually no provisions to help low-income families. The unfinished business of welfare reform is a substantial commitment by the federal government to create living-wage jobs, offer job training, and provide high-quality child care to enable low-income parents to raise their families out of poverty. The Block Nurseries represent one effective strategy for accomplishing this. By providing the resources for neighborhood people to create high-quality child care programs on the Block Nurseries' model, the government can simultaneously create jobs, strengthen neighborhoods, and transform lives.

Battling "the System"

On the first day of the 2000–01 school year, the chancellor of New York City's public schools visited Central Park East 2, an alternative public school in East Harlem. A parent of a second grader was alarmed to see him, thinking it was better for the school to be left alone by the central bureaucracy. "The Board of Education has a policy," she told the chancellor in the hallway. "It destroys anything that works!" (Hartocollis, 2000).

Bureaucracies have a well-deserved reputation for undermining good programs. This seems absurd. We laugh at the parent's comment to the chancellor. But there is a method to the madness. In a recent conversation, Tony Ward recalled a "Peanuts" cartoon: Linus is happily playing with some toys. Lucy comes in and says, "Hey! Gimme those toys!!! Everything's Mine! Mine! Mine!" As she walks away, she flips him a rubber band. "Here, I guess you can have this rubber band. Have fun with that." Linus takes the rubber band and stretches it up and down and this way and that and soon he's having a wonderful time. Suddenly Lucy appears. "What's going on here?! Gimme that!" She snatches it from him. "I didn't mean for you to have *that* much fun."

"So the schools were the rubber bands that society left us," Tony observes, "and when we began to have too much fun, SNATCH!"

Losing their rubber bands when they begin to have too much fun—that's what it means to be poor in a class society. "The system" that destroys good programs is not simply bureaucracy, if by that we mean a tangle of arcane regulations or offices of tired city workers resistant to change. "The system" is the whole array of institutions enforcing policies that serve the interests of the influential and wealthy few at the expense of the vast majority of people, especially the poor. Bureaucracies do exactly what they're supposed to do: control the people who are getting the short end of the stick.

The story of the Block Nurseries and the campaign for community-controlled day care is a classic example. I have described the attributes of the schools that set the stage for people changing their lives. Those same features led the parents to "get uppity" with the Division of Day Care. Bringing new families into the Block Schools had always been a process of neighbors reaching out to neighbors. Under Day Care it became "intake," a procedure in which agents of a bureaucracy investigated people and filled out forms. The parents' response was outrage. This simply didn't accord with the respect to which they had become accustomed. And since they were allied with other parents in an organization with strong leadership, they did not have to put up with it. They could say no and fight a principled battle against oppressive social policies and practices.

Moreover, the Block Nurseries' struggle with the Day Care bureaucracy was not taking place in a vacuum. Other parent-controlled centers were springing up around the city, fueled by parents' growing need for child care, their desire to improve their children's education, and their yearning for participation in a small neighborhood organization they could help shape. Like parents at the Block Schools, parents at these centers wanted exciting classrooms for their children, parent control, comprehensive services for families, and the possibility of work (paid or volunteer) in close proximity to their children.

By 1969, the infrastructure to support effective replication of this "community model" of day care was taking shape. Bank Street College's Day Care Consultation Service was providing technical assistance to help new groups develop sound educational programs. The Block Nurseries were available as a model program, demonstrating how well parent-controlled centers could work and challenging day care policies inconsistent with their vision. The Committee for Community-Controlled Day Care was organizing community groups around the city to build a political constituency for community day care. Given the time, these organizations, working together, could have nurtured and sustained hundreds of high-quality, neighborhood-based centers around the city.

And in fact, as we have seen, the Block Nurseries and the day care re-form movement won some impressive victories against the bureaucracy. The Block Nurseries' effectiveness in these advocacy efforts resulted from their authenticity and from the respect with which they generally treated public officials. They were authentic in the sense remarked on by Alice Graves and Dianne Morales: They were down-to-earth people from East Harlem with no other agenda than to maintain the effectiveness of their programs.

Demanding to be treated with respect, they treated others with re-spect—even the bureaucrats who were undermining their program. Under the leadership of Dorothy, Judi, Sonia, and Tony, they developed demands that were concrete and achievable; they articulated those de-mands clearly; they maintained good relationships with public officials; and they consistently strove for win–win solutions. While usually respect-ful, thoughtful, and patient, they were willing to stage demonstrations when necessary. And they allied themselves with the more confronta-tional and militant Committee for Community-Controlled Day Care, tak-ing part in Committee-sponsored demonstrations and lending their hands to strengthen the Committee's work.

There was always a tension between the parents' narrow focus on their schools and the leadership's insistence that they join forces with others to fight city agencies if they wanted to survive. But if the par-ents' insularity made them vulnerable, it was inextricably tied to their strength, reflecting as it did their singular focus on running the best possible program for their children.

There was another reason that the Block Nurseries and day care re-formers were successful in fighting city agencies between 1968 and 1972. During that time, day care was a contested issue; policy-makers questioned current practice and disagreed with each other about what ought to be done. This breakdown in consensus about day care policy had many causes: the growing number of women with young children entering the workforce, the civil rights movement, the availability of uncapped money for expan-sion of day care, the work of day care reformers over many years, concern among right-wingers about the growth in the welfare rolls, and Mayor Lindsay's strategy of creating super-agencies (like HRA) to challenge os-sified city bureaucracies.

All of these developments unsettled New York City's day care pro-gram and gave activists some leverage. If the Block Schools ran into oppo-sition from Muriel Katz, they could go above her to Mitchell Ginsberg, head of HRA. For a time Ginsberg's successor, Jule Sugarman, even encouraged demonstrations so that he could fund more centers.

This is not to say that the advocacy work of the Block Schools and the Committee was insignificant. Although top-level officials in the city—the

Mayor, the Commissioners of HRA and ACD—were committed to change, they needed grassroots pressure and ideas.

But absent the array of favorable conditions described above, the campaign would have made little headway with the strategies it was using. For the city bureaucracies weren't able to make the most important of the rules; their job was to carry them out. The Block Schools and the campaign for community-controlled day care learned that the hard way in 1973.

With the civil rights movement waning, a recession deepening, and a Republican in the White House, the political climate changed. Funds for day care and other social services were capped and cut. The federal and state governments issued new guidelines that greatly restricted day care service. The Agency for Child Development and the city, sincerely committed to day care reform but dependent on Washington and Albany for funds, had to comply with restrictive new rules and budget cuts. The party was over: Lucy came and snatched the rubber band.

The campaign for community-controlled day care mounted no effective resistance because it lacked clout in the places that counted: Albany and Washington. Advocates couldn't organize to override Nixon's veto of the Child Development Act. They couldn't stop him and his Congressional allies from capping Title IV-A. They couldn't prevail on the state legislature to increase day care funding or change the eligibility and fee rules.

And so the government abandoned the "community model" of day care—the bright vision of hundreds of parent-controlled day care centers serving the real needs of children and their families in neighborhoods around the city—several years after its birth. By cutting classroom staff, eliminating the family workers, and restricting eligibility to very poor people who were in training, seeking work, or working, the system pushed day care toward what we might call the "employers' model," since it does little more than serve employers' interest in having a low-cost, compliant workforce. Only persistent, sophisticated organizing by Tony and his colleagues at the Day Care Forum and Child Care, Inc., has prevented the system from completely reducing day care to the "employers' model." Today centers have some "wiggle room," but, as Vivienne observes, for a center to be more than a babysitting service, its people have to find additional resources and surmount an array of bureaucratic obstacles.

This story holds several lessons for local advocates and practitioners.

- Advocates need to figure out who ultimately has the power to allocate resources and make decisions about the policies they are trying to change, and then shape their strategies accordingly. Both Tony Ward and Dorothy Stoneman learned this lesson well. Sizing up the situation with day care in the mid-1970s, Tony saw that the state legislature was the key player, with lots of control over day care policy and funding. (The federal government also had tremendous influence, of course; but Tony judged that given his resources he would be able to have a bigger impact in Albany than in Washington.) He therefore decided to focus his day care advocacy efforts on the state government—with great success. Dorothy saw that if she wanted to spread her ideas about youth development around the country, federal funding would be necessary; so she has worked extensively with Congress and with the Department of Housing and Urban Development to win substantial federal appropriations for youth development programs on her YouthBuild model.

- Local practitioners need to give active support to local advocacy efforts, even though staff may feel they already have their hands full simply trying to run a good program. Examples are the strong role the Block Nurseries played in the movement for community-controlled day care; and, more recently, the letters and phone calls the schools generated in support of the campaign for universal prekindergarten. Persistent organizing and advocacy is the only way to hold onto past gains and push the system to yield more.
- Local programs and advocacy efforts are greatly influenced by the national context. Title IV-A, passed during 1967 when the civil rights movement was still flourishing, provided the material support for the campaign for community-controlled day care. As the civil rights movement waned, so did federal support for day care. When Nixon capped and cut day care funding, he dealt day care reformers in New York City a major blow. Local activists need to stay informed about national developments to avoid being blind-sided. Even more important, they need to join in efforts to influence federal policy, as Georgia McMurray did in organizing her successful campaign against Caspar Weinberger's oppressive day care regulations. The National Center for Children in Poverty and the Children's Defense Fund are good sources of information about developments in Washington that affect children and about actions local advocates and practitioners can take to influence federal policy.

Dream Deferred

What has it accomplished—the tremendous amount of loving effort that has gone into creating and sustaining these parent-controlled schools in East Harlem?

The Block Schools are part of the radical democratic tradition, based on the conviction that all people ought to live in dignity and have a say in the decisions that affect their lives. This rich legacy of people's resistance and insurgency runs throughout American history and has found many forms of expression—from slave revolts to abolitionism, from Henry David Thoreau to Rosa Parks.

Inspired by the civil rights movement, people at the Block Schools worked to make the radical democratic vision real within their organization and fought to spread it to the world beyond. Their schools have touched thousands of families. And they helped lead a campaign that produced a dramatic expansion of day care services in New York City.

But while they and their allies can count a number of successes, they failed to achieve their audacious goal of changing governmental policy to promote wide-scale, high-quality implementation of the "community model" of day care. By addressing the real needs of families and fostering citizen participation at the grassroots level, the creation of day care programs on the Block Nurseries' model in neighborhoods throughout the city would have represented a significant "people's victory." It was not to be.

The deferring of that dream, marked by the letter Judi Macaulay sent to the Agency for Child Development announcing the Block Nurseries' surrender in the 2105 struggle, was a profound disappointment. And that was only one of many setbacks poor people would endure in the years to come.

Does their failure to achieve their ambitious agenda in the wide world mean that the Block Schools are significant only on a personal level, that their impact consists only of the thousands of lives they touched directly? Not at all.

"Urging the possible a little further than at first it had wanted to go," the dreamers at the Block Schools thought unconventionally, created boldly, and inconvenienced themselves mightily. They experienced wonderful moments of triumph, and wrestled with defeat. Formed in this crucible, the life changes many people experienced at the Block Schools were not only personal, but political—in the broad sense of that word. Life change at the Block Schools was not only about increased earning power, professional skill, self-esteem, and happiness—important as those things are. It was also about being part of a determined and resourceful group of people who were making a difference in the world, discovering the special skills and talents they had to contribute, and realizing that joining with others to fight for a better world is a wonderful way to live. The Block Schools inspired, nurtured, and trained dozens of people who became teachers and leaders in the struggle for social justice and have stayed faithful to this calling throughout their lives.

Anna Rivera, Carmen Gonzalez, Donna Benton, Peggy Walton, Rosie Gueits, Sonia Medina, and Toni Perez, all of whom appear in our story, are among many parents who began as volunteers and went on to become educators, imbued with the high expectations for children and commitment to parents instilled by the Block Schools. It's likely that none of them would have become educators if the Block Schools hadn't touched their lives. Together, they have served New York City children and their families with great dedication for a total of more than 190 years.

After leaving the Block Schools, Tony Ward spent nearly 20 years as the leading organizer and advocate for day care in New York State and founded an organization, Child Care, Inc., that continues to play a leading role in promoting high-quality day care. After leaving Child Care in 1994, Tony became executive director of the Carnegie Corporation's Task Force on Education in the Primary Grades. Three years later, after completing his work with the Task Force, he decided to become a teacher. He is now in his third year of teaching first grade in a public school in the Washington Heights section of Manhattan.

Through her work in creating the Youth Action Program and then YouthBuild, Dorothy Stoneman has helped shape national policy on youth development. For several years now, her efforts have produced annual appropriations from Congress of $40 million dollars for programs on the YouthBuild model. In 1996 Dorothy received a MacArthur "genius" award.

Lois Goldfrank went on to become a leader in multicultural education in California. The librarian and media specialist at Bay View Elementary School in Santa Cruz, she created a multicultural resource guide and conducted workshops for teachers throughout the state.

Susan Kosoff has been on the faculty of Wheelock College in Boston for the past 30 years. In 1981 she founded the Wheelock Family Theater and is its producer and a frequent director. The aim of this acclaimed multicultural and intergenerational theater is to make theater accessible to nontraditional audiences.

Now in my twentieth year as executive director of Educators for Social Responsibility Metropolitan Area (ESR Metro), I co-founded the Resolving Conflict Creatively Program, a collaboration of ESR Metro and the New York City Board of Education, which has supported thousands of teachers in providing regular instruction in creative nonviolent conflict resolution to hundreds of thousands of young people in the New York City public schools.

Dorothy, Lois, Susan, Tony, and I are among many professionals who worked at the Block Schools and, influenced by what we experienced there, have gone on to make significant contributions in a variety of settings around the country.

The Block Schools were born in a "mountaintop time." Although we may seem to be deep in a valley now, the Block Schools' dream—of creating parent-run child care centers in low-income neighborhoods as part of a substantial societal effort to eliminate poverty—is only deferred, not dead. We will need a miracle to turn things around for poor people in this country, but miracles are possible. In my lifetime, I have witnessed several, including the end of apartheid in South Africa and the dissolution of the Soviet Union. "Miracles" like those are possible because of lots of nitty-gritty, behind-the-scenes work by so-called ordinary citizens—folks like you and me. The future is open and we will help create it. What are our tasks during this "valley time"?

One is to sustain our organizations. Organizational work can seem tedious and unglamorous, especially compared with the thrill of participating in a movement. But it's essential. Child Care, Inc., the East Harlem Block Schools, ESR Metro, the Wheelock Family Theater, the Youth Action Program, YouthBuild—these organizations are among thousands across the country that not only serve the people but engage them in authentic communities where they have a voice.

Beyond their intrinsic value, organizations such as these are valuable because they help form the base for social movements. In his compelling study of the origins of the civil rights movement, Aldon Morris (1984) shows that although they may have seemed spontaneous, the mass protests that characterized the movement were the product of activists working through organizations. He describes how the African-American churches became the movement's institutional base, and how the NAACP made a critical contribution by developing local leadership and keeping the flame of resistance alive through years of harsh repression.

Building leadership is a second crucial task. We have seen that at the Block Schools this happened organically as a natural outgrowth of the struggle to create and sustain the schools. Looking at the Block Schools of the 1960s and 1970s from our perspective 25 years later, it's clear that what people were *becoming* was as important as what they were *doing*, for most of them had more than 30 years of productive work time ahead of them. To the extent that their experiences during those years helped them understand reality, deepened their commitment, and enabled them see how they could be most effective, they would serve well for years to come.

The Block Schools paid an unusual amount of attention to developing their adult staff, especially the parents; and the pay-off was great. The lesson is that as we go about our work—waging our campaigns, running our programs, teaching our courses, putting on our plays—we must not lose sight of the people working alongside us. In the midst of hectic lives, we need to help each other reflect on the experiences we're having in our social change work, analyze what's going on beneath the surface in society and politics, and learn "people's history," drawing inspiration and insight from the long line of visionaries, justice seekers, and peacemakers who have come before us. Acknowledging that the personal and political go together, we also need to pay attention to the quality of our personal relationships, building in time for emotional support and mentoring. By transcending daily pressures to make our organizations learning places as well as workplaces, we're making one of the best contributions we can to the struggle for justice.

Working through an organization to accomplish something big in the world is inevitably an adventure—replete with fascinating characters, compelling stories, and useful insights. Although a celebrity-obsessed society may seem to place little value on our remembrances—we're unlikely to pull down $8 million advances for our memoirs as Hillary Clinton did!—our experiences, if we can relate them well, have much more to offer society in the long run. And so another of our tasks is to write down our stories so that they can be shared, discussed, and celebrated for the inspiration and wisdom they contain. That has been my purpose in writing *A School of Our Own*.

Finally, we need to "carry it on," as the song says, moving ahead, even if we aren't always certain that we're going in the right direction. One thing *is* sure: We won't get out of the valley if we stand in one place. This means lending our hands and voices to efforts to create a new grassroots movement—for economic fairness. The primary objective of this early stage of movement-building is to bring such realities as poverty, economic insecurity, the gross disparities of wealth and income, and corporate dominance of the political process to public awareness as critical societal issues—not only for economic justice, but for democracy itself. The "Growing Divide" workshops of United for a Fair Economy, the protests against the World Trade Organization, the anti-sweatshop campaigns, Nader's 2000 run at the presidency—these are examples of efforts of activists to shake the country out of its long slumber. We need to stay informed about what activists are doing, support them where we can, express our disagreement when we must, enter into the conversation about what will be the most effective strategies for raising public awareness, and take action ourselves, finding effective ways to educate folks within our own spheres of influence.

The road will be long and hard. But we'll make good friends along the way. And if the past is any guide, we also will have our share of surprises. Every era, whether mountaintop or valley, offers a unique set of barriers and possibilities. The obstacles are usually all too familiar. But the opportunities have a habit of turning up in the most unexpected places. Who could have predicted that the refusal to serve coffee to four college freshmen at a Woolworth's lunch counter in Greensboro, North Carolina, on February 1, 1960, would ignite the civil rights movement? Or that on a June evening in 1965 a group of Puerto Rican mothers in East Harlem would find that they had the opportunity to start their own schools?

References

Child poverty fact sheet. (2001, June). National Center for children in poverty. *cpmcnet.columbia.edu/dept/nccp/ycpf*

DeParle, J. (1999, December 30). Bold effort leaves much unchanged for the poor. *New York Times.*

Freire, P. (1970). *Pedagogy of the oppressed* (M. Ramos, Trans.). New York: Herder and Herder.

Hartocollis, A. (2000, September 8). Schools try to smooth the bumps on day 1. *New York Times.*

Horton, M. (with Kohl, J. & Kohl, H.) (1998). *The long haul: An autobiography.* New York: Teachers College Press.

Metropolitan Briefs. (1973, March 31). Day-care protest snarls traffic. *New York Times.*

Morris, A. D. (1984). *The origins of the civil rights movement.* New York: Free Press.

Perlmutter, E. (1973, March 27). Mothers seize day-care offices to protest new form. *New York Times.*

Schorr, L. (1997). *Common purpose: Strengthening families and neighborhoods to rebuild America.* New York: Doubleday.

Steinfels, M. O. (1973). *Who's minding the children?: The history and politics of day care in America.* New York: Simon & Schuster.

Ward, A. (1979, February 15 and 22). The political economy of day care in New York City. *WIN Magazine*, pp. 8–15, 32–33.

Index

About the Author

Tom Roderick is executive director of Educators for Social Responsibility Metropolitan Area, a post he has held since 1983.

In 1985, Tom co-founded the Resolving Conflict Creatively Program (RCCP), nationally recognized as one of the most effective and sustained school-based conflict resolution programs in the country. In addition to the RCCP and other programs on conflict resolution and intercultural understanding, ESR Metro has projects on economic justice and prevention of nuclear war.

The civil rights movement drew Tom into the field of education. He worked for the Northern Student Movement, establishing tutoring programs in New Haven, Akron, and Philadelphia, before coming to New York City in 1965 to attend Bank Street College of Education. After his year at Bank Street, he taught third grade at Public School 92 in Central Harlem for two years. From 1968 to 1975 he served as teacher-director of the East Harlem Day School, the elementary school of the Block Schools.

Tom has a B.A. in history from Yale University and an M.S. in education from Bank Street College. He lives on the Upper West Side of Manhattan with his wife, Maxine Phillips, and his daughters, Emma Rose and Anne Marie.